CW01283966

HONG KONG POLICE
INSIDE THE LINES

From Cultural Revolution to Umbrella Movement

CHRIS EMMETT

EARNSHAW
BOOKS

Hong Kong Police: Inside The Lines
By Chris Emmett

ISBN-13: 978-988-8552-21-4

© 2018 Chris Emmett

HISTORY / Asia / China

EB112

All rights reserved. No part of this book may be reproduced in material form, by any means, whether graphic, electronic, mechanical or other, including photocopying or information storage, in whole or in part. May not be used to prepare other publications without written permission from the publisher except in the case of brief quotations embodied in critical articles or reviews. For information contact info@earnshawbooks.com

Published by Earnshaw Books Ltd. (Hong Kong)

CONTENTS

ACKNOWLEDGEMENTS	VI
PREFACE	VII
PART 1: NARCOTICS BUREAU	1
PART 2: MUTINY (OR NOT)	69
PART 3: SHA TAU KOK	85
PART 4: BOAT PEOPLE	133
PART 5: FLYING TIGERS	181
PART 6: UMBRELLA MOVEMENT	233
EPILOGUE	287

ACKNOWLEDGEMENTS

I WISH TO thank ex-colleagues from the Royal Hong Kong Police, and the post-colonial Hong Kong Police Force, who contributed their time and stories to this work. Without their help, this book would not have been possible.

Keith Braithwaite
Martin Cowley
Jim Elms
Fung Yiu-ming
Mike Howard
Gilberto Jorge
Andy Kennedy
Guy Shirra
Barry 'BJ' Smith
John Turner
Ken Wellburn
Dick Williamson
Steve Wordsworth

Not forgetting those who have asked me to safeguard their privacy but whose contribution was equally important.

PREFACE

THERE IS A BOOK inside every policeman. Some tell of humor and comradeship, some are sad and tragic, others are about conflict and adventure. In truth, a police career has all this but sadly, many of these stories go untold. I wrote my first book, 'Hong Kong Policeman,' shortly after I retired. When people ask why I wrote it, I tell them I did it by accident. It was meant to be an after dinner speech but after two days of listing all I wanted to say, the book just followed naturally.

In my first book, I wrote about the colorful and sometimes crazy things that happen to a young man who finds himself in an adventurer's playpen like Hong Kong. In this latest volume, I wanted to show a more serious side of what it means to be a police officer in this amazing city. So, I asked several ex-colleagues to share some stories with me. What I received was a remarkable catalogue of events taken from Hong Kong's modern history. The Narcotics Bureau arrests the owner of Hong Kong's biggest newspaper for trafficking in twenty-nine tons of opium and heroin. Another ex-colleague tells of shady dealings by America's federal narcotics agents. There are eye-witness accounts of the 1967, cross-border shooting that left five Hong Kong policemen dead. There is a confrontation between the Hong Kong Police and the Vietnamese army at Hanoi airport. A counter-terrorist officer tells of his battle with criminals armed with hand grenades and a Kalashnikov rifle. For the first time, officers involved in the Umbrella Revolution tell what it was like on the police side of the barricades.

These are stories of courage, determination and professionalism told by officers who were there. Most have let me use their real names; a few have asked that I preserve their privacy.

I hope that in these pages, I do them all justice.

PART 1
NARCOTICS BUREAU

CHAPTER 1
THE BROTHERS

UNDERCOVER DRUG BUYS. I hate them, I detest them. They always go wrong. But I'm a detective inspector in the Royal Hong Kong Police Narcotics Bureau, and my drug buys are not allowed to go wrong. Back in my drug squad days, I didn't mind risking ten dollars to nail a street dealer. Now, the show money isn't ten dollars, it's a briefcase full of crisp, five-hundred dollar bills. I have counted them. Twice. The briefcase contains more money than a detective inspector earns in a year. And whose signature is on the government treasury's receipt? Mine.

I'm working with Sham Shui Po division's drug squad. Their informant swears he can deliver two kilos of number four heroin. Number four looks like talcum powder and is up to ninety percent pure. And that's a problem. General Orders say only the Narcotics Bureau can handle a case this size, but Sham Shui Po wants to keep the case so we compromise. They can keep it, but only under Narcotics Bureau supervision.

So here I am, running a bloody drugs buy.

The sergeant's name is Hon Tak. He's a typical drug squad sergeant: sensible, competent, self-assured. We are in a two-roomed apartment in a rundown tenement off Yen Chow Street. The lights are dim. The airconditioner doesn't work. I have been in this sweatbox of a bedroom for two hours. Sweat stings my eyes. My shirt is sodden. The informant sits in the corner, quiet and sullen. One piece of advice: never, ever trust a narcotics informant. I do not like narcotics informants and I particularly do not like this one. I do not know why I don't like him, I just don't.

I have planted two microphones in the living room; one wired to a cassette recorder in the bedroom, the other is a backup wireless transmitter. For the tenth time, I order Hon Tak into the living room to test the microphones. He rolls his eyes but steps through the door.

Hon Tak has cast a young constable called Bobby Jai — Little Bobby — as the buyer. Bobby Jai is living the role: bubble perm hairstyle, skin-tight shirt, gold chains, mirror sunglasses. There are five targets, all young and cocky. Bobby Jai brings one of them to the apartment. He wants to see the money. I stay in the bedroom while Bobby Jai comes into the bedroom and takes the briefcase. The target counts the money then hands over a small packet of white powder. Bobby Jai tells him he has a junkie in the bedroom who will test it. In the bedroom, I run the powder through the field test. Positive. Time to do the deal. The target leaves, saying he will bring the goods soon.

An hour passes. Nothing. We swelter in silence. The radio crackles. The observation post reports two targets have approached Bobby Jai.'

'Two? Do they have the stuff?' I ask.

Hon Tak speaks into the microphone. 'OP, over.'

Silence.

He checks the channel and volume control. 'OP, over.'

Silence. He shakes his head.

Shit. Communications are down.

Then, 'This is OP, over.'

I exhale. Comms are back.

'Kui dei yau mo foh ah?' — *Do they have the stuff?*

The reply crackles back. 'M ching choh,' — *Not sure.*

Minutes later, the main door opens. Now there are two targets with Bobby Jai. There are raised voices. Hon Tak clamps on the earphones. A growl rises in his throat. 'Hei yau chi lei,' — *Dammit*, he says. 'They change the plan.' Now he is whispering. 'They want to do the trade in a car.' His lips are thin. 'They say, bring money downstairs. They want to drive to Sai Kung and hand over drugs there.'

CHRIS EMMETT

I pause. Is there a way round the change? No. It isn't safe. I make a chopping motion across my throat. 'Kill it,' *I say.* 'We'll arrest the two in the living room. The OP can take the others.'

Hon Tak gawks at me. His voice is a hard whisper. 'Ah sir. Two kilos of number four. Two kilos!' *His eyes glitter. I have seen it before. First there is the adrenaline-filled hours when nothing happens. Then there is action. It grips you and then there is only the case. Nothing else matters. It is a madness and now I see it in Hon Tak. He wants the two kilos. He wants it with every strand of his being.*

'We follow them to Sai Kung,' *Hon Tak urges me.* 'We follow them close.' *His words come fast and urgent.* 'Bobby Jai *is good man. All are good men.' His eyes are pleading.* 'Ah-Sir, trust me.'

And I want to trust him. I want those two kilos. I want the targets. I want the case. My heart thuds. My breath rasps. Two kilos! There is silence. I pause. I suck in a breath. Then, 'Kill it,' *I say again.* 'Make the arrests.'

Hon Tak shakes his head and turns away. He speaks into the radio. Scorn drips from his voice. 'Lai sai kui dei.' — *Arrest them all.*

I step into the living room. Standing with Bobby Jai *are two young men. Their eyes widen at the sight of a Westerner.*

'MO YUK!' — *DON'T MOVE! I shout. They gape at each other, then at me. I wave my warrant card.* 'CHAI YAN.' — *POLICE.*

It hits them. They turn to the door but Bobby Jai *blocks the way. All color drains from their faces. One covers his face with both hands.*

'I find out where the drugs are,' *Hon Tak says. He glares at the two targets.* 'Gan mai lei,' — *follow me. He moves to the bedroom.* Bobby Jai *bustles the targets in after him. They shut the door.*

Minutes later, Hon Tak is back. He is massaging his fist. 'Bastards,' *he snarls.*

'I couldn't risk...' *I start to say.*

Hon Tak shakes his head. 'Robbery,' *he growls.* 'Bastards. There is no two kilos. They just want the money.' *He gives the informant a look that would turn fire to ice.*

The informant cowers back into a corner. His voice is thin and

wheedling. 'M gwan ngoh si, sah-jin.' — *Nothing to do with me, sergeant.* 'M gwan ngoh si.'
There is no two kilos. There is no number four heroin. For a moment, failure crushes down on me. Then there is relief. I smile. I almost laugh. A robbery. A fucking, bloody robbery.
   Undercover drug buys.
   I hate them. I detest them.

Who would not want it? Four months paid holiday back in England with travel expenses also paid. It was an outdated colonial policy that went back to Queen Victoria's time but it was such a great little perk that no one had bothered to fix it. In Victoria's days, Britain's Colonial Office feared their overseas civil servants might take a liking to the relaxed lifestyle of their local subjects. They might even forsake their stiff collars, don grass skirts and, as they say, go native. The antidote to this was the long home leave. Every three years or so, colonial civil servants shipped themselves back home and spent months reconnecting with their roots. Like I say, who would not want it? Well, me for a start. Do not get me wrong, there was nothing wrong with England in 1977. In fact, everything was right. The weather was wonderful, there were street parties to celebrate Queen Elizabeth's Silver Jubilee and to top it all, Virginia Wade won the Wimbledon's lady's tennis championship. England was a happy place but it was boring. My old mates had all married and moved away. The pubs closed at 11 p.m. and on Sundays, it seemed that everything closed. So, it was with some relief that in July that year, I stepped off the airplane at Kai Tak airport and reveled in the sweltering summer heat. In my pocket was a letter from the Police Personnel Wing, I was to report the Narcotics Bureau offices in Police Headquarters where I would receive my duty assignment.

   In Hong Kong, nothing had changed. The Star Ferry made its progress back and forth across the harbor, the Hong Kong

Island trams trundled along the same old routes and as always, the Central business district sidewalks were so crowded, they were impassable.

I was happy with my new posting. The Narcotics Bureau worked office hours and since the arrest in 1974 of drug baron, Ng Sik-ho, the drug scene seemed quiet. At least, that is what I thought. But as it turned out, the drug scene was very unquiet. For years, the Narcotics Bureau had been investigating two brothers who ran a syndicate far larger than that of Ng Sik-ho's. The brothers were society darlings; one a leading entrepreneur, the other a newspaper mogul of the old school. In Hong Kong's harbor and out on the South China Sea, the brothers shipped in their cargos of opium, morphine and heroin. On the streets, they kept their lieutenants in line with a mix of handsome pay and the threat of vicious beatings. The brothers controlled the narcotics' sea lanes. They were supreme in their trade. They felt invulnerable.

Then, it all started to unravel.

The motorboat was underpowered. Even in the inner harbor's light chop, it dipped and wallowed. The engine grumbled and the exhaust slipped in and out of the water, making a *wallawallawalla* sound. Perched on a stool, the helmsman squinted through a salt-crusted windscreen. Behind him, an awning of yellow tarpaulin covered a passenger compartment that at a push, could seat about thirty passengers. Today, there were just three passengers. In a way, they were co-workers, but they did not speak. Lo Ting-shu glanced at the other two. Each wore faded shorts, grubby vests and rubber sandals. Deep lines scored their faces. Their skin was dark, almost black. Sinewy muscle covered their arms and shoulders. *Coolies*, Lo thought. One was Ah Pang, the other was Ah Chak and that was all he cared to know about them. They seemed calm, almost as if they did not understand the risks they were taking. The brothers had recommended them. Good men, the brothers said. Good men who would keep the shipment safe. Lo shook his head. *Safe*. Nothing and no one was *safe*. No one except the brothers. The brothers were safe. Safe in their fancy offices while others took the risks.

The brothers: the eldest, Ma Sik-yu; the youngest, Ma Sik-chun. Two brothers, each straddling two different worlds. Ma Sik-yu: in one world, a respected merchant, in the other, the head of Hong Kong's biggest narcotics syndicate. Ma Sik-chun: owner and chief editor of Hong Kong's most popular newspaper. In his other world, he was his brother's chief enforcer. The elder brother, Sik-yu, was quiet and thoughtful. He was not prone to anger but if something displeased him, he became cold and silent, like a snake. As for Sik-chun, it was hard to imagine that he and his brother were of the same blood. He was hearty and quick to laugh. Every head waiter and nightclub doorman knew his name. He drank the finest brandy, ate the best food and always had a pretty girl on his arm. Everyone was his friend, but in the time it took to flick a light switch, the laughter could fall silent, the eyes would narrow and his voice would take on a guttural edge.

Lo Ting-shu had been lucky — for him, everything had gone smoothly. Not so for everyone. Sometimes, shipments were lost. The police, the revenue, rival drug syndicates, it was all part of the business. But younger brother Ma Sik-chun did not see it like that. Where some put losses down to bad luck, the younger Ma saw betrayal. Betrayal by design or by incompetence, it did not matter. Betrayal was betrayal and deserved punishment. There were people to take care of such matters but Ma Sik-chun liked to deal with them himself. Forget breaking news stories, forget fawning society divas. For Ma Sik-chun, real power lay in the smell of fear and cries of pain.

'*Do la,*' — We're here, the helmsman called.

Lo Ting-shu stood and grabbed the tarpaulin's braces as the boat rolled, threatening to throw him to the deck. Ahead, a ship's superstructure towered above them. A Polish flag hung from a staff at her stern railing. Below it, in bold print were the ship's name and home port.

Ustka

Gdańsk

The motorboat edged round Ustka's stern to where a cargo lighter hugged her side. D-shaped iron rungs, welded to the lighter's hull made a ladder onto the deck. Lo Ting-shu nodded to Ah Pang and Ah Chak, then he grabbed onto a rung and let the motorboat's deck drop away. He clambered onto the deck and waited for the other two to follow. Men crowded around the lighter's cargo hold. They peered upwards, expectant. An overseer spoke into a handheld radio. Above them, there was a puff of black smoke and a diesel engine growled into life. A derrick boom swung a cargo net out from Ustka's deck. Steel cable squealed through pulleys and the derrick lowered the net into the lighter's hold.

Lo Ting-shu, Ah Pang and Ah Chak crossed the deck to where a temporary pilot staircase allowed movement between the two vessels. To the work gangs, they were just another overseer and two laborers. As they stepped onto the Ustka's main deck, no one paid them attention. Lo Ting-shu led the way aft and they slipped through a door leading into the superstructure. They entered a corridor. Caged lamps lit their way. The walls were of riveted iron, painted off-brown. The floor was of some rough, non-slip material. A painted signboard read:

Kwaterach Oficerów

(Officers' Quarters)

Lo Ting-shu had been here before. He continued on until he came to a door marked with the number 6. He knocked and in an instant, the door opened. The man who appeared was short and had a pinched face. The braid on his shirt epaulettes marked him as an officer. He was new and Lo did not like new people. New people were an unknown. Unknowns were a danger.

The officer hunched his shoulders and leaned forward. He looked left and right, checking the corridor. 'You, Mister Ma?' he asked in a half whisper.

Lo did not answer, instead he pulled a slip of paper from his pocket. It was half of a Thai banknote, cut diagonally.

'You wait,' the officer said. He stepped back into his cabin and rummaged around in his locker. 'Ah. I have.' He handed a similarly cut banknote to Lo.

Lo aligned the two halves, then nodded. 'Where goods?' he demanded.

'You have my American dollars?' the officer asked.

Lo showed him a wad of American dollars. 'First goods,' he snapped. 'Then money.'

The officer stepped into the corridor and locked the door. 'Come, come,' he said. 'We get now.'

He led them back to the main deck then through another door. They were on an ill-lit landing at the top of a flight of iron mesh stairs. The officer led them down one flight, then another, then two more. The stairwell smelled of salt and old diesel. Their footsteps clattered off the stairs. At the bottom of the stairwell was a watertight door. The officer spun the locking wheel and it *clanked* open. He stepped through and pulled a lever on the wall. There was an echoing *humzz* as arc lights flickered into life. They were in a cavernous hold that stretched four stories above them. Canvas netting secured cartons and crates.

'Number three hold,' the officer said. 'All this for Yokohama. No Hong Kong customs come here.' He led them to a locker at the far end of the hold. He opened it and there they were: two industrial plastic bags, each the size of a cement bag.

Ah Pang wrestled one of the sacks from the locker and laid it on the hold's floor. Lo pulled out a pocket knife and cut along the top seam. He reached in and pulled out what looked like a mottled house brick. He weighed it in his hand. It felt smooth and slightly oily. It weighed about three pounds. Three pounds of top grade Thai morphine. All Lo had to do was to get it to the safe house, then it was up to the boss to refine and distribute it.

'Thirty-five bricks,' the officer said. 'Is good?'

Lo nodded. *Is good.* Refined and bulked out with caffeine, a three-pound morphine brick made fifteen pounds of number three heroin. Number three: it looked like instant coffee granules. The quality varied by the batch and most addicts made the safe choice of smoking the stuff. Some, but not all. Some were stupid enough to inject it. Again, Lo weighed the brick in his hand. Thirty-five bricks this trip. Forty bricks three weeks ago. In three weeks' time, thirty or forty more. And three weeks after that. And three weeks after that. And every three weeks for as long as they all stayed safe.

Yes, he thought. *Is very good.*

South of Macau, the fishing junk sheltered in the lee of Siu Wan Shan Island. The China coast lay sixteen miles northwest. To the south, there was only open sea. Lung Chau-man spread his feet wide and cast his eyes across the water. He did not like what he saw. The wind was gusting from the north and white foam flecked the sea's surface. There was a grey-green tinge to the water and above him, the clouds were scudding low and fast. *There will be a squall,* he thought. His crew squatted on the deck, silent and sullen. He scanned the horizon. *Where is it?* Yesterday, he had been on station all day but the boat had not arrived. Now was late afternoon on day two. Soon, the light would start to fail and there was a squall coming.

The weather and the failing light were not his only problems. Three days ago, a detective from the police Narcotics Bureau had come to his home. He had been friendly, cheery even. In exchange for information, the detective promised money and protection. He gave Lung a business card with his name and phone number. Lung had laughed in his face, ripped up the card and ordered him to leave.

HONG KONG POLICE: INSIDE THE LINES

Tan Wu, the youngest crew member scurried to the side railing and peered into the distance. He let out a small cry, *'Ho chi yau suen,'* — Looks like a boat. He clambered up onto the railing and steadied himself on the mainmast standing line. He grinned and beckoned Lung Chau-man to him. *'Yau suen! Yau suen!'* he cried, and pointed into the deepening gloom. *'Goh do.'* — Over there.

'M'yeh suen ah?' — What kind of boat? Lung growled.

'Yu Suen,' — Fishing boat, Tan Wu answered. The other boat was still a half-mile off. It was battling towards them against a sea driven by a freshening wind. As it drew closer, Lung saw a boat with a hull that lay deep in the water, showing little in the way of freeboard. Aft, there was a three-storey deck house that gave the vessel a top-heavy look. The look was deceptive. The design marked it as a deepwater fishing trawler from Thailand. This ungainly little vessel had crossed a thousand miles of ocean just to make this meeting.

'Yue bei,' — Get ready, Lung ordered.

Tan Wu leapt down from the railing and pulled a bright orange flag from a deck locker. He knelt by the foremast, clipped the flag onto a foremast halyard. *'Dak la,'* — Ready, he said. Lung nodded. Tan Wu hauled the flag up the foremast where the wind caught it. In an instant, an orange flag fluttered from the trawler's forward derrick. Lung resisted the urge to go out to meet the trawler. *He can come to us,* he decided. In the island's lee, the cargo transfer would be easier.

Ten minutes later, the two vessels were side by side. The hulls ground together. The mooring lines groaned but held. The trawler's crew pulled hessian sacks from their hold and passed them across the gunnels to Lung Chau-man's crew. There was no need to check their contents. Each sack had a smell unique to this particular cargo. It was a heady blend of aniseed and licorice. Once smelled, never forgotten.

Opium.

It was done. Fifteen thousand *taels* the man in Macau had told him. Fifteen thousand, just over half a ton in the foreigners' measure. Lung Chau-man cast off the lines and the boats drifted apart. Not one word had passed between the two crews. The Trawler's engine grumbled. She spat a puff of black smoke from her stack and wallowed briefly in the swell as she pointed her bow to the west.

Lung ordered his crew to stow the sacks below, then gunned his engine. The junk shuddered as it left the lee of the island. The wind sighed through the standing lines and stinging spray swept the deck. The hull boomed as it shouldered into a roller. Lung set a course for Macau. *Macau. Why Macau?* His orders were to moor close to the Praya Grande and wait for the Macau contact. The contact would check the cargo then clear it for shipment to Hong Kong's Yau Ma Tei typhoon shelter. *Too many steps; too many people.* The Thais knew what he was carrying, the people in Macau knew, so did the Hong Kong people. *Too many people.*

'Yau suen.' Tan Wu was standing at the prow, feet planted wide. The spray had plastered his hair flat against his head. He backhanded salt water from his eyes. '*Yau suen*,' he called again.

Lung squinted through the gloom and the spray. Another boat was on an intercept course towards them. He spun the wheel, taking a more easterly course that would see him pass behind the boat. The boat changed course towards him. It was coming on fast. *Police? Customs?* No, they were outside Macau waters. The boat was nearer. Not police; not customs. *Chinese Coast Guard?* No. It was a fishing junk. There were men on the raised stern decking. The boat closed to within twenty paces of Lung Chau-man's stern then skewed round to match his course. Lung gave his engine more throttle but the other boat was overhauling him. The distance between them closed. A man at the boat's stern raised a loudhailer to his lips.

'Ting suen.' — Heave to.

Lung cupped his hands to his mouth. '*Wei, lo yau*.' Hey, old friend. '*Fung long lei,*' — there's a squall coming. '*Jun fai, faan O Mun.*' — Quick, get back to Macau

'*Ting suen.*' The man nodded to a crew member who disappeared below decks. Seconds later he was back, holding a rifle. He worked the bolt and raised the rifle to his shoulder. There was a CRACK. The rifle bucked and the railing near Lung Chau-man splintered.

'*Mo gong yeh. TING SUEN.*' — Don't talk. HEAVE TO.

Lung Chau-man's mind raced. If he cut his engine and came about, the other boat would overshoot. In the confusion, he might just stay ahead of the chase until darkness fell.

Aboard the other craft, the man with the rifle again raised it to his shoulder.

'*TING SUEN.*'

It was no good; there was no escape. Lung Chau-man cut the engine and let his boat wallow to a standstill. Moments later, hard-faced men jumped aboard and lashed the two craft together. The man with the rifle took up position at the bow where he could command the whole vessel. No one gave any orders. Each man worked with quiet purpose. The last to cross was short and slim. He wore baggy britches of black cotton and a black tunic buttoned to the throat. His hair was unkempt on top but close-cropped at the back and sides. He stared into Lung Chau-man's face with eyes made large by thick, horn-rimmed spectacles. '*Di haak bin do?*' — Where's the black stuff? he demanded. His voice bore the nasal accent of a mainlander.

'*M ji lei gong mat.*' — No idea what you're talking about, Lung Chau-man snorted. He reeled back as the man slapped him hard and fast across the cheek.

'*Mo hoi wan siu,*' — Don't joke around, the man snarled. He made a show of sniffing the air then he grinned, showing gold-capped teeth. '*Wah! Ho heung.*' — Wah! Something's very fragrant.

There was no denying the aniseed-licorice smell of opium

drifting from the hold.

Lung sucked in a breath *'Ging go lei,'* — I'm warning you, he said. *'Ni di haak hai Ma si hing dai ge.'* — This black stuff belongs to the Ma brothers.

'Gong choh,' — You're mistaken, the mainlander chuckled. *'Ni di haak hai ngoh ge.'* — This black stuff is mine.

He turned and snapped orders to his men. They pulled open the main hatch and piled the sacks back onto the deck. Within minutes, the hold was empty. As the sea thieves' boat pulled away, Lung Chau-man pondered his next problem. He must explain things to the brothers. There would be demands for compensation. It would be hard to come up with the money but Lung would find it somewhere. The wind picked up and he shuddered but not from the cold. There would be beatings, questions and more beatings. Was his family safe? Now he wished he had not thrown away the detective's business card. What was his name? Fan? Fu? No, it was Fung. Fung yiu-ming and Fung Yiu-ming had promised to protect him. For a moment he hoped it might be true but it was no use. Detective Fung Yiu-ming could not protect him.

No one could protect him.

Hong Kong Police Headquarters stood at the junction of Arsenal Street and Gloucester Road, just across the road from the China Fleet Club. There were two buildings in the headquarters' complex. Caine House had been there since the 1950s. It was eight floors high and was a typical 1950s design: square and featureless. The secretive Special Branch occupied most of the lower floors and on the top floor was the clubby, Gazetted Officers' Mess, reserved for superintendents and above. Many said that late nights at the mess were to blame for the force's more perplexing policies. Sandwiched between 'The Mess,' and 'The Branch,' was the fifth floor, the Police Commissioner's domain. There, the Commissioner, his deputies and his heads of departments hammered out force polices and priorities. The fifth floor had an ambience all of its own. As soon as the elevator doors slid open, a heavy silence descended on anyone who ventured in. On the fifth floor, people spoke softly and walked with a gentle tread.

Just across the compound was May House. Opened in 1973, it stood twenty storeys high and was modern by the standards of the day. A high-speed elevator whisked me up to the Narcotics Bureau offices. The Bureau occupied May House's ninth and tenth floors, the Intelligence Wing was on the ninth floor and the Operations Wing on the tenth. The superintendent in charge of the Operations Wing was Dick Williamson. Always well-dressed and impeccably groomed, he was an urbane man in his thirties. Some described him as cheery but the easy-going charm belied a shrewd intellect. His secretary was *Mary Jai* — little Mary. She had served the Bureau for longer than anyone could remember and was a great favorite.

The Operations Wing had three sections, each dealing with different aspects of the narcotics trade — one dealt with local distribution, another with exports and the third with importation and manufacturing. Keith Braithwaite was the detective chief inspector in charge of the Import and Manufacturing Section. He was tall and slim with fair hair and clear blue eyes. He was soft-spoken and had an air of quiet unflappability. Two inspectors worked for him. Tam Chung-shing, nearing retirement, was the steady type, quiet but with a great depth of wisdom and experience. By contrast, Detective Senior Inspector Fung Yiu-ming was all energy and flair. My first impression of Fung was of an immensely likeable man with a bouncy personality and a permanent smile. Later, I would discover this cheerful and modest man was full of surprises.

There is nothing a police officer likes more than getting credit for good work. Around the world, police forces have systems for commending a job well done. A nice result from good, but generally routine work, will earn a line or two in an officers' service record. Someone who shows initiative above normal expectations might receive a formal commendation from his commanding officer. Next step up is the Police Commissioner's commendation. It is a sign of outstanding performance and is very rare. Rarer still is His Excellency the Governor's commendation. It is easy to spot a uniformed officer who has earned one of those. He or she wears a red lanyard looped around the left shoulder and fixed to the left breast pocket. In a police region of two to three thousand officers, less than half a dozen will wear the red lanyard. During his Narcotics Bureau service, Fung Yiu-ming had earned three of them.

After a welcoming chat, Keith Braithwaite told me I had some reading to do. No surprise there, I braced myself for the usual tsunami of files, but it was not to be. Braithwaite unlocked a cabinet and handed me a single file. I had expected a pink file jacket stamped with the word, CONFIDENTIAL. This file was different, it was a brownie-orange color and graded, SECRET. Braithwaite showed me to an empty office and closed the door behind him as he left. On the first page, two photographs stared back at me. They were the kind of bland photographs found in passports or identity cards showing two men with heavy jowls and blank expressions. One photograph bore the title, Ma Sik-yu; the other, Ma Sik-chun, alias Ma Yik-shing. Their father had been a minor drug dealer and had introduced his sons to the trade. Taking things up a notch, the brothers invested in legitimate businesses, which made useful covers for their drug dealing. The elder brother, Ma Sik-yu, posed as a well-to-do merchant while the younger brother, Ma Sik-chun, founded a newspaper called the Oriental Daily News. At the same time, he set up an illegal lottery called *Tse Fa*, based on the American numbers racket. Every week, Ma personally drew the winning numbers. If there were too many winners, he would draw them again. Ma published the winners in his newspaper and riding on the back of the *Tse Fa* lottery, the Oriental Daily's circulation grew until it became Hong Kong's best-selling newspaper.

By now, both brothers were successful businessmen. They could have stepped back from the drugs trade but their narcotics dealing had become a major enterprise. They had contacts in Thailand from where they regularly shipped in supplies of morphine base and raw opium. Once landed, their transport network took the raw materials to secure warehouses and from there to backroom refineries. After that, the wholesale side of the business passed the finished product to freelance street dealers. Some said that if Henry Ford had been a drug dealer, he would have changed his surname to Ma.

Background intelligence is one thing; evidence is another. The file was crammed with lists: lists of names, lists of shipments landed, lists of known chemists. There were cases where the police had seized drug shipments belonging to the brothers and had even made arrests. But there was no evidence. Fung Yiuming and Tam Chung-shing visited fishermen suspected of drug smuggling and tried to persuade them to become witnesses against the Ma brothers. They dug up useful information but could not persuade anyone to give evidence. The investigation juddered to a halt.

Then, as I was reading myself into the case, everything changed.

Just after midnight, the tide turned and worked with the Pearl River's natural flow to push the fishing junk further south. Lo Ting-shu had done the trip more times than he could remember and he adjusted the helm to compensate. No morphine bricks on this trip; tonight his cargo was snakes. *Snakes*. That is what they call mainlanders who come illegally into Hong Kong. *Snakes*, they hide in the grass and crawl along the ground until danger passes. But tonight the snakes were not hiding in the grass, they were hiding in the hold of Lo Ting-shu's junk. A dozen of them, silent, fearful and judging from the smell, more than a little seasick. To the north, Lantau Island was a dark mass against the night sky. Lo Ting-shu planned to pass south of Lamma Island then slip unnoticed into Aberdeen harbor. But first he had to dodge Hong Kong's Marine Police. Now he was clear of the river delta, he switched on his navigation lights. Hong Kong police launches had good radar and a boat running without lights was an instant target.

Dead ahead were the lights of another boat. It was about a mile away, too far for Lo to make out if it was coming towards him or heading away. The lights became clearer. Green on the left; red on the right. The boat was heading towards him. *Police?* Maybe; maybe not. Best take no chances. He eased back on the throttle and made a slow turn toward the Soko Islands. If he risked the hidden reefs and got close inshore, the island might clutter any police radar. He fought the urge to gun the engine and turn sharp towards the shore. Any sudden moves would draw suspicion.

The other boat was nearer. The lights were brighter and Lo could make out the sparkling phosphorescence of a wake. The boat was coming on fast. Now he could hear the burble of a powerful marine engine. A searchlight winked on. A dazzling finger of light probed the water's surface. It touched Lo's deck and sought him out at the helm. He turned away his head and shielded his eyes with his forearm. A metallic voice bellowed at him.

'TING SUEN.' – HEAVE TO.

For a moment, Lo considered making a dash for the Sokos. He could ground the boat and make a run for it. Instantly, he dismissed the idea. The shoreline was rugged and boulder-strewn. Even if he got clear, the islands were just tiny lumps of scrub and rock. Come daylight, they would have him.

The police launch was alongside. Crewmen were standing by with grappling lines. *'SUI GING GIM CHA.'* – MARINE

POLICE INSPECTION. *'TING SUEN.'*
Lo Ting-shu cut his engine and even before both craft came to a stop, police crewmen had stepped across onto his deck. The last across was a middle-aged police officer. The insignia on his shirt marked him a station sergeant. He stood before Lo with his fists on his hips and his feet spread wide against the sea's motion. A slow smile of recognition spread across his face. *'Lo Ting-shu Sin Saang,'* — Mister Lo Ting shu, he said, his voice mocking. *'Nei ngou ye.'* — You're up late. *'Yau m'yeh foh ah?'* — What's your cargo?
'Mo yeh, Si Sah Wong sir.' — Nothing Station Sergeant Wong, sir.
The station sergeant snapped an order and crewmen opened up the main hatch.
Three years, Lo thought. Three years in prison for human trafficking and that was in the lower courts. If the police took him to a higher court, he could get seven. It was time to call on his insurance. *'Si Sah Wong!'* he called.
'Dim ah?' — What?
'Mo Yeh.' — Nothing. Now was not the time. When they got back to shore, Lo would speak to an inspector and ask for his freedom. There was a good chance the police would grant it. They would grant it because Lo Ting-shu had something to give them.
Something very valuable.

Even over the telephone, the Marine Police detective superintendent did not sound happy. 'It's bollocks,' he snapped. 'We've been after this bugger for years and finally, we've got him. Got him good.'
Braithwaite waited for him to finish. 'You've arrested him on an illegal immigration charge?' he asked. 'Not narcotics?'
'Smuggling illegal immigrants,' the superintendent answered. 'He insists on talking to Narcotics Bureau. Won't say why. Just

says over and over, "Talk NB. Talk NB. Talk NB."' He sighed. 'I'm telling you, it's bollocks. Waste of time. Leave him to us.'

Braithwaite gave it a moment's thought. 'Can't do any harm to send someone over,' he said. 'If it's bollocks, we've lost nothing.' He put down the phone. The prisoner's name was Lo Ting-shu and Braithwaite had a niggling feeling he might have something important to say. Or perhaps not; perhaps he was just trying to dodge the people trafficking charge. Braithwaite called Tam Chung-sing into his office. Tam was steady and reliable. He could spot a fraud in a heartbeat. Braithwaite told him to get to Marine Police Headquarters, speak to the prisoner and find out what he had to say.

That afternoon, Tam telephoned Braithwaite. He was bringing Lo Ting-shu back to the Bureau and if what Lo had told him was true, the trip to the Marine Headquarters had been worth it.

Back at the Bureau, Lo had a lot to say. He told of his personal dealings with the Ma brothers and with their nephew, Ma Woon-yin. He spoke of the Polish Ocean Lines sailing officers who brought in the morphine base. He knew the land couriers and the warehouse keepers. He knew the syndicate's Bangkok-based morphine and heroin supplier. He would make a formal statement but only in exchange for certain assurances.

Braithwaite checked Lo into a nearby hotel. He organized twenty-four hours a day protection for Lo and his family and arranged a living allowance for them. He got authority to promise Lo that nothing he said would be used against him. In time, Lo would want immunity from prosecution and Braithwaite was sure he could arrange that. Over the next few days, Tam Chung-sing and Fung Yiu-ming questioned Lo. They drilled down into the workings of the Ma syndicate. Not once did Lo trip up over dates and events; not once did he contradict himself. Braithwaite, Fung and Tam came round to one view.

It was not bollocks.

HONG KONG POLICE: INSIDE THE LINES

Back at the Narcotics Bureau, Lo Ting-shu gave form to the Ma brothers' morphine and heroin business. He knew the Thai contacts, the sea couriers, the land couriers, the storerooms. He had their names, their home addresses, their workplaces. He knew which shipments they had handled. He had a fair idea of who could be persuaded to become a crown witness. The investigation was back on track. Things could not get any better.

Then they got better.

Fung Yiu-ming revisited the fishermen suspected of involvement in the opium side of the business. He was not optimistic, the fishing community was a closed circle. Then, out of the blue, Lung Chau-man, took up Fung's offer of protection. It did not take long to find out why. After having his opium cargo hijacked at sea, two men had bundled Lung into a car and taken him to a rundown office building in Yau Ma Tei. For the rest of the day, they interrogated him. There were beatings and threats against his family. That evening, Ma Sik-chun, owner and editor of Hong Kong's biggest newspaper, turned up. Lung felt sure the beatings would stop and at first, Ma had been his affable self but that did not last. When Lung denied any fault, Ma joined in on the beatings. It was fists and kicks and elbows. When he cried out, they stuffed a rag into his mouth and beat him again. Body, face, arms, legs, the face again. They beat him until his body was a mass of pain, then they beat him some more. The next day, they released him but the threat remained. Return the opium or neither Lung nor his family would be safe.

It was like a row of dominos collapsing. One information source led to another, then another, then another. Braithwaite drew up a list of target addresses. They included homes and workplaces, the homes of close friends and mistresses. It was shaping up as a big operation. To hit everywhere at the exact same time would take nearly one-hundred detectives. Braithwaite divided the targets into two categories. List one: arrest and charge. List two:

offer immunity and turn as witnesses. Two names topped the arrest and charge list: Ma Sik-yu and Ma Sik-chun.

After years of investigation, it was all coming together. I checked and rechecked the cases linked to the Ma brothers. I prepared draft criminal charges. During an eight-year period, the brothers had trafficked in twenty-nine tons of opiate narcotics. In the prices of the day, the cash value was $600 million or US$120 million. Raid plans were drafted and redrafted. Legal advice taken and reviewed. Suddenly, it was done. We were ready to go.

Then Ma Sik-yu boarded a flight to Australia.

It was just one of those things. Word was, Ma had placed his son in a prestigious Australian boarding school and had gone with the boy to get him settled in. So we sat on our hands and waited.

And waited.

Ma Sik-yu did not return to Hong Kong. After installing his son in school, he left for Taiwan and there he stayed. There were the inevitable questions. Was he tipped off? If so, by whom? If someone had tipped him off, the suspect pool was small: the investigating officers, a few senior police officers, and one or two barristers in the Attorney General's chambers. Younger brother Ma Sik-chun, and nephew Ma Woon-yin, were still in Hong Kong. Why had they not joined Sik-yu in Taiwan? The family was close. It was unthinkable that Sik-yu would have said nothing to them. The only explanation was that the rest of the family did not share Sik-yu's worries. Ma Sik-yu's sojourn in Taiwan was not unique. Years earlier, a major drug dealer named Ng Sik-ho had inexplicably fled Hong Kong for Taiwan. He stayed there for six months before returning to Hong Kong.

But we could not wait six months. We had two witnesses under protection and were canvassing others. The more people we spoke to, the more people would know something was happening. With each day's delay, the chances of a leak increased. With or without Ma Sik-yu, we had to move.

HONG KONG POLICE: INSIDE THE LINES

So we moved.

Time: just before midnight. Place: the Narcotics Bureau conference room. Every chair taken. People standing two deep against the walls. Cigarette smoke thickened the air. The room bubbled with chatter. The air conditioning struggled with the late summer heat. These were just the raiding team commanders. In the headquarters canteen, one-hundred detectives waited for orders.

Chief Superintendent Jack Johnson sat at the head of the table. Flanking him were the Operation Wing's Dick Williamson and Keith Braithwaite. There was instant silence as Braithwaite called the meeting to order. Jack Johnson spoke a few words of welcome then handed the meeting back to Braithwaite. The briefing was short. Braithwaite ran through the details of the case. There were gasps when he identified the main targets. Lying in neat stacks on the conference table were twenty-eight A4 sized envelopes. These were the raid packs. Each contained details of a target address, the name and photograph of a target individual, and assorted instructions such as vital timings and key telephone numbers. One by one, Braithwaite read out names of team commanders. As each acknowledged, I handed them a raid pack. The main target address was the Ma family home. It occupied three floors of a Prince Edward Road apartment block. Within these three floors was a network of connecting doors and staircases. What had once been a collection of individual apartments was now a sprawling family mansion.

'The time now...' Braithwaite checked his watch. '...is zero-zero-twenty hours. You may brief your officers then head out to your designated areas. All raids are to take place at the exact time mentioned in your raid pack. From now on, strict security discipline. No one makes any telephone calls, no one to absent themselves, no matter how briefly. Questions?'

There were a few questions then the raid commanders filed

out. Earlier, communications engineers had installed extra telephones in the conference room. As the raid commanders filed out, Narcotics Bureau detectives filed in to staff what was now the operation's command centre. I sat with Johnson, Williamson and Braithwaite. There was some attempt at small talk but mostly, there was just silence. Across Hong Kong Island, Kowloon and parts of the rural New Territories, raiding parties were moving into place. There was nothing left for us to do. Success or failure depended on the operation plan being right. And there being no leaks. I checked my watch. Zero-one-fifteen. Less than an hour since the briefing. It would be a long night.

Zero-four-thirty. All attempts at small talk had long since ended. The ashtrays were full. The rubbish bin overflowed with plastic coffee cups. Our eyes were red; our throats nicotine sore. My heart jumped as a telephone jangled. A constable snatched it from its cradle. We gathered round him.

'*NB. Bin wai?*' — NB. Who's that? He grabbed a pen and bent over a note pad. '*Dak...dak...sau do...*' — Okay...Okay...got it. He put down the phone. 'Number three raid party reports target address secure. One arrest.'

Now we were smiling. It was just one result but things were moving. More telephones jangled. The room filled with telephone chatter. The results came in fast. *Target premises secure. Target individual detained.* It was as if hours of silent tension had never been. So far, every raid had come up gold. A constable had a telephone to his ear. He stood and waved for us to join him. 'Prince Edward Road raid party reporting,' he called.

Prince Edward Road — the Ma family home. Braithwaite shushed everyone into silence.

The constable gave a thumbs-up sign. 'Ma Woon-yin, in custody,' he said. We grinned at that. We had Ma's nephew. The constable's brow furrowed. '*Joi gong.*' — Say again. He shook his head and looked up at Braithwaite. 'Ma Sik-chun not present,' he said. He turned away and spoke into the telephone. '*Hai m hai jan ge?'* — Is that right? It was. The raiding party had missed Ma Sik-chun. They had seized his passport and his Hong Kong identity card but where was the man himself?

'Not to worry,' I said, trying, and failing, to sound chirpy. 'There's still the newspaper office and his...er...lady friend.' Minutes later, the raiding parties tasked to visit Ma's mistress and his newspaper offices reported in. He was not there. Where the hell was he? Ma Sik-chun was the Bureau's biggest-ever target.

And we had missed him.

There was some good news. Of our potential witnesses, all but one agreed to give evidence for the crown. While narcotics officers took their statements, I sent out a 'flash' wanted notice to all police stations. I issued a press release urging anyone who knew Ma's whereabouts to get in touch. The police newspaper, 'Off Beat,' had a recent photograph of Ma. It was publicity shot, taken when he and the Deputy Police Commissioner had opened a new boy scouts' centre. Before I circulated it, I asked one of our crime scene photographers to trim it down so that it showed only Ma's head and shoulders.

The press loved it. 'Why did the police let him go?' they crowed and we had no answer. It was journalistic treasure. In one story, they could have a dig at the police and a rival newspaper. At exactly nine o'clock next morning, I put Ma on the Immigration Department's stop list. Marine police checked the harbor typhoon shelters and impounded Ma's two luxury yachts. Mid-morning, a solicitor telephoned me. 'Your raiding party seized Mister Ma's Hong Kong identity card,' he said, a bit too pompously for my liking. 'I am on my way to your office now,' he continued. 'Have it ready for me.'

'Certainly,' I answered. 'But I prefer to hand it to him in person.'

The line went quiet and there was a *click* as he hung up on me.

CHRIS EMMETT

We trawled Ma's favorite restaurants and night clubs. We checked his friends, acquaintances, business associates. Nothing. It was as if Hong Kong's most famous son had evaporated. Then, on day three, Ma's solicitor telephoned Jack Johnson. Ma Sik-chun would surrender to the Narcotics Bureau.

Ma arrived with his lawyer just after ten o'clock that evening. He was a smiling, swaggering picture of self-confidence. Dick Williamson and Keith Braithwaite received him then passed him over to me. Through a Chiu Chow dialect interpreter, I read him the charge — trafficking in dangerous drugs, namely heroin, morphine and opium. I administered the formal caution that starts with the words, *you are not obliged to say anything...* Throughout all this, Ma just nodded and smiled like a contented Buddha.

With legal formalities done, Williamson and Braithwaite left me to it. One of my constables fingerprinted and photographed Ma and I arranged with a nearby police station to have him detained overnight. By now, the press had got wind of the surrender. For the first time, the confidence fell from Ma's face. He implored me to let him leave Police Headquarters without handcuffs. General orders were clear, arresting officers had to handcuff all prisoners but I reasoned that Ma had surrendered and if he did make a run for it, there was nowhere he could hide. I agreed and we took the lift to the ground floor. And on the ground floor there was utter chaos.

I should have known better. The Police Public Relations Branch had placed a few barriers to form a press compound and assigned two constables to keep order. Those two constables had no chance. As soon as the lift doors opened, a photographer vaulted over the barrier and sprinted into the lift lobby. In his haste, he lost his footing and skidded across the floor. The constables pleaded with the press to stay behind the barriers but it was a lost cause. Photographers swarmed around us, shouting, jostling, elbowing each other aside. Camera flashes sparkled.

HONG KONG POLICE: INSIDE THE LINES

A television crew pushed their way through, their spotlight blinding. There were shouted questions but the racket was so great, no one could make them out. Ma smiled and waved like a Hollywood celebrity. We forced our way through and Ma and myself boarded a waiting police car. As we edged forward, a photographer threw himself across the car bonnet. A constable dragged him off then we were away, across the compound and through the main gate.

As we left the press behind, Ma Sik-chun buried his face in his hands and wept.

Some say the mark of a good detective is in the number of informants he or she is running. That is true, but only to a point. Detectives who get the services of good informants are on their way to carving a reputation for themselves. However, in their zeal, some fall into simple traps. First: be it drugs, burglary, or any other crime, the better the information, the deeper the informant is involved in it. Second: the informant has been playing the game for a long time and has learned a few street smarts. Third: informants are not out to forge a better society, they have an agenda. Fourth: street-wise, agenda-driven informants care only about themselves. The upshot is that sometimes it is not the detective running the informant, it is the informant running the detective. They do this for all kinds of reasons: to distract attention from themselves or to get close to confidential police information. Triads actually like to be seen with the police, it adds to their aura of untouchability. More than a few police careers come to a screeching halt when informants slowly but inexorably draw their handling officer closer and closer to the line until at last, they cross it. Despite this, I was quite pleased with my new informant. To be honest, I had not recruited him myself; rather, the Bureau had assigned him to me. His name was Ng Sik-ho.

Before the Ma brothers, there was Ng Sik-ho. Since a bad

run-in with triads, his nickname had been *Bai Ho* — Limpy Ho. A few years earlier, the Narcotics Bureau had arrested him on charges of dealing in twenty-five tons of opium and two tons of morphine. Never proven, but well-known, was his involvement in Amsterdam's *China White* heroin trade. There were suspicions that Ng had ordered at least one murder, but again, there was no proof. Ng received a thirty-year jail sentence and ended up in Stanley Prison's high security wing. As far I was concerned, Ng Sik-ho was old news. At least he was until word came from Stanley Prison. Ng Sik-ho had done business with the Ma brothers and now, he wanted to speak to the Narcotics Bureau.

There were three of us: Ng's lawyer, a Narcotics Bureau interpreter, and me. A prison officer escorted us though a series of double-gated enclosures that led into the high security wing. The wing was a jail within a jail and was home to Stanley Prison's hard cases. Here were the murderers, the armed robbers, the triad bosses and the drug barons. The main security gates opened onto a small compound where a group of inmates were playing volleyball. They were having a good time and if not for their prison garb, they would have looked like any group of weekend sportsmen.

Inside the main block there was a stark reception area. An unsmiling prison officer checked our identity documents and ticked our names off a list clamped to his clipboard. He opened my briefcase and rifled through my hoard of blank statement forms. He showed us into a side room then left, locking the door behind him. The walls were plain. The floor was smooth concrete. There were two doors. The one through which we had entered led back to the reception area. Another, on the opposite side of the room, led to the cellblock. There was an oily rattle and the cellblock door swung open. And there he was. He was shorter than I expected but despite a distinct limp, he walked with an air of easy confidence. Without waiting for an invitation, he sat on the chair opposite me. He nodded a greeting then looked me over with a cool gaze.

I had a preliminary script written in my police notebook. The interpreter read it over in Chinese. It stressed that the Attorney General would not offer any reduction in Ng's jail term in exchange for his evidence. Ng smiled at that. We both knew it was bullshit but it would be the first question Ma's defense lawyer would ask.

Ng spoke. His voice was quietly rasping. The interpreter translated. 'He says he understands and is willing to give evidence.' The interpreter lowered his voice. 'He wants you to guarantee you will not use anything he says against him.'

The question threw me. It was perfectly reasonable but what if Ng admitted anything serious. What if he owned up to a homicide?

Ng read my thoughts. A light smile hovered around his lips.

'I can guarantee that,' I said, after a brief pause.

Ng nodded. This time his smile was real and open. 'Cigarette?' he asked in English.

I fished out my pack of Marlboro and shook one out for him. He drew heavily on the cigarette then spoke again.

'He says he will give a statement,' the interpreter said.

I took a statement form from my briefcase and smoothed it out on the tabletop. 'Let's start with how he got into the drugs trade,' I said.

The answer to that question filled the first page of what turned out to be a sixty-page witness statement.

If the British colonials left anything to their former colonies, it was a legal system rich in pageantry. Bewigged judges decked out in crimson, dominated the court from their elevated benches. Behind them, Hong Kong's royal crest reminded everyone that their Lord or Ladyships represented the power and majesty of the crown. Dark wooden paneling covered the walls. In the well of the court, wearing black robes and horsehair wigs, sat the court officials and contending barristers. Everyone stood and bowed as the judge entered. The judge bowed in return and only then did the court's business start. Pomp and splendor aside, it was serious stuff. For the defendant, it could be life-changing. Even before the trial started, there was a lot to get through. The judge and lawyers had to study the evidence and key legislation. They looked at records of past cases. Had there been previous judgments? More importantly, had the appeal courts ruled on the meaning of this word or that turn of phrase? The time consumed was huge; the costs eye-watering. Often, it seemed the wheels of justice turned exceeding slow. Court diaries were full for months in advance and allotting court time was an imprecise science. A clock-watching judge does not serve the interests of justice, so trials frequently overran. Trying to juggle all this was the judiciary's administration wing. By and large, they did a pretty good job, but the last thing they needed was a no-hope case that wasted everyone's time and money. The High Court needed a filter and the magistrates' courts delivered that with something called a committal hearing.

Each Hong Kong magistrate was a full-time professional who had worked as a barrister for at least seven years. From time to time, they had to oversee committal hearings. Committals did not decide on guilt or innocence, they just considered if there was enough evidence to put to a jury. As a junior detective inspector, I had done several. I had gathered the witness statements, expert certificates, and lists of physical exhibits then served them on the defendant and the magistrate, giving them enough time to prepare for the hearing. I say *hearing*, but most committals were just paper exercises. Sometimes, the prosecutor, the defendant or the magistrate might insist that a particular witness appear in person. I have called witnesses to give verbal evidence if I suspected they might change their stories. Magistrates sometimes did the same to clear up any contradictions. Defense lawyers, on the other hand, like to keep their strategy to themselves so it is rare for them to ask for verbal testimony. After a bit of practice, I could present a paper committal in half a day. Not so with Ma Sik-chun's committal. That was to take four weeks and end in a storm that people still talk about today.

Central police station has stood on its site in Hollywood Road since the 1860s. It has high ceilings and deep verandas running the building's length. From Hollywood Road, a ramp leads to an enclosed compound that had once been a small parade ground. At the compound's north-west corner, is Victoria Prison. At the north-east, a flight of stone steps led to the Central Magistracy's main entrance.

The committal hearing started in late November. Representing the crown was Senior Crown Counsel, James 'Dingo' Ruly. There were ten defendants and all had lawyered-up. Ma engaged Edward Lyons, a London Queen's Counsel who was also a member of the British Parliament. The defense team demanded copies of all witness statements and interview notes. We delivered them in a big steel trunk but because some concerned existing operations, we had partially redacted many of them. Lyons QC *harrumphed* and puffed up like an angry turkey when he found that one statement was a just a mass of black. Only the witness' name showed.

On the morning of the hearing, we left Lai Chi Kok Prison in convoy. First, a police Emergency Unit Land Rover, next the prisoner van transporting all ten defendants. I and two constables followed in an unmarked car. Bringing up the rear was another Emergency Unit Land Rover. In the morning traffic, it took nearly an hour to reach Central police station. The press surged around the prison van as it slowed to turn onto the Hollywood Road entrance ramp. As the last police Land Rover passed, a constable stepped out and shut the compound gates. The prison van stopped at the bottom of the courthouse steps and constables armed with shotguns surrounded it. A few selected press photographers waited on the staircase. The prison van doors opened and a handcuffed Ma Sik-chun was first out. He wore a light grey suit and a white shirt, open at the neck. My constables and I escorted him up the stairs. He smiled at the press then we whisked him into the court.

The magistrate was His Worship, John Griffiths, a scrupulously fair and polite man. He had set aside the month leading up to Christmas for the hearing. Our witnesses were all co-conspirators who had agreed to become crown witnesses. You can never trust a turned witness. There is always a chance that during the trial, they will recant their original statement. We wanted to get them in the witness box early. If they were to renege, best that it happen during the committal hearing rather than in front of a jury.

Our case had two legs: chief courier, Lo Tung-shu was the main witness on the morphine and heroin side. On the opium side, most of the witnesses were fishermen. Edward Lyons QC got himself excited when the fishermen seemed to be mixing up their dates. I whispered to Dingo Ruly that they were using the traditional Chinese calendar, which varied from the western calendar by as much as two months. In Chinese, the words used for both systems are exactly the same and the interpreter was translating the dates as though they were the western system. Dingo rose to his feet and offered to explain the problem.

'I need no help from the prosecution,' Lyons bristled.

So Dingo shrugged, sat down and let him get on with it. The best part of a morning passed before we had the chance to clarify things. His Worship was not a happy magistrate.

Ng Sik-ho was what we call in the trade, a star turn. Neatly dressed in a business suit, he spoke of his dealings with both Ma brothers. Through intimidation and manipulation, the brothers had insinuated themselves into all levels of Hong Kong's drug business. At one point, they held a monopoly on all syndicated street trade. Ng allowed himself a smile as he described how he and other major dealers sabotaged the operation by inflating their costs and reducing retail prices. For months, Hong Kong had the world's only loss-making narcotics trade.

Then, it was all over. John Griffiths retired to his chambers to consider the evidence, Ma Sik-chun and the others went back to Lai Chi Kok and we Narcotics Bureau officers went for a drink. The next day, we were back in court. There were no surprises. Griffiths found there was enough evidence to put before the High Court. He set the case down pending a trial date.

Lyons rose and made an application for bail. The other lawyers, more in hope than expectation, did the same. The submissions took more than two hours. Griffiths disappeared back to his chambers, which I supposed was to make it look as though he was giving it some serious thought. Edward Lyons went off to another appointment. Dingo and I went for cups of tea. Later that morning, John Griffiths was back in court. I sat next to Dingo and waited for the inevitable.

'I have considered these bail applications very carefully,' Griffiths said.

Sure you have, I thought.

'And I am minded to grant bail,' Griffith continued.

That got my attention. I gaped at Dingo Ruly. He rose to his feet. 'I...*er*...Your Worship...Did I hear correctly?'

'You did, Mister Ruly,' Griffiths said. 'Defendant one, Ma Sik-chun.' He peered at Ma over the rim of his spectacles.

Ma stood. He seemed as confused as the rest of us.

'Mister Ma, you are released on cash bail of five hundred thousand dollars. Also, you will require two other people to stand surety, each in the same amount.'

Half a million Hong Kong dollars, US$100 thousand. Ma was grinning. I half expected him to pull the money from his back pocket.

'Mister Ruly,' Griffiths inclined his head towards the prosecution team. 'Do you wish to address me on the issue of bail conditions?'

'I do not, sir,' Ruly snapped. 'The crown will not be party to this. We object to any suggestion of bail.'

Griffiths was unruffled. 'I have granted bail,' he said. 'If you check the Magistrates Ordinance, you will find that once made, the decision is not open to objection nor is it open to appeal.'

Griffiths laid out bail conditions. Ma Sik-chun must report to his nearest police station twice a week; once on Tuesday and once on Saturday. That was that. Ma's friends and family thronged around him. For now, Hong Kong's most significant drug dealer was a free man.

And there was nothing we could do about it.

From time to time, Ma's solicitor called me, reminding me of my duty to look for evidence supporting his client's innocence. I promised I would, but to be honest I did not make it a priority. I hoped Ma would forget to report to his nearest police station and thus break his bail condition. Alas, he was as good as gold. I asked our new chief superintendent, Mike Flanders, to put Ma under twenty-four hour surveillance. He said no. I could not blame him, a police surveillance operation is a big job. A surveillance team needs at least four officers, each taking a turn on point. Three shifts a day brings the number up to twelve and there has to be a forth team to cover leave days. Factor in mobile surveillance teams when the target decides to use his car and you get an idea of the operation's scale. Even with everything in place, surveillance is strictly short term. Sooner or later, usually sooner, a streetwise target will realize what is happening.

No breach of bail conditions; no surveillance. The man was free to do what he wanted and we had no idea what that might be. Then in July, we had a visitor. His name was Tan Bing and he claimed to have an offer that would help everyone.

Tan Bing was a small-time drug dealer and had been a prosecution witness in the Ng Sik-ho case. I expected he would arrive with a lawyer but he was alone. I met him in the lift lobby and took him straight to Mike Flanders' office. Dick Williamson joined us. As we sat around a coffee table sipping tea, I triggered a tape recorder linked to a microphone under the table. Through an interpreter, we made some small talk, then Tan Bing got down to business.

'Would you like elder brother, Ma Sik-yu to return to Hong Kong?' he asked.

Indeed we would.

Tan leaned forward and lowered is voice. 'Ma Sik-chun can arrange it.'

A sting operation! My pulse quickened.

Flanders took his time to answer. 'And how will he do that?'

Tan Bing smiled. 'If you agree to drop all charges against Ma Sik-chun, he will persuade his brother to return.'

What? I hissed my disdain and earned a reproving look from Flanders.

Of course, it was nonsense. The realization grew on me that it was not only nonsense, it was desperate nonsense. It could mean only one thing.

Ever the polite host, Flanders thanked Tan for taking the time to speak to us and promised to give the offer some thought. Meeting over, I escorted Tan back to the lift lobby then went back to join the others. Les Howard, the superintendent in charge of the Intelligence Wing was there.

'What do you think?' Flanders asked.

'He's going to jump bail,' I snapped back. 'This was a last ditch crack at slipping off the hook.' I shook my head. 'Last ditch and desperate.'

'Suggestions?' Flanders asked.

'Surveillance,' I answered.

'Never work,' Les Howard said. 'He'll be expecting it. Waste of resources. I'll have to take them off other operations.'

Les Howard was right but there were other issues in play.

I chose my words carefully. '*If...when...*he skips town, everyone will ask why he wasn't under surveillance.'

In that instant, I knew I had clinched it. Flanders frowned and nodded. I had my twenty-four hour surveillance. But there is a saying: *'You're damned if you do and damned if you don't.'* I should not have felt so pleased with myself. As things turned out, we were damned no matter what we did.

At last, we had an idea of how Ma Sik-chun spent his days. He rose late and took a light meal in a teahouse near his home. Sometimes he visited a local park, then filled the rest of the day meeting friends and business contacts. Every Tuesday and Saturday morning, he went to Kowloon City police station and signed the bail reporting register. I was keen to see if Ma met up with any known narcotics personalities. If he had, it would have been good reason to revoke his bail. No such luck. Every evening, at around ten o'clock, he went to the head office of his newspaper, the Oriental Daily News. At four the following morning, the day's edition was ready for distribution and Ma would leave, sometimes for home, sometimes for an upmarket nightclub where he would bask in the company of friends and hangers-on.

It could not last. In early September, the overnight team watching Ma's home received a flask of tea and a bag of cakes. Courtesy of Mister Ma, the delivery man said. The operation was blown, as we knew it would be. Mike Flanders called a hurried meeting. Should we keep the surveillance in place? I was torn. There were operations going short of vital surveillance support but Ma's trial would start in just a few weeks. Overt surveillance might deter him from jumping bail. Even if it did not, there was always that obvious question: *Why did the police not keep an eye on him?*

The surveillance stayed in place. On Tuesday, September 19, Ma signed the Kowloon City police station bail reporting register.

He spent a leisurely day with friends and at ten that evening, went to the Oriental Daily's office. At four the next morning, delivery vans took that morning's edition to distribution points across Hong Kong, Kowloon and the New Territories. The surveillance teams waited for Ma to leave and go about his normal routine. They waited until daybreak. Ma did not appear.

We went to Ma's Prince Edward Road home. Neither Ma Sik-chun nor his nephew, Ma Woon-yin were there. They're visiting friends, their family said. Which friends? Not sure. Where do the friends live? No idea. It got worse. We did the rounds of the other defendants. By day's end, we listed half of them as missing. We had our response all planned out. First, revoke their bail. Next, a flash teleprinter message to all: arrest Ma and the other bail jumpers. We had a list of target addresses, if Ma was still in Hong Kong, we would have him. But what if he was not? I prepared Interpol Red Notices, requiring member states to arrest Ma and the others and hold them pending extradition. The notices needed an arrest warrant and that is where everything shuddered to a halt. Ma was not in breach of his bail conditions. Sure, he had slipped the surveillance, no doubt in the back of a newspaper van, but that meant nothing. On Tuesday, he had signed Kowloon City police station's register, which was all that his bail conditions required. If he failed to sign in by midnight on Saturday then, and only then would he would be in breach. For now, we could do nothing.

By Wednesday morning, I had done all the necessary paperwork. The rest of the day dragged by. Thursday passed in misery. Friday was worse. I have never known a Saturday to pass so slowly. At one minute past midnight, I telephoned the Duty Officer at Kowloon City. Ma had not reported in. I called the Narcotics Bureau hotline desk and asked them to send out a teleprinter message, confirming the local wanted notice. Even as it went out, I knew in my heart of hearts that Ma was long gone.

Tomorrow was Sunday and the courts would be closed. By the time I got the warrants, Ma Sik-chun would have had a five-day head start.

On Monday I filed the papers. With arrest warrants signed and sealed, I sent out Interpol Red Notices for all our missing defendants. On Tuesday, the bail sureties turned up with briefcases full of five-hundred dollar bills. They wore grubby singlets, faded shorts, rubber sandals and smug expressions. They gave their occupations as street hawkers.

The press were all over us. First question: 'Why did you not have him under surveillance?'

Answer: 'We did.'

Next question: 'So, why did you let him go?' Even today, newspapers looking back on the case use phrases like, '...Ma Sik-chun jumped bail despite *supposedly* being under round-the-clock surveillance...'

Like I said, *'You're damned if you do...'*

Ma Sik-chun eventually surfaced in Taiwan, which is an Interpol member but which has no extradition treaties with anyone. We pressed Taiwan's Interpol station to execute our Red Notice but nothing happened.

Back home, Ma Sik-chun's son, Ma Ching-kwan took over the family's newspaper business. Untouched by his father's drugs dealing, Ching-kwan built the business into today's Oriental Press Group. It is an ultimate irony that where the drugs business made his father a multimillionaire, the Oriental Press Group made Ma Ching-kwan a multibillionaire. Today, he is one of the world's richest men.

Elder brother, Ma Sik-yu died in 1991, at the early age of 55. In 2014, Ma Sik-chun's lawyers applied to Hong Kong's high court to have his arrest warrant revoked. The Justice Department admitted that the passage of time meant there was little chance of a conviction. Nonetheless, the court rejected the application, stating it would send the wrong message to offenders and to the public. The warrant stayed in force until Ma Sik-chun's death in June, 2015. He was 77 years old.

After their flight, neither brother ever left the island of Taiwan. They died in exile.

CHAPTER 2
FEDS

MIKE HOWARD WAS not normal. That is not to say he was abnormal. He spoke with an English west-country burr, had an open face and was quick to laugh. He was not overly tall but he had a solid build that lent him an air of casual immovability. He played centre in the police rugby side and spent most lunchtimes working the power lifting stations in the Police Headquarters' gym. What was not normal about Mike Howard was his police background.

For most Hong Kong police inspectors, the career path was pretty standard. After basic training there was command of a patrol sub-unit doing day-to-day beat duties. Next, a spell in the paramilitary Police Tactical Unit. After that, it was anyone's guess. Some went to the Emergency Unit, which was a mobile patrol division, trained and equipped to handle any and all emergencies. Some became motorcycle cops in the regional traffic branch. Others went back to their old stations where there were cozy nine-to-five jobs. For the more adventurous, there was the divisional drug squad. There might even be a chance to become a detective.

Mike Howard's career background was different. In September 1977, he had completed basic training. That was it. When he stepped out of the elevator and into the Narcotics Bureau offices, he still had his graduation parade haircut. Howard was part of a plan to bring fresh faces into specialist units. That is, fresh faces untainted by yesteryear's corruption. At first, there was

HONG KONG POLICE: INSIDE THE LINES

some doubt but it was soon clear that the selection process did not involve pulling names from a hat. If the new boys lacked anything, it was the grizzled, hard-assed copper look that any half-decent crook could spot in a heartbeat.

Howard's boss was Mike Dunn, a youthful detective chief inspector with apple-cheeks, tousled hair and bright eyes. He was in charge of the Bureau's anti-distribution section. The section sometimes worked with overseas police agencies like the United States Drug Enforcement Administration, the Royal Canadian Mounted Police and Australia's Federal Police.

Howard took command of a team of four detectives, all young. Their clothes were fashionably casual and they wore their hair just touching the collar. The sergeant was Ben Lo. 'Welcome to Team 3, sir,' he said. His English carried just a trace of an accent. He introduced the three constables: Tony, cheerful and dressed in the casual elegance favored by junior managers. *Kwan Jai*, slim with an earnest face. *B Jai*, quiet but with an underlining air of toughness.

Howard's office was on the south side of the building, overlooking the police married quarters. Next door to his office was the Bureau's hotline room. The hotline was a publicly listed phone number that people could use to call in narcotics information. Good idea on paper but in reality, callers were mostly pranksters, crazies or vengeful neighbors. Having said that, the room had its uses. There was a key rack for the Bureau's fleet of decrepit Ford Cortinas and a dog-eared register for signing vehicles in and out. There was a small table, a kettle and one of the blurriest television sets known to electrical engineering. It was something of gathering point and there was always a clamor of conversation seeping through the plasterboard walls.

'Not the best office,' Dunn breezed. 'But it'll do for now. Give it a year or so and we'll get you properly settled.' He paused. 'I've a nice little investigation for you,' he said. 'I'll get the confidential registry to send you the files.'

Later, a clerical assistant appeared at the door, pushing a battered tea trolley. It had two fixed trays: an upper tray for a tea urn, cups and saucers, and a lower tray for biscuits and on special days, cakes. But there was no tea urn, no cups, no saucers and definitely no cakes. Instead, there were files, dozens of them, all with bright pink covers stamped, CONFIDENTIAL. The clerk flashed a smile and unloaded them onto Howard's desk. There were thick files, thin files, hardbound and softbound files. Attached to some, were sub-files. There were surveillance reports, intelligence briefs, personality files and correspondence files. By the time the clerk had finished, they covered Howard's desk. Some of the piles were a couple of feet high. They swayed and threatened to topple onto the floor. Howard slumped into his chair and pulled a file from the nearest heap.

Amphetamines.

Doctors often prescribed amphetamines as a pick-me-up. They were certainly not Hong Kong's party drug of choice. So, what was the problem? The problem was that Tokyo's partygoers could not get enough of the stuff. We are not talking about the little capsules handed out on prescription. The Tokyo party crowd wanted the bootleg version — a chemical of dubious quality, dissolved in solution and injected into a vein. Effect: euphoria, increased sex drive, hyper-alertness, sense of invulnerability. Of course, drug highs are like gravity — what goes up, must come down. Amphetamine lows included, anxiety, paranoia, mood swings and depression.

In the West, amphetamines' street names were: speed, throttle or whizz. The Japanese called it simply, *shabu* — stimulant drugs. For the Tokyo police, *shabu* was a serious business but in Hong Kong, the law put amphetamines on a par with having antibiotics without a doctor's note. For Hong Kong drug couriers, it was a sweetheart deal: maximum profit and, in Hong Kong at least, minimum risk. No prizes for guessing that Hong Kong was Japan's main supply source for *shabu*. Almost every other week, a letter bearing a Japanese postmark wafted into the Narcotics Bureau registry. 'Feel free to share operational intelligence,' they invited. 'Advise of progress,' they demanded. That and other, ever-so-polite ways of saying ...*get honorable ass in gear and do something*...

Then, it all changed. Japanese arm-twisting pushed Hong Kong's law makers into action. In short order, amphetamines became an honest-to-goodness narcotic. From that moment, anyone dealing in illicit amphetamines risked a life sentence. Still the letters came and the Narcotics Bureau had no answer. There was no operational intelligence and certainly no progress. The Bureau had not a whiff of a case.

Nothing.

The United States consulate stood on the downhill section of Garden Road, which connected the swanky homes on Victoria Peak to the swanky office blocks in Hong Kong's business district. For an address so close to the city centre, the consulate had a pleasant setting. Trees and shrubbery lined nearby roads. The Botanical Gardens were within walking distance and the nearby St. John's Cathedral had tranquil sitting-out areas. Just across the road from the consulate was the downtown terminal for the Peak Tram. Every day, the little funicular railway took tourists and the occasional commuter, up an eye-poppingly steep slope to Victoria Peak. There, a lookout point offered stunning views across Hong Kong's harbor.

The tram's downtown terminus occupied the ground floor of the unremarkable St John's Building. The upper floors were a haphazard collection of offices and apartments. Tucked away on the first floor was an anonymous suite of offices. The door was always closed and there was no brass plate identifying the occupants. The offices belonged to the Hong Kong station of the United States Drug Enforcement Administration, DEA for short. The DEA agents were a sociable crowd, particularly when there was something to celebrate. Today was such a day. Three members of the Thai parliament had decided to boost their income by dabbling in the import/export trade. To be precise, they planned to export several kilograms of heroin from Thailand into Hong Kong. The DEA station in Bangkok picked up on the plan and tipped off Hong Kong's Narcotics Bureau. With the three parliamentarians tucked away in Lai Chi Kok Prison, the DEA put the beer on ice, broke out the Pringles and gave Mike Dunn a call.

The DEA's main squad room was a jumble of desks. On one wall was a photograph of President Jimmy Carter. On another was a notice board crammed with dog-eared bulletins and photographs of the DEA's most wanted. By the time Dunn and Howard arrived, the place was a hubbub of good cheer. There was laughter and rowdy banter. A beefy New Yorker with a bear-trap handshake introduced himself. 'Buzz Ziegler,' he said, and thrust a chilled Budweiser at Howard.

Dunn raised his voice above the clamor. 'Where's Herman?' he asked. 'Mike should meet him.'

Ziegler nodded to a corridor leading off the squadroom. 'Be gentle,' he said. 'He's having a rough day.' He put his head close to Dunn's. 'Head office.' He furrowed his brow and nodded as though those two words explained everything.

Dunn led Howard to where a door stood open, revealing a neat office. There was a desk at which a man sat sifting through papers. On the wall behind him was a crest bearing the DEA's emblem of an eagle in flight. In a corner, an American flag hung from a short flagstaff. A sign on the desktop announced, 'Herman Chang. Special Agent in Charge.'

Dunn tapped on the door. Herman Chang stood and walked from behind his desk. 'Hi, Mike,' he said. His accent was South California. 'Who's this?'

Dunn introduced Howard.

'Delighted,' Chang said. His handshake was firm but his smile seemed forced. 'Sorry,' he said. He shook his head and waved a dismissive hand. 'Sorry,' he said again. 'I'm a bit distracted.' He lowered his voice. 'Washington.'

Dunn raised an eyebrow. 'Washington?'

Chang took a sheet of paper from his desk. Its letterhead bore the US Department of Justice crest. 'Priorities. Budgets,' he sighed. 'Asia's yesterday's problem. Central and South America are the new hot spots.' He rolled his eyes. 'Or so decrees some smart-assed college boy in the Department of Justice.' He dropped the paper onto his desk. 'They want our Japan office to scale down. First Japan; next, Hong Kong.' He shook his head. 'But that's not your problem. It's mine. Mine and Tokyo's.' He sucked in a breath then brightened. 'Not to worry,' he said. 'All we need is a good case. Just one. Do you know what? I'm guessing there'll be one real soon.' He draped his arm over Dunn's shoulder. 'C'mon. I promised you guys a celebration.'

Later, back in his office, Howard checked his 'correspondence in,' tray. It was empty save for a letter bearing Tokyo's Metropolitan Police crest. He sighed and laid it aside. He unlocked his file cabinet and pulled out the latest intelligence cover. He reread it, hoping the patron saint of narcotics officers would reveal something new. Nothing. The Bureau needed a case and needed it soon.

There is a saying: everything comes to those who wait. And so it was that a case did indeed come along. But when it did, there were some who wished it had not.

Mary Jai, Dick Williamson's secretary smiled up at Howard. 'You can go in,' she said.

'Ah, Mike. Come in, come in.' Williamson waved Howard to a chair. The office was not particularly large and the furnishings were simple but it had spectacular views over the harbor. 'I never tire of this view,' he said. 'How much do you think a private landlord would charge for an office with this view?'

Howard had no answer.

'More than my salary,' Williamson chuckled. 'More than ours combined, I think.' He shuffled through some papers. 'Ah, here it is.' He selected a sheet of paper, headed CONFIDENTIAL. Howard squinted at it, trying to read it upside down.

'SPOC — Syndicate Penetration Operations Committee,' Williamson said at last. 'They've come up with some information. Well, something and nothing really. Probably nothing.'

'Sounds interesting,' Howard answered, at a loss to say anything else.

'I've a job for you,' Williamson said, tapping the paper. 'Looks like something's happening in Kowloon Tong. According to this, it's a possible heroin refinery.' He stressed the word, *possible*. 'Fancy taking a look for me?'

Howard thought he had misheard. 'A refinery? Me?' His face clouded. 'I've only been here two months.'

Williamson waved away Howard's doubts. 'You have to start somewhere,' he said. 'Who's your sergeant?'

'Ben Lo,' Howard answered

'Ah yes of course,' Williamson said. 'Ben. Good man.' He leaned across the desk. 'I may as well come along. I'll make my own way and meet you there. Don't worry, it'll be your case. Or it will be if there's actually something there.'

Back in his office, Howard thought things through. Putting together a refinery case was a huge job. Police witnesses, experts, exhibits. It was like a three-dimensional jigsaw. It all had to slot together perfectly or the defense would shred it. Still, there were positives: Sergeant Ben Lo was a steady sort and Dick Williamson would be there to guide him. All Howard had to do was get into the target address and detain anyone he found. Then it was a matter of going through a check list of experts and operational support officers. God help him if he missed one. It was complex, but so long as he took things slow and steady, there was no reason to worry. Yes, slow and steady does it, he thought. It would be fine.

What could go wrong?

Immediately, it went wrong. Always eager for a bargain, the police had bought a fleet of bottom-of-the-range Ford Cortinas. They had an anonymous black paint job and because there was no air conditioning, detectives had to ride around with the windows open. It all screamed: *warning – cop car*. They had manual gearshifts mounted on the steering column, which flummoxed the Bureau's drivers. One driver, *Ah Boh*, solved the gearshift problem by driving everywhere in second gear, which did nothing for the Cortina's service life.

At nine that evening, Howard returned to Police Headquarters and met his team. The tough looking B Jai collected the Bureau's Ingress Facilitator System, namely a four-foot long crowbar and a massive sledge hammer.

There was only one car key left on the rack. Ben Lo grimaced. 'Number four car,' he groaned. *'Laap saap.'* – Rubbish.

Which it was. Howard slipped into the driver's seat and turned the ignition key. At the third attempt, the engine fired and started to clatter like a cement mixer. Howard wrestled the gear shift into first and they were off. Seconds later, the Cortina gave a cough and hiccupped to halt just short of the main gate. A wisp of blue-grey smoke curled from the beneath the hood.

Beyond the gate, there was the flash of a passing taxi. Sergeant Ben Lo sprinted after it shouting, *'Wei, dik si.'* – Hey, taxi. *'WEI!'* The taxi squealed to a halt. Ben and Howard clambered into the front seat, the constables jammed themselves into the back, trying to look inconspicuous with the crowbar and hammer.

The driver scowled when Ben told him they wanted to cross the harbor to Kowloon. *'Gwoh hoi yiu bei chin,'* he grumbled. – I have to pay to cross the harbor, *'Faan lai, joi bei chin.'* – And I've to pay to get back.

'Fong sam,' – Don't worry about it, Ben Lo told him.

The driver hunched over the wheel and spent the journey

muttering under his breath. A half-hour later, they pulled off the Waterloo Road expressway and into the tree-lined streets of Kowloon Tong. The driver stopped at the end of Fessenden Road and tapped the meter. *'Gwoh hoi. Doh yee saap man.'* — Crossing the harbor. Twenty dollars extra.

Howard counted out the money, the driver crunched the taxi into gear and was gone.

This was Kowloon Tong, a tranquil suburb of low-rise apartment blocks and stand-alone houses. Trees lined narrow avenues, lanes and crescents. This was home to bankers, lawyers, doctors and the occasional crook or two. At the peak of his stardom, Bruce Lee had lived less than a mile from where they now stood. Dick Williamson was waiting for them. He said his hellos then pointed to a gated complex. Inside the walls stood two apartment blocks, each eight stories high. Marble gate posts flanked the entrance to a cramped car park. The gate stood open.

'Merry Court,' Williamson said. 'Our target is block one, apartment eight-oh-two. It's on the top floor.'

Howard sent *Kwan Jai* to check for lookouts. He returned a few minutes later. *'Mo yeh'* — Nothing, he said.

'It's all yours,' Williamson said. 'Go get it.'

Kwan Jai stayed behind to watch for anything thrown from the windows. Howard, Sergeant Ben Lo, Tony and *B Jai* moved through the car park and into the lift lobby. The lift was in use. They waited, eyes fixed on the floor indicator. *Fourth floor, third, second, first, ground.* There was a muted chime and the doors slid open. A middle-aged couple gawked at them.

'Wei, Jo mat yeh loh chui?' — Hey, what's the hammer for? the woman demanded.

B Jai gave her a toothy smile. *'Jing din si.'* — Television repairs.

They boarded the lift and the doors slid shut. Their target was on the eighth floor so Howard pressed the button for the seventh. The lift reached the seventh floor and they found themselves in a neat lobby. Off to one side, a door led to a staircase. Inside the stairwell, the stairs were bare concrete and the lights were unshaded neon. Grime streaked walls that had once been white. The smell was of damp plaster and old dust. As they moved up the stairs, the hammer clattered against the wall. In the narrow stairwell, it sounded like a wrecking ball. They paused, watching, listening. Howard signaled them to move on. Now, he saw that each apartment had a rear door leading onto this staircase. *Damn!* He would have to place a guard in the stairwell. The plan was to use the hammer on the main door then storm in, loud and fast. A flurry of *what ifs*, washed over Howard. *What if* the door was barricaded? *What if* there were guards ready to put up a fight? With one constable downstairs and another on the staircase, the raiding party was down to just three men.

They stepped into the eighth floor lift lobby. There were two apartments. Which one? Eight-oh-one or eight-oh-two. Eight-oh-two. Yes, he was sure.

Maybe.

'*Ah Sir*, I knock the door now?' *B Jai* whispered.

'Sure. Go ahead.'

B Jai waved Howard aside and hefted the sledge hammer. The crash of iron against lock rang against the lobby walls. Something clattered against the floor on the other side of the door. Where there was once a lock, there was now a splintered hole. The door swung open. The three of them barreled into a spacious living room.

'*CHAI YAN!*' — POLICE!

The lights were on. They paused. There was a smell. It was like a hospital emergency room mixed in with a leaky gas main. It stuck in the nostrils and prickled the eyes.

'*YAU MO YAN AH?*' — ANYONE HERE?

Silence.

'*NGOH DEI SO DUK.*' — WE'RE THE DRUG SQUAD. '*CHUT LAI.*' — COME OUT.

Silence.

CHRIS EMMETT

They moved from room to room. Kitchen — no one. Bathroom — no one. A toilet door stood open — empty. Master bedroom — no one. They opened the last door and a chemical haze burned into Howard's throat. Tears filled his eyes. In the middle of the room stood a table. On it was a mishmash of glass and steel equipment. There were flasks, retorts and bottles. Some of them stood alone, others hung from spindly stands and clamps. Glass and rubber tubing connected them. A scummy liquid boiled in a bulbous flask. Underneath it, blue flame jetted from a Bunsen burner. Beneath the table, a gas cylinder fed the burner. Teetering on the table edge was a glass bottle containing a clear liquid. Against a wall, salt-like crystals spilled from a polythene bag. Next to it stood a plastic jerry can. A two-bar electric fire glowed in a corner. Howard reached under the table and found the gas cylinder's cut-off valve. He pointed to the electric fire. 'Switch that off,' he ordered.

Ben Lo shook his head. 'Better to leave it, sir,' he said. 'Lots of fumes. One spark and *boomph*.' With his hands, he made the shape of a growing mushroom cloud.

'Well, well.' Dick Williamson was standing in the doorway. 'Seems there's something after all.'

Howard grinned. 'My first heroin refinery,' he said.

Ben Lo frowned. 'Not heroin,' he said. 'I don't know what it is, but not heroin.'

'*Ah Sir.*' B Jai handed a collection of passports to Howard. 'These are in the living room.' There were six of them. They had maroon covers embossed in gold with a winged beast and the words THAI PASSPORT in English and Thai script. Howard thumbed through them. All bore different names but their photographs were of the same man. He was East Asian, possibly Thai or Chinese. He had a fleshy face and a comb-over hairstyle that failed to hide a receding hairline.

'Fake,' Howard snorted.

Ben Lo took one and tested the paper between his thumb and

forefinger. 'If they are fake, they are good ones,' he said. 'I will bag them up as exhibits.' He moved from room to room, opening the windows. 'I will tell Tony to call Kowloon Control from the watchman's station,' he said. 'They can send some uniforms to search the rooftop, stairwells and utility rooms.' He paused. 'Should he ask for forensic chemist to come?'

'Yes,' Howard answered. 'And Identification Bureau for photographs and fingerprints.'

Ten minutes later, Ben was back. 'All *gau dim*, sir.' — 'all fixed. 'Chemist and IB are on the way.'

Proper management of a crime scene is crucial. The scene is a hoard of hidden treasure but a moment's carelessness can render it useless. The case officer must keep a written log of all comings and goings. Who entered? When did they arrive? When did they leave? Did he or she take anything away? If yes, what? Later, police witness statements must match the crime scene log exactly. The trick is never to rush. Follow-up enquiries may take days, weeks or even years but the crime scene is here and it is now. It is a pristine snapshot in time. Once the detectives leave, the snapshot is gone. They may revisit the scene but never again will it be pristine. Detectives control the crime scene, but it belongs to the experts. There are experts who locate fingerprints, and scientific evidence experts can build the profile of a suspect from cigarette ends, bed sheets, hair brushes and all manner of day-to-day items. Those scratches on the door hasp: are they wear and tear or signs of a break-in? A ballistics expert can tell which is which. If detectives find a housebreaking tool, the same expert can match it to the damage.

The photographer and fingerprint specialist arrived but had to wait until the forensic chemist declared everything safe. The chemist was Ron Edgely, a down-to-earth veteran of narcotics investigations. He shuffled around the equipment table. 'A bloody bomb factory, this is,' he growled. 'Smelled it as soon as I came in. Ether and some kind of acid. It was on the boil, you say.'

'And there was an electric fire,' Howard answered.

Edgely shook his head. 'Good job you didn't touch any switches,' he growled. 'One spark and the whole lot would have gone up. It's a bloody, buggering bomb factory.' He pulled on a pair of latex gloves and knelt by the plastic bag that was leaning against the wall. He gave it a prod. '*Hmmm*. Crystalline,' he mused. 'Not morphine. Not heroin base.'

'Then what?' Howard asked.

'Can't be absolutely certain,' Edgely said. He stood and slapped dust from his trousers. 'It looks like ephedrine but I don't have a field test for that. Not much of it around.'

'Ephedrine?'

'I'll know better when I get it back to the lab. But that...' He nodded to the bag. 'I'm pretty sure is ephedrine. Starting point for amphetamine. Yes, if I were a gambling man, I'd put a week's pay on this being an amphetamine refinery.'

A school exercise book lay on the table. Edgely picked it up and thumbed through it. His eyebrows arched. 'Knew it!' he chortled. 'It's step-by-step instructions for making amphetamines.' He took another walk around the equipment table. A touch here, a sniff there. 'All cooled,' he said at last. 'Tell the scene of crime team they can start.'

The fingerprint man signed in and dusted the obvious places: door handles, cabinets, kitchen work surfaces. He dusted the exercise book and lifted several prints. The photographer had already started. Police photographers know how to walk a magistrate, judge or jury, through the crime scene. He had started at the car park entrance then moved on to the ground floor lobby, the eighth floor lift lobby, and the broken front door. He signed in and Howard walked him through the apartment: the lounge, the corridor leading to the bedrooms, the door to the impromptu laboratory. Finally, Edgely walked him around the equipment, directing which shots to take.

'Nearly there,' Edgely said. 'Bring in your exhibits officer and

HONG KONG POLICE: INSIDE THE LINES

I'll tell him what to seize. Chemicals and any equipment with residue must come to me.' He peeled off his gloves. 'Looks like the process was about two-thirds done. I doubt there's any finished product but there's plenty of evidence for a manufacturing charge.' He raised an eyebrow. 'All you have to do is find the bugger.' He turned and headed for the door. 'You've a busy night ahead,' he said over his shoulder and was gone.

And busy it was. Howard's team bagged the chemicals and took extra care to safeguard any liquids. They tagged each item of laboratory equipment. They went through the flat, seizing receipts, letters and documents. 'Boss,' Ben Lo called. He held out a collection of photographs. All were of the man in the passport photographs. There were pictures of him with friends and some who looked like family. There were pictures of him with three different women.

'He's a busy boy,' Howard quipped. 'Log them in and bag them.'

Dawn was a creeping grey light as they loaded the last of everything onto a police van. Back at headquarters, it all had to be checked into the Bureau's exhibits store. Later that morning, Howard had his first break. The apartment's management company came up with a tenancy agreement. The signatory was a Mister Peter Yau-leung Wong. When he leased the apartment, he had provided a copy of his Hong Kong identity card. The photograph on the ID card was the now familiar picture of a man with a fleshy face and a comb-over hairstyle. Howard put out a wanted notice to all regional control rooms and police stations. That done, there was urgent paperwork, notably the forms needed to accompany exhibits to the forensic laboratory. Lunchtime came and went. He had been awake for more than thirty hours.

'You look dreadful,' Mike Dunn chirped.

'Never felt better,' Howard groaned.

Dunn lowered his voice. 'Intelligence Wing reckons they have something on your boy but they're being coy.'

'They're always bloody coy,' Howard sniffed.

'No, no. Whatever it is, it's got them agitated,' Dunn said. 'They're in a real spin. Give it a day or two. We'll see what happens.'

Give it a day or two; why not? Howard checked his paperwork, he had done all the urgent stuff. He locked away the case file and headed home. He did not know it, but Peter Yau-leung Wong was already making ripples. Soon, those ripples would grow into a tidal surge.

And when that happened, some people would be in desperate need of lifejackets.

The Chinese have many wise sayings. In police work, one of them goes, 'If the boss is happy, you will be happy.' The other side of that coin is, 'If the boss is unhappy, you will be downright miserable.'

In overall command of the Narcotics Bureau was Chief Superintendent Jack Johnson, better known as 'Jolly Jack.' Two days after the raid, Howard received a summons from Johnson's office. The word was out: Jack was decidedly unjolly. Johnson's secretary greeted Howard and almost immediately, a light flashed on her intercom. 'You can go in,' she said in a half whisper.

Howard sucked in a breath and stepped into the office. Johnson was tall and slender, with a bald pate and a bulbous nose. He gestured to a chair and Howard sat, unsure what would come next.

'Give me a moment,' Johnson growled. Then, half to himself, 'They must think we're stupid.' He held up a hand in a gesture that signaled, *say nothing*. He picked up his phone and dialed. After a moment, someone answered. Johnson's voice was cracked glass. 'I'd like to speak to the special agent in charge please,' he said.

There was a pause.

'Yes, that's right, special agent Herman Chang.'
Another pause.
Johnson's eyes narrowed. 'Tell him he has two choices,' he snapped. 'Choice one, he can come to the phone. Choice two, he can explain to the Consul-General why my officers are executing a search warrant in the DEA office.'

A longer pause. Then, 'Ah, Herman, thank you for taking my call.' Johnson was silent for a moment as Chang returned a pleasantry or two. 'I need to you talk about a man called Peter Yau-leung Wong,' Johnson continued. He punched a button on the phone console and Herman Chang's voice crackled over the speaker.

'...doesn't ring any bells, Jack. What's your interest?'

'We want to speak to him about an amphetamines refinery.'

'Ah... that is... how can *we* help?'

'An amphetamines refinery in Fessenden Road, Kowloon Tong,' Johnson persisted.

On the other end of the line, Chang stifled a cough. 'Look Jack,' he said. 'I... er... don't want there to be any misunderstanding between us.'

'No misunderstanding, Herman, no misunderstanding at all. You know what you have to do. So do it.'

'I don't follow you, Jack.'

'I give you two hours, Herman. After that, it's between London and Washington.' Without waiting for an answer, Johnson slammed down the phone. He glared at Howard. 'Did you get that?'

'Yes sir,' Howard answered but to be frank, he did not get it at all.

'Good,' Johnson said. 'That's all for now.'

Howard stepped into the anteroom where Williamson was waiting to go in.

'Ah, Mike,' Williamson said. He seemed as cheerful as ever. 'Can I take it the boss has spoken to you?'

'Not really,' Howard answered. 'What the hell's going on?'
Williamson flashed a wolfish grin. 'What indeed?' he said. 'Don't worry. Soon, all will be clear.'
'Mister Williamson, you can go in now.'
Williamson stepped towards the door but paused and turned to Howard. 'Soon,' he said. 'Very soon.'

Indeed, the order came very soon. Howard was to get himself down to the DEA office where Herman Chang would deliver to him one Peter Yau-leung Wong. Howard was to arrest Wong for the offense of manufacturing a dangerous drug, namely amphetamines.
'Get him back here,' Johnson ordered. 'Then take a statement from him immediately. *Immediately.* Understood?'
'Understood,' Howard answered.
Fifteen minutes later, a stone-faced Buzz Ziegler showed Howard into Herman Chang's office. Chang sat behind his desk, his face expressionless. Lounging in a chair facing him was another man. He had a fleshy face and a comb-over hairstyle. He stood at Howard's approach and extended his hand. His lips curved in a smile. 'Peter Wong,' he said. 'I'm sure we can work this out.' He was doing his best to speak with an American accent but beneath the West Coast drawl, was the voice of a streetwise Hong Konger. He extended his hand but when Howard refused to take it, he shrugged and turned to Herman Chang. 'Seems this guy's in the dark,' he said. 'Does he know?'
Chang said nothing.
'Peter Yau-leung Wong?' Howard asked.
'That's me.' Peter Wong spoke as though Howard was offering an invitation for tea and biscuits.
'Peter Yau-leung Wong,' Howard said. 'You are under arrest for manufacturing a dangerous drug, namely amphetamines.'
Wong rolled his eyes as if he were on the receiving end of a prank.

'You are not obliged to say anything,' Howard said. He moved behind Wong and handcuffed him. 'But anything you do say will be taken down in writing and may be given in evidence.'

'Yeah, yeah. Whatever,' Wong said. 'See you later, chief,' he called to Herman Chang as Howard hustled him from the room.

Back at his office, Howard sat Wong down and removed the handcuffs.

Wong massaged his wrists. 'So, when do I get out?' he asked.

Howard rummaged around in a desk drawer and found a blank statement form. 'Name. Age, Address.' He demanded.

Wong leaned forward and rested his forearms on the desk. 'Look,' he said. 'Let's stop playing games. This case is not going to court.'

'Name. Age. Address,' Howard said again.

Wong leaned back and looked at the ceiling. 'Peter Wong,' he sighed. 'Chinese name, Wong Yau-leung. Thirty-seven years old. Address? Fessenden Road, if you like.'

Howard filled in the statement form's personal details section. He looked at his watch, wrote the time and date then put his own name under the 'Statement taken by' section. In the main body of the statement, he wrote:

'I am Peter Yau-leung Wong. I wish to make a statement. I have been told that I am not obliged to say anything unless I wish to do so. Anything I do say will be taken down in writing and may be given in evidence.'

He passed the statement to Wong and tapped the preamble. 'Read that.'

Wong bent over the statement then sat back. 'Okay. It's read.'

'Do you understand it?'

'Yeah.'

Howard handed Wong his pen. 'Are you willing to sign it?' he asked.

'Sure, why not?' Wong signed the preamble. 'Can I go now?' he asked.

'Let's talk,' Howard said. 'Better still, you talk; I'll write.'

And talk he did. Peter Wong was what the DEA called a *cooperating individual*, which meant he was a paid informant. 'How much does the Hong Kong Police pay you?' he asked.

Howard told him.

'You're with the wrong outfit,' Wong said.

Wong talked and talked. The more he talked, the more his confidence grew. He was like the drunk at the end of the bar, eager to impress with his knowledge and importance. 'They send me all over Asia,' he said. 'That's why I need the passports.'

'You agree the fake passports are yours?' Howard asked.

'Fake? *Fake?*' Wong scoffed. 'The United States Drug Enforcement Administration does not fuck about with fakes.' He glanced over his shoulder then lowered his voice. 'The DEA's Bangkok office had a word with the folks in Thai immigration and *hey presto...*'

'The setup in Fessenden Road was impressive,' Howard said. 'I'm guessing you've done this before.'

Wong shook his head. '*Nah,*' he groaned 'It was my first try at *whizz.*' He gave a humorless chuckle. 'They told me what to buy then helped me set everything up. They talked me through the business. *Jeez!* I'm no scientist. It took all day. Even then, I had to write it down.'

'They?' Howard asked.

Wong looked at Howard as though he were a dullard pupil struggling with a lesson. 'Yes,' he said. '*They. Them. Those people.* The DEA.'

Howard read through the statement. 'That will do,' he said. At the end of the statement, he wrote:

'I have read the above statement and it is true to the best of my knowledge and belief. I have been told I can add, alter or correct anything I wish.'

Howard read the passage over to Wong. 'Do you understand?' he asked.

'Yeah, yeah. All clear,' Wong said.

Howard slid the statement across his desk. Wong read then signed it. 'So, have you got it yet?' Wong asked. He paused, waiting for an answer. When none came he spread his arms and looked around the room as though he were addressing an audience. 'You can't charge me.' he said. 'You can't. If this goes to court, I'll blow the game wide open. Our friends in the consulate won't like that. No *sir*. They won't like it at all.'

He's right, Howard thought. The consulate would not like it; Washington would like it even less. But that was not Howard's problem. The problem belonged to the people in the anonymous office suite in St John's Building. He picked up the phone and told Sergeant Ben Lo to bring the Bureau's camera and fingerprint pad. As soon as Ben Lo arrived, Howard went to the registry office and collected a formal charge sheet. He paused at the door then went back for some spare copies.

After all, typing was not his strong suit.

The day after his arrest, a stunned-looking Peter Yau-leung Wong stood in the dock of Central Magistracy's number one court, His Worship Mister Paul Corfe presiding. The courtroom was the picture of colonial dignity. Wood paneling covered the walls and the magistrate presided from a leather-bound chair set upon an elevated bench. On the wall behind him was Hong Kong's colonial crest. At the prosecutor's table, Mike Howard checked his papers. His Worship peered at Howard over the rim of his spectacles. 'Is the prosecution ready?' he asked.

Howard stood. 'Detective Inspector Michael Howard of the Police Narcotics Bureau, Your Worship.'

Corfe held a fountain pen, poised to take notes. 'And what may I do for you this morning, Inspector?'

'We ask for a week's remand in police custody, sir.' Howard made to sit down.

'Not so fast, young man,' Corfe said. 'Why should I remand

him in *police* custody? Indeed, why should I not release him on bail?'

'I... this is a serious offence, sir. There are a large number of exhibits, all requiring forensic examination. The defendant is a flight risk and may have access to falsely issued travel documents.' Howard paused. 'And...'

'*And*, Inspector?

Howard took a breath. 'And we believe the defendant was working with others.'

Corfe bent over his legal pad, made his notes then sat back. 'Thank you, Inspector. You have made yourself most clear.' He turned to Wong. 'Mister...' He glanced down at the charge sheet. '...Mister Peter Yau-leung Wong?'

Wong stood and smoothed down his hair. 'Yes,' he mumbled. He squared his shoulders and spoke more forcefully. 'That is, yes, Your Honor.'

'The police want to keep you in their cells for a week. Do you have anything to say about that?'

'I do,' Wong said. 'You need to know, sir that I work for the United States Drug Enforcement Administration.'

Paul Corfe blinked, then bent over his legal pad and made a careful note. He put down his pen and inclined his head towards Howard. 'That is something of a development, Inspector,' he said. 'You may wish to contact the United States Consulate.' To Wong he said. 'Your relationship with foreign powers means nothing to this court. You will remain in police custody for seven days.' He beamed at his court clerk. 'Next case, please.'

Later that day, Jack Johnson called the US Consulate. Rumor has it that his language was not overly consular. It was a glum-looking special agent Herman Chang who arrived at Johnson's office. Waiting for him was Dick Williamson. Williamson had with him a wad of police statement forms. To save time, he had already filled in Chang's personal details. At the top of the first page, he had written a brief preamble that ended with the words:

'.. I have been told that I am not obliged to say anything unless I wish to do so. Anything I do say will be taken down in writing and may be given in evidence.'

Williamson led Chang into Jack Johnson's office and closed the door.

Howard could only wait, but he was sure orders would soon come to prepare a fresh charge. A fresh charge that would name Peter Wong and one other. In a spare moment he drafted it out:

'You, Peter Yau-leung Wong, together with _____ did manufacture a dangerous drug, namely amphetamines, in Flat 802, Merry Court, Fessenden Road, Kowloon, Hong Kong. Contrary to Section 6 (1)(a) of the Dangerous Drugs Ordinance. Chapter 134 Laws of Hong Kong.'

He left the co-defendant's name blank, although he knew exactly who it would be.

A day passed. No orders.

Howard called the confidential registry and told the clerk the case reference number. 'Has Mister Johnson finished with the file?' he asked.

'Wait one,' the clerk answered and the line went quiet. After a while, the clerk was back. 'The file's not here,' she said. 'It's with Mister Stewart.'

'Oh. I see. Thanks.' Howard put the phone back onto its cradle. Assistant Commissioner Bertrand T Stewart. The DCI: the Director of Criminal Investigation, Hong Kong's most senior detective. Of course, it made perfect sense. With something so sensitive, the DCI had to see the file. It had probably gone all the way up to the Police Commissioner, maybe even higher.

The telephone rang, breaking Howard's thoughts. A musical voice sounded through the earpiece.

'Mister Howard, this is Mister Stewart's secretary. Would you please come up to his office?' There was a pause. 'Mister Stewart would like to see you immediately.'

Howard took the elevator up to the nineteenth floor. *This is it,* he thought. *These are the orders.*

The secretary smiled up at Howard. 'He says you're to go straight in,' she said.

Howard tapped on the door then went in. The office was large. On the wall behind the desk was a map of the colony. Covering the other walls were plaques and certificates. There were photographs of Stewart at conferences and police gatherings around the world. There were photographs of him receiving awards: the Colonial Police Medal, the Queen's Police Medal, the Governor's commendation. The man himself was hunched over his desk, writing a note on a file's minute sheet. He glanced up at Howard and used his pen to point to a chair. He signed the note, closed the file and dropped it into his 'out' basket. He lay down his pen, pinched the bridge of his nose then leaned back.

'Well, my lad,' he said. 'Seems you've kicked over a hornets' nest.'

Howard cleared his throat then sat in silence.

Stewart reached into his 'in' basket and pulled out another file. 'I'm sure you know what this is,' he said, laying it on the desk. 'I've been on the phone all morning. I've spoken to a lot of people, all of them a darn sight more senior than me.' He tapped the file with his forefinger. 'This is a good case you've got yourself,' he said. 'But it's given the Commissioner a headache, His Excellency the Governor a headache and no doubt, there's a headache or two in Washington D.C.'

'They brought it on themselves, sir,' Howard said. 'The boss has taken a cautioned statement from Herman Chang. I can have the charge sheets ready in...'

'There will be no charge sheet,' Stewart said. 'At least not for Herman Chang.'

HONG KONG POLICE: INSIDE THE LINES

'Sir?'

Steward leaned forward and his eyes bored into Howard's. 'I said, you will be laying no charges against Herman Chang,' he said.

Howard reached across the desk as if to retrieve the file. 'Herman Chang's clearly implicated,' he said. 'There's enough evidence. There's even a statement under caution...'

'There *was* a statement under caution,' Stewart answered. 'That statement is now with me and that is where it stays.' His voice softened. 'Tokyo's been leaning hard on the DEA, so our Herman Chang had it all planned out. Regular shipments to Japan; regular tip offs to the Tokyo police. Well, he outsmarted himself. Last night, Herman Chang boarded a flight back home.' Stewart looked at his wristwatch. 'About now, he's crossing the California coast.' He allowed himself a smile. 'No doubt he's feeling quite sorry for himself.' The smile dropped away. 'No one's happy with this, but it's official: there is no Herman Chang, at least not as far as this case is concerned. ' His words became precise and deliberate. '*And there is no DEA involvement.*' He pushed the file back towards Howard. 'You've done well,' he said. 'There's your case. Now get on with it.'

Howard felt numb. For a moment, he considered arguing the case, but Bertrand T. Stewart was not one to pick a fight with. Howard collected the file and headed back to his office.

Let us be frank, drugs raids are a buzz. But after the buzz, comes the drudgery of the paperwork.

The first bit of paper to arrive was the forensic chemist's report. It showed that Howard had seized seven pounds of ephedrine, six pounds of perchloric acid and a lot of other chemicals. It was enough to make fifty-one pounds of amphetamine, which, when you think about it, is a shedload of *whizz*. To put it in money terms, the wholesale price was about US$2 million. By the time it hit the Tokyo streets, the value would have gone up to US$30 million. The glass retorts, flasks, funnels and tubing all had traces of either the base chemicals or the finished product. No question, the apartment was an amphetamines refinery.

The rest of the paperwork came in. It was Peter Yau-leung Wong's signature on the apartment's tenancy agreement. His fingerprints were on the laboratory equipment and on the notebook detailing the refining process. The refining instructions were in Wong's handwriting. There were credit card receipts for the equipment and chemicals. The cards belonged to Peter Yau-leung Wong. It all amounted to a man who was either not very bright or who was supremely confident in his untouchability.

Howard put the reports in the case file, wrote up his covering report and sent everything off for legal advice. The advice was a formality, Peter Wong's future looked none too rosy.

The case went to trial the following March. Wong's defense was a triumph of imagination over credibility. He claimed that a friend by the name of Tommy Chan was researching cures for cancer, rheumatism, arthritis and asthma. At a crucial moment in his research, Tommy had run out of funds. His landlord evicted him and his credit dried up. To help out, Peter Wong used his credit card to buy all the chemicals and equipment that Tommy said he needed. With Tommy's laboratory shut down, Peter Wong let him use a room in the Fessenden Road apartment. Peter Wong had been crushed to learn that his friend Tommy was a narcotics chemist and not a research scientist. To strengthen his *bone fides*, Wong repeated his claim that he was a DEA agent. He was wasting his breath. No one from the DEA came forward to support him.

The jury did not buy it. It took next to no time to reach a unanimous verdict: guilty. The judge was in a quandary. Manufacturing narcotics carried a maximum penalty of life imprisonment, but amphetamines had been on the narcotics schedule for only a short time. Had Wong appeared in court just ten months earlier, he would have got away with a fine. His Lordship announced a short adjournment and retreated to his chambers. Having given the matter some thought, he returned and delivered his sentence; three years in prison.

From the look on Peter Wong's face, he was finding it hard not to dance a jig around the dock.

A few weeks after the raid, an invitation arrived. The DEA's Hong Kong station had a new boss, which was as good a reason as any for a party. Howard went along and judging from the *bonhomie*, you could have thought there had never been a problem. When the time seemed right, he asked about Herman Chang.

'Last I heard, he was searching rust buckets on the Mexican Border,' came the answer. Those were the last words ever spoken about Herman Chang.

Well, almost the last. I made a Freedom of Information request to the DEA Headquarters in Springfield, Virginia. I asked the Agency about Special Agent Herman Chang's involvement in the Fessenden Road amphetamine case. The DEA's reply was prompt but not too helpful:

> '...we have decided to neither confirm nor deny the existence of such records...This should not be taken to mean that records do or do not exist...'

And that, as they say, was that.

In the coming years, Mike Howard arrested Peter Yau-leung Wong three times. At one point, Wong took out a contract to have Howard murdered. Wong's career came to a crashing *finale* during one of Howard's combined operations with Australia's Joint Task Force. Howard gave evidence against Wong in Australia's High Court. The verdict was guilty; the sentence was sixty-four years.

Mike Howard worked in the Narcotics Bureau for another twelve years. During his thirty-four year police career, he moved up the promotion ladder, finally retiring with the rank of detective superintendent. Now, he works with an international bank and travels the world, investigating fraud, money laundering, terrorist financing, human trafficking, and many other financial crimes.

But he never learned who it was that shut down his investigation into the DEA's very own amphetamine refinery.

HONG KONG POLICE: INSIDE THE LINES

PART 2
MUTINY (OR NOT)

HONG KONG POLICE: INSIDE THE LINES

CHAPTER 3
MUTINY (OR NOT)

THE NEWSPAPERS said it was a police mutiny. A television station ran an editorial condemning the police mutiny. So, who can blame the public for believing it? After all, Police Commissioner Brian Slevin, did not deny it, and neither did Hong Kong's Governor, Sir Murray MacLehose. Even today, there is always someone ready to mention the 1977 police mutiny. But let me tell you right now, there was no mutiny.

I know because I was there.

Back then, people said the Royal Hong Kong Police was the finest police force money could buy. It was hurtful but to be honest, we brought it on ourselves. Police corruption had been a problem since the 1840s. By the 1960s, some police divisions worked like criminal corporations. At the heart of police corruption, was a senior non-commissioned officer, normally a staff sergeant. There were two grades: the most senior was the staff sergeant class 1 and after that came the staff sergeant class 2. Officially, their job was to be a communication bridge between the junior and senior ranks. Police divisions like Wanchai, Sham Shui Po, Mong Kok and all the rest, each had two class 2 staff sergeants. One served in uniform, the other was a detective. Further up the chain, in the Regional Headquarters of Kowloon, Hong Kong Island, New Territories and Marine, were the class 1 staff sergeants.

Uniformed staff sergeants wore a crimson sash draped from

HONG KONG POLICE: INSIDE THE LINES

right shoulder to left hip. In their starched uniforms and gleaming leatherwork, they looked magnificent. Their rank insignia was a silver crown worn on the sleeve. It was like the insignia worn by army sergeant majors. In everyday police jargon, the staff sergeant was, 'The Major.'

Magnificent as they were, the real power lay with the detective staff sergeants, the legendary, 'D Majors.' Chief among them was Class 1 Detective Staff Sergeant Lui Lok. He was one of five staff sergeants dubbed, 'The Five Dragons,' who coordinated corruption within their police regions. Some say that when he retired in 1968, Lui Lok was worth a cool HK$500 million, then worth more than US$80 million.

Every week, the divisional class 2 staff sergeant sent a junior sergeant to do the rounds of the brothels, massage parlors, gambling dens, opium divans, blue movie theaters, unlicensed taxi operators and anything else the police felt they could lean on. The sergeant-cum-bagman collected squeeze money from them and distributed it throughout the division. The constables got the smallest share and the superintendent running the station supposedly got the biggest. I use the word, *supposedly* because everyone knew it was the staff sergeant who was the big winner. To keep the statistics healthy, operators paying squeeze money took turns to receive prearranged raids, better known as, *'jo hei.'* — a theatrical act. There were arrests and even cash seized. Then, with an alacrity that would have done a DHL courier proud, someone fronted up with the bail money. The next day everyone went to court, pleaded guilty and the person who had paid the bail, turned up to pay the fines.

Corrupt police always found ways to excuse themselves. We are in control, they would say, the criminals know who the boss is, we make sure things don't get out of hand. And there was some truth in that. Corrupt police did indeed keep a handle on things. Even in corrupt divisions, there was no profusion of vice and gambling, and major crimes were rare. When serious crime did happen, the staff sergeant's underworld contacts saw the offenders locked up in no time. It was an upside-down logic that suggested corruption actually benefitted society. With a kind of contrived morality, corrupt divisions did not tolerate anyone going freelance. So, where brothels and illegal casinos operated openly, it was darn near impossible to fix even a parking ticket.

I make it sound far worse that it was. Not every division was corrupt and inside corrupt divisions, not every officer was on the staff sergeant's payroll. In the parlance of the day, it was like a bus. You could get on the bus and ride in comfort. You could stay off the bus and get hot and sweaty running alongside. However, it was a really, really bad idea to stand in front of the bus.

The police also had no monopoly on corruption. Want to jump the queue for public housing? No problem, you could always find a helpful housing officer. Applying for a restaurant license? A few hundred dollars would get you a hygiene certificate. Everyone joked that the Fire Services wanted cash before turning their hoses on and even more cash before turning them off. Driving licenses, building permits, liquor licenses, all came at a price. Everyone knew what was going on, it was just part of day-to-day life. Hong Kong in the early 1970s was a city rooted in cynicism.

Trying hard to fight it was the Police Anti Corruption Branch. The Branch had doorstep-thick files on police and civil service corruption. They were desperate to make cases but they were up against a culture of the satisfied customer. So long as payments received and services given met expectations, witnesses were in short supply. Another problem was that both bribe giver and bribe taker committed an offense. For the Anti Corruption Branch to bring a case, one party to the bribe needed immunity from prosecution. This made for what the courts called *tainted witnesses*. Tainted witnesses had an agenda, namely to save their own skins. Without clear and separate evidence supporting their testimony, tainted witnesses were next to useless.

Then it all changed. On May 14, 1971, Hong Kong introduced the Prevention of Bribery Ordinance. Along with accepting illegal payments, it became a criminal offense for government servants to own unexplained wealth or enjoy a lifestyle not in keeping with their salaries. There was no need to prove the wealth or lifestyle came from corruption. Instead, it was for the defense to prove it did not. Crucially, the ordinance did away with the idea that witnesses who were party to a bribe were tainted.

This posed a problem. Juries are notorious for putting fair dealings ahead of legal niceties. How would they react to witnesses who were clearly looking out for themselves? Government law officers had the answer. The Prevention of Bribery Ordinance was a perfect fit for Hong Kong's District Courts. The District Court was a uniquely colonial institution where a judge, sitting without a jury, can impose prison sentences of up to seven years. Where juries might sideline legal complexities, a judge cannot. If the law tells his honor to accept the unsupported evidence of a tainted accomplice, that is what he must do.

Unsupported accomplice witnesses and the burden of proof shifted onto the defense. It sounds harsh but the scale of the problem called for drastic measures. In cynical Hong Kong, many thought it just a show. After all, corruption was as much a part of Hong Kong as late night shopping and summer storms. But even in Hong Kong, there are times when the shops close early and the summer skies stay blue.

At first, it seemed nothing had changed. There were no dawn raids and the District Court benches did not groan under the weight of an increased caseload. That is not to say the Anti Corruption Branch was idle. They dusted off their files and looked afresh at their targets. There were plenty to choose from but one in particular took their eye.

Chief Superintendent Peter Fitzroy Godber was the force darling. Revered by many, feared by some, he was a hardcore working copper. Off duty, he was humorous and lively. In 1973, he was nearing retirement but as second in command of the tough Kowloon police region, he was a happy senior officer. Hong Kong's Kai Tak airport was in Kowloon and Godber held an airport security pass allowing him access to all restricted areas. It was a nice little perk, particularly when meeting friends arriving from overseas.

Just a few months before leaving the force, Godber received transfer orders. He moved to Police Headquarters to coordinate the latest fight crime campaign. The new job was no real challenge and it gave Godber plenty of spare time to manage the odds and ends involved in winding down to retirement. On June 4, just a few weeks before his retirement, he entered the Deputy Commissioner's office to attend a routine meeting. His colleagues were grim-faced but so what? There was always some crisis or other. In that, he was right. The Deputy Commissioner handed Godber a written notice. As he read it, Godber's heart raced and for a moment, he could not catch his breath. He slumped into a chair and gawked at the Deputy Commissioner. The Deputy glared back. The notice came from the Anti Corruption Branch and it listed overseas bank accounts, all traced back to Peter Fitzroy Godber. The accounts held more money than Godber had earned in his whole career. He had twenty-eight days to explain where it had come from.

In Godber's car, anti corruption officers found lists of brothels and illicit casinos. At his home were documents pointing to more wealth. Tucked away in the kitchen freezer was a bundle of cash totaling HK$400,000. It was double the amount that Godber earned in a year. The Police Commissioner immediately suspended him from duty. Until they could formally arrest Godber, the Anti Corruption Branch had no legal power to seize his passport. Instead, they placed him on the Immigration Department's stop list. Any attempt to leave Hong Kong would mean instant arrest. It was a textbook operation. Well, almost. The anti corruption detectives had made one mistake. It was

HONG KONG POLICE: INSIDE THE LINES

only a small mistake but as it turned out, its effect was seismic. They forgot to seize Godber's airport security pass. In his new post, Godber did not need a pass. He should have handed it in when he left Kowloon but he did not.

Four days after receiving the unexplained wealth notice, Godber paid cash for a first class, airline ticket to the UK via Singapore. He went straight to the airport, checked in his luggage, then clipped the security pass to his shirt. He calmly bypassed the immigration checks, boarded his flight, accepted a complimentary glass of Champagne, and was on his way home.

Back in Hong Kong, a community made cynical by decades of open corruption, looked on in dismay. There could be only one explanation: the Royal Hong Kong Police had let Godber go.

Governor MacLehose's reaction was immediate. There would be a new anticorruption body, one that was independent of the police. He commissioned the very able Jack Cater, to take charge. Just eight months after Godber's flight, Hong Kong's Independent Commission Against Corruption brought its first case. Hoping to dodge a traffic ticket, a driving instructor had offered a small bribe to a police constable. The constable reported it to the ICAC and an astonished driving instructor found himself in the dock.

To ordinary police officers, the new anticorruption body was a bit of a joke. Shortly after I took over the Hong Kong Island drug squad, the ICAC arrested my predecessor. My mates teased me mercilessly.

'They'll have a file on you,' they quipped.
'I hope the photo's nice,' I fired back.
'Check your office for microphones.'
'No need, I found plenty at home.'

While we joked, Jack Cater built his ICAC from the inside out. The first recruiting drive drew more than eight thousand applicants. In the United Kingdom, advertisements appeared in the Police Federation magazine, inviting experienced detectives to join Hong Kong's ICAC. Before long, the jokes turned sour.

Investigators targeted the corrupt sergeants-cum- money collectors. In exchange for immunity, they turned against their corrupt colleagues. *Tainted witness*, defense counsels cried, but District Court Judges brushed the concerns aside. The lawyers demanded jury trials but the courts would have none of it.

The ICAC was cleaning things up. Corrupt police syndicates shut up shop. The *jo hei* raids stopped. Unlicensed taxi drivers stuck to known customers. Illegal casinos laid on extra watchmen to warn of police activity. Vice outlets became wary of new clients.

Most police officers accepted the need for change but what happened next was hard to take. It started with a piece of routine administration. Every month, the Government Treasury pays police salaries into officers' bank accounts. The Treasury then sends each officer a slip showing his or her basic salary, plus any special allowances and minus any deductions. There is nothing secret about police pay and so the slips do not come in personalized envelopes. Instead, they come into the police unit's central mailroom and the clerks pass them on to the individual officers. In one station, a sharp-eyed clerk noticed that some new constables received a special allowance. A quick check of ICAC's employment terms revealed that the allowance topped up the constables' salary to ICAC pay levels. Then, in Police Headquarters, an inspector fresh out of basic training, dropped his warrant card. The reception desk constable retrieved it and hurried after him. The constable noticed that the card did not bear the police crest. As the inspector snatched it from him, the constable caught a glance of the Chinese characters, 廉政...He had seen them before. They were part of the title, 廉政公署, a stylistic form projecting honest and unselfish public office. It was the Chinese name for the Independent Commission Against Corruption.

In canteens and officers' messes; in briefing rooms and firearm loading bays, officers asked, 'Who's watching? Who's listening? Is it him? Is it you?' That *click* on the phone, was it a bad line or something else? That man in the cinema queue, did I see him yesterday at the supermarket? Was it him at the taxi rank?

To the general public, it seemed that the ICAC had a bottomless source of new cases but in fact, they were marching back in time. Current cases gave way to cases that were years old. Then ten years old, then they were even older. The number of serious cases was fewer; the number of minor cases increased. And where were the building inspectors, the public health officials, the driving examiners and the rest to balance off the police who were being named? More police officers appeared before the District Court. More tainted witnesses gave evidence. A climate of fear crept through the police force. Would these witnesses offer up the innocent with the guilty just to settle old scores?

In street markets, restaurants and bars, off-duty officers pretended not to hear the sneering asides. Wives and girlfriends learned to do the same. School bullies made life miserable for police officers' children. There were the rumors: police officers left for hours in frigid ICAC cells; a senior ICAC investigator handy with his fists. The press picked up on the mood. The headlines read, 'POLICE MORALE AT ALL TIME LOW.'

Police officers are a stoic lot. Every day, they put on their uniforms and get on with the job. They would have put up with the sarcastic comments and the bad press but there was one thing that pushed them over the edge. That was the way senior management dealt with the problem. Or to be more accurate, did not deal with it.

In those days, the Hong Kong Police had a paramilitary culture. Inspectors and above were officers; sergeants and constables were the rank-and-file. No staff association spoke for the lower ranks. They had no say in pay negotiations, working conditions or welfare. Grievances had to go through the chain of command. Of course, no commander would admit his unit had a morale problem. It was a system that quarantined the Police

Commissioner from bad news. From Commissioner Slevin's office in Caine House, everything looked fine. As the press continued to report poor police morale, Assistant Commissioner Paul Grace appeared on television. Morale has never been higher, he declared. Talk of poor morale came from a few malcontents who were just, 'whining in their beer...'

While Slevin was congratulating Paul Grace for a job well done, a group of rank-and-file officers met at Wong Tai Sin Police Married Quarters. They came up with a nine-point petition that included an end to what they saw as ICAC oppression and, more importantly, formal recognition for a rank-and-file staff association. They phoned a few likeminded colleagues and invited them to meet the following evening at the Police Sports and Recreation Club. The idea was to bounce around a few ideas and come up with a way to put things to the Commissioner.

In a force where down-up communication barely existed, it was astonishing how quickly messages moved when travelling sideways. The following evening, so many police officers turned up, the club bar could not hold them. By the time a function room had been opened up, numbers had swelled even more. Finally, everyone moved onto the sports field. Estimates put their numbers in the thousands. Among the constables and sergeants were dozens of inspectors, both Chinese and British. The press arrived. Camera flashes popped. Television crews set their sights on an impromptu speakers' platform. As a speaker read out each of the nine demands, there were roars of approval. But how would they make the Commissioner listen? They had no voice.

The next day, four thousand police officers turned up in the plaza in front of City Hall. They were part of a police force that numbered 17,500. The officers formed into groups of about two hundred, then marched to Police Headquarters. The plan was to talk to the Commissioner, but they did not know if he would see them. If he refused, then what? There was no plan B.

I was in my office when I heard them. A roar that would have rivaled an England goal at Wembley. My officemate sat upright. 'My God, what was that?'

We moved to the window.

'*Jesus.* There are thousands of them,' my officemate said.

The compound was filling up as more and more people streamed through the Arsenal Street gate. All were in plain clothes but the uniform officers were distinct with their short hair.

The office door opened and another colleague poked his head around the jamb. 'Word from Jack Johnson,' he said. 'Anyone who wants to join them, can go.'

The elevator lobby was packed. The elevator doors *pinged* open but there was no room for anyone to board. The stairwell was not so crowded but progress was slow. Outside, the compound was a mass of people. There was no shouting, no chanting, no raised fists, just a rumble of anticipation. The press filled the steps leading to the Caine House lobby.

A loudhailer squealed. A middle-aged detective addressed the crowd, his voice scratchy. I strained to hear but could not catch all he said.

'He says Commissioner has agreed to meet them,' a voice behind me translated.

Five, long-serving sergeants climbed the steps and disappeared into Caine House.

We waited.

It was Friday and the following day would be the weekly meet at Happy Valley racecourse. Around the compound, people unfurled newspapers and checked the pundits' tips. An hour later, the delegation nudged the press aside. The loudhailer squealed again. '*Gok wai tung si.*' – Colleagues. 'CP *paai jun ngoh dei ging chat dui yun jo kap hip wooi.*' – The CP has recognized our Junior Police Officers' Association.'

A great roar drowned out the rest of his words. People raised their arms and applauded. There were cheers, smiles, laughter. A stranger pumped my hand. The delegation leader raised a hand for silence. *'Gok wai, teng jue.'* — Everyone, listen. As he spoke, his voice cracked. With each pause, there were more cheers.

'My God,' my translator gasped. 'This... this changes everything.'

One hundred and thirty years of military style staff relations were gone. There would be no more rank-and-file. From now on, constables and sergeants would be junior police officers. A properly constituted association would speak for them on matters of pay, service conditions and welfare. Concerning the other demands, the Commissioner promised to look into them and make a statement later. The loudhailer fell silent. Singly and in groups, everyone left. There was no formal end to the gathering, it just faded away. Within half an hour, the compound was empty. It should have been a perfect day but as the saying goes: when something looks perfect, some prat will come along and screw it all up.

We wandered back to the Narcotics Bureau on a cloud of good will. At lunchtime, it seemed the whole Bureau wanted to watch the midday news on the hotline room's blurry television set. We cheered as the voiceover reported the formation of the new police association. The camera showed everyone leaving the compound, laughing and chatting. The announcers' voice became somber. As the gathering at Police Headquarters ended, dozens of officers had broken away from the main group and gone to the ICAC offices in Hutchinson House. There were shots of a crowded lift lobby, raised fists and shouting. The camera shook, the picture tilting at crazy angles. It focused on a broken ICAC signboard. There was a jagged crack in a glass pane. Someone kicked out at an ICAC officer. A hand grabbed the necktie of another.

Behind me a voice gasped, *'Wah! Jo mat yeh ah?'* — Wah! What are they doing? Another voice, angry this time. *'Chi lan sin.'* — Fucking crazy. Their voices filled the room, questioning, cursing, disbelieving, angry.

That evening, television news broadcast the scenes over and over. An ATV newsroom manager read out an editorial. It condemned what it described as violent demands to curb the ICAC's fight against corruption.

The next day, newspaper headlines bellowed, 'POLICE MUTINY!' Relegated to the inside pages was the story of a young Kowloon City constable, shot in the stomach during an armed robbery. Governor MacLehose called a meeting with the Police Commissioner, the Commander of British Armed Forces, the Attorney General and heads of key departments. They bunkered themselves in the Central Government Offices and set about hammering out a solution. There was no shortage of questions, but because nobody had a clue what had happened, there was little by way of answers. While the police carried on their duties as normal, MacLehose and his advisers talked of sending troops onto the streets to maintain law and order. No one thought to speak to the police staff bodies, particularly the newly-convened Junior Police Officers Association.

A week later, Governor MacLehose announced his decision. It was Saturday and I had not kept an eye on the news. That evening, I was at my usual place in the Hermitage bar's police corner when one of the regulars strode in waving a copy of the South China Morning Post. 'Amnesty!' he declared. 'I can't believe it. Bloody amnesty!' He laid the newspaper on the bar top and we crowded around it, jostling for a better look.

Of course, he had not got it completely right. There was an amnesty alright, but it was conditional: no amnesty for serious corruption cases, no amnesty for suspects who fled overseas, no amnesty for suspects who had been interviewed as part of an ongoing investigation. We read it again. The bar was silent then someone half-whispered, *'Fuck me.'*

And that was it. There was no jubilation, no sense of victory. It grew on me slowly. There would be no more listening for that unusual *click* on the telephone. No more wondering why my old sergeant had invited me for morning tea. No more sideways glances at new colleagues. No more sideways glances at me.

No more mistrust, *period*.

The Deputy Police Commissioner took personal charge of investigations into the attack on the ICAC offices. Police detectives went through the ICAC reception CCTV footage but most attackers were canny enough to avoid the cameras. Among the crush of people, the police identified one ex-policeman and nine serving officers. They charged the ex-policeman with affray and he served three months in prison. The nine police officers were dismissed from the force.

Of a force numbering 17,500, four thousand officers attended the Police Headquarters gathering. Not one of them was absent without leave. No beat went unpatrolled, no traffic ticket went unissued, no crime went unrecorded.

So, why did Governor MacLehose and Commissioner Slevin allow reports of a police mutiny go unchallenged? No one knows for sure but among frontline policemen and women, there were plenty of theories. Top of the list was that the incident left both the Governor and the Commissioner looking incompetent. For MacLehose, badly advised by his Police Commissioner, suggestions of ineptitude must have stung. Allowing the press to run with the mutiny story was a useful distraction from the real issues, which were the Commissioner's fitness to command and the Governor's inability to connect with his community. These failings were career breakers but by staying silent, MacLehose and Slevin survived the crisis.

Even today, people believe the gathering was a protest against corruption enforcement. It was not. Sure, corruption was the catalyst, but the main issue was the disconnect between junior and senior officers. Junior ranks believed that senior force management had little idea of the problems they faced on the ground and, worse, that they did not care. To some extent this was true and the lack of direct dialogue exacerbated things.

At last, junior police officers took their rightful place at the negotiating table. Their pay and conditions improved. The force offered extra training so that junior officers might better advance through the ranks. The recruiting office saw a surge in applications. Since 1977, the Hong Kong Police has almost doubled in size. Now, it is one of best trained, best disciplined and least corrupt of the world's police forces. As with any force, the Hong Kong Police has its problems. The complaints office receives reports ranging from rudeness to criminal assault and there is some lingering corruption. From time to time, there is dissatisfaction with pay and conditions. There has even been another mass meeting at the Police Sports and Recreation Club.

But take it from me, there has never been a police mutiny.

PART 3
SHA TAU KOK

HONG KONG POLICE: INSIDE THE LINES

CHAPTER 4
RED WIND — BLUE STEEL

In 1965, China was back on track. The disaster that was the Great Leap Forward lay in the past. Under the guidance of three reformers, Deng Xiaoping, Liu Shaoqi and Zhou Enlai, the nation was on the cusp of a social renaissance. In these three men, there beat the hearts of true communists, but they knew it took more than slogans to drive growth. Under their reforms, farmers shared ownership of the land they worked, factory workers earned proper wages and the store shelves were relatively full. In cities like Shanghai, women visited beauty parlors and dressed in western fashions. In universities and other centers of thought, intellectuals considered how best China might take her rightful place in the world. Some even whispered of contact with the West.

From the sidelines, Mao Zedong saw the reformists chipping away at his revolution. Just one year earlier, a Kremlin palace coup had toppled his ally, Nikita Khrushchev. In Beijing's Zhongnanhai, Mao's acolytes picked up on Mao's fears and simply echoed them back to him. The darker the rumor, the more attention Mao paid it.

It all came to a head with a stage play. Wu Han was a rock-solid party man and back in 1959, he had written a play called, '*Hai Rui Dismissed from Office.*' It was a historical drama about an honest official, dismissed for criticizing a corrupt emperor. At first, Mao gave it fulsome praise but in 1965, his growing mistrust took new meaning from Wu Han's words. Could the honest official symbolize an army general, purged after criticizing Mao? If so, who was Wu Han's corrupt emperor?

Mao's wife, Jiang Qing, set about cleansing China's art movement of anything and anyone she judged disloyal to party, state, and more importantly, to Mao Zedong. Sensing a shift in the power base, hardliners gathered round her. Jiang decreed that the three so-called reformers, Deng, Liu and Zhou, were counter-revolutionary. Her followers clamored to agree. Officials close to Deng, Liu and Zhou, found themselves out of favor; doors once open, slammed shut.

There was a new mood in the capital, a sense that things had become too cozy. With prompting from above, Beijing's youth were first to act. Students boycotted classes. In big character posters pasted on the walls of universities and schools, they denounced their college administrators. Jiang Qing's supporters passed among them, handing out crimson armbands. Picked out in gold in China's new, simplified characters, was the legend 红卫兵 — *Hongweibing* — Red Guard.

The Red Guards set about demolishing the 'four olds': old customs, old culture, old habits, old ideas. They sacked churches, mosques and Buddhist temples. They burned sacred texts and Confucian writings. They marched north and south, first to the Beijing suburbs then beyond to the countryside, towns and cities. They were like rowdy children free of constraint. They could go where they wished, do what they wanted. Schools and universities closed. Waving copies of Mao's little red book, the Red Guards hauled officials, teachers, and intellectuals before jeering crowds. They humiliated and beat them. Fear washed through China like a spring flood. Friend denounced friend; son denounced father.

Mao ordered the People's Liberation Army to support this new revolution he had engineered. The world's largest army stepped into the mix. Some local military commanders issued weapons to the Red Guards and sent troops to support their purges. But what or who was revolutionary? No one had defined it. The young men and women Red Guards struggled to find their own meaning for the word. The more they discussed it, the more they disagreed. Fault lines within the movement cracked, then broke. Now it was Red Guard denouncing Red Guard. Solidarity marches turned into street brawls; street brawls turned into gun battles. China descended into a crazy civil war where no one knew where the spiritual dividing lines lay. The death toll rose into the hundreds of thousands.

A bewildered populace looked on as the nation was torn apart.

About forty miles from Hong Kong, across the Pearl River delta, lay the Portuguese enclave of Macau. Apart from its legal gambling casinos, Macau was a sleepy little place. It had a pleasant Mediterranean feel and compared to Hong Kong, life was leisurely. In Macau, there was always time to linger over lunch. A second bottle of rosé? Why not? It should have been idyllic, but in 1966, this unhurried lifestyle became Macau's undoing. It started over something and nothing. A citizens' group applied to build a private school. The license was not forthcoming and reminders went unanswered. For Macau, this was business as usual, so the citizens decided to forgo the tiresome matter of licensing and proceeded to build their school regardless. After all, who could object to a new seat of learning? Sadly, no one counted on the power of bureaucratic indignation.

When word of unauthorized construction filtered back to the Municipal Council, the authorities bristled and decided to act. Police moved onto the site and arrested the school officials. Construction workers, seeing their pay packets threatened, intervened but found themselves on the business end of police batons. This greatly displeased the local residents who wanted to place their children at the school. They gathered at the building site and promptly received the same treatment as the construction workers. The press, keen to follow up on anything that departed from Macau's sleepy news days, flocked to the scene. Before long, they added their numbers to the walking wounded.

Macau's communists, seeing a chance to show their revolutionary credentials, marched on the governor's official residence. For two weeks, crowds camped outside the residence, singing revolutionary songs and chanting Maoist slogans. Tiring of the disturbance, His Excellency ordered their arrest. Far from fixing the problem, this inflamed the wider public. They rampaged through the streets, defaced statues, broke into government offices and destroyed public records. The governor declared martial law but by the time authorities restored order, eleven people were dead and another two hundred injured.

Undefeated, the communists started a protest called the three no's: no taxes, no service and no selling to Macau's Portuguese residents. Overnight, shops, restaurants and other service providers refused to serve Westerners. Portuguese enterprises saw their business dry up. The number of people refusing to pay taxes was so great, the authorities could do nothing about it. Macau's governor capitulated and a senior official signed a statement of apology. That day, everything changed. The Portuguese flag still flew over government buildings, Portuguese remained an official language and Portugal still appointed the enclave's governor but Portugal's absolute dominion had ended. Henceforth, Portugal would administer Macau only with China's consent.

In Hong Kong, the communists rejoiced and made their plans.

Mao's Cultural Revolution did not storm into Hong Kong, it rather slipped in through an open door. At first, it was just a hearts and minds campaign. Pictures of a benevolent Mao appeared outside left-wing schools, trade union offices, communist banks, department stores and other businesses that just wanted to hedge their bets. Mao's Little Red Book was on sale, as were badges bearing his image. Everywhere, there were banners promoting Mao's thoughts. In the main, they were harmless: *'The Sun is Chairman Mao; the Sun is the Communist Party'* and *'Successfully march under the Shining Glory of the Party's Socialist Construction.'* It was pretty bland, but with Hong Kong being a British colony, it was only a matter of time before the posters became more robust. More and more, they condemned British imperialism but as ever, Hong Kong life went on, business thrived and all seemed well.

At first, none of this caused sleepless nights for the police, but bit by bit, the rhetoric became more fiery. In May 1967, a labor dispute at a Hong Kong plastic flower factory turned ugly. There were clashes and police arrested twenty-one strikers. Trade unionists made rowdy protest outside police stations and were arrested. This was what Hong Kong's leftists had been waiting for. Demonstrators carrying Mao's Little Red Book poured onto the streets. They chanted Maoist slogans and threw stones at the police. Spurred on by left-wing activists, noisy protests turned into running street battles.

The Police Commissioner dusted off his mobilization order. Immediately, the Royal Hong Kong Police changed from a civil police service to a paramilitary security force. Station commanders activated well-practiced contingency plans. They opened their emergency control rooms and powered up the radio networks. They took men off normal beat duties and formed them into riot companies. Heavily-armed units called Light Striking Forces patrolled the streets. They carried full riot gear and within minutes, could link up with other units to confront the disorderly mobs that popped up without warning. In Hong Kong's business district, the Bank of China mounted loudspeakers on its roof and pumped out streams of Maoist rhetoric. The newly-formed Committee Against Hong Kong British Persecution, set about organizing demonstrations that became more and more violent. The police answered barrages

HONG KONG POLICE: INSIDE THE LINES

of stones with barrages of teargas. Chanting demonstrators thronged to the Governor's residence. They waved placards and plastered the gates, guard posts and fences with posters. There were strikes in key services, particularly public transport. Bit by bit, the leftist chipped away at society's fabric. Bit by bit, they sought to bring Hong Kong's colonial era to a shuddering end.

The Hong Kong Police prefers the term, 'internal security operation' to 'riot suppression.' It has a managerial ring and looks much better in the press. Today, Hong Kong Police internal security training lies with the Police Tactical Unit, better known as 'The Blue Berets.' But before there was a Tactical Unit, there was the Police Training Contingent. In 1967, the PTC was just a training establishment. Its job was to take officers away from day-to-day policing, train them in riot control then return them to their parent divisions. The idea was that police divisions would have a pool of officers trained to deal with major disturbances. As far as internal security plans went, it was a good one, which was fortunate. Soon, China's Cultural Revolution would test the Hong Kong Police to its limit.

The PTC base was at Volunteer Slopes, just a few miles from Hong Kong's border with China. It was an old army barracks, vacated nine years earlier when the army moved somewhere better. There was a drill square, firing ranges, an assault course and a good-sized canteen. The accommodation was basic, just a collection of corrugated iron huts clustered around a low hill. The huts had been painted silver to reflect away the summer heat and from the air, they looked like a collection of drinks cans, half buried on their sides.

Superintendent Ken Wellburn commanded the contingent's Delta Company and he was well-pleased. Things were definitely looking up. Six weeks earlier, he had watched the arrival of Delta Company's core staff. There were six probationary inspectors, three sergeants and twelve corporals. They had looked like children arriving on their first day at school, quiet and nervous. And who could blame them? For some, PTC was a make-or-break posting. The job revealed hidden strengths, but it also exposed hidden weakness. PTC could bring out an officer's best but it also saw some high-flyers wilt under the spotlight.

I must make special mention of the company staff sergeant. In police parlance, the staff sergeant was, 'The Major,' and he was the key man. Lost equipment? Speak to The Major. Is a troublemaker spreading dissent? Speak to The Major. The armory constable reports he is short a round of .38 ammo. Speak to The Major. The Major was a man of boundless wisdom and resource. Delta Company's Major was a solid boulder of a man. He was always resplendent in a starched uniform with a crimson sash of office draped from right shoulder to left hip. As the sergeants and corporals stepped through the PTC gates, The Major met them with an iron glare. After the last man had lowered his eyes and made his way to the Non-Commissioned Officers' barracks, the major turned to Wellburn.

'The NCOs and I understand each other, sir,' he said. Then he turned and strode away.

Training started with a three-week command course for the inspectors, sergeants and corporals. The training staff led everyone through the basics of riot drill, crowd management, leadership, operational planning, instructional technique and field craft. There was live firing of all weapons. There were sessions in the gym. There were cross-country runs under a tropical sun. Day by day, Wellburn's doubts began to evaporate. The inspectors were all young and keen to show what they could do. Under the glare of Delta Company's Staff Sergeant, the sergeants and corporals went at it like Rottweilers. In the evenings, Wellburn and his inspectors retreated to the officers' mess. The mess was a place of boozy companionship and tall stories. Over a few beers, Wellburn learned more about his six inspectors than he did during a whole day under training. Three were Chinese. They were quiet and professional. The other three were British. Inspector Adam Keen was bright but not sure if his future lay with the Hong Kong Police. Mark Freedall was quiet and reflective. He had a love of poetry and in his spare hours, often sat by himself with notebook and pen. Martin Cowley was clever and humorous. He had an eye on becoming a detective and Wellburn suspected that if any of them made the police their life's career, it would be Cowley.

Command training done, Delta Company's constables arrived. There were more than ninety of them. They were not hand-picked, nor were they volunteers. Ideally, everyone in the Hong Kong Police had to attend PTC at least once in their career. This worked well for divisional commanders who saw the unit as great way to get rid of troublemakers. As a result, Delta Company was a collection of mixed blessings. There were many solid workers, but there were also backsliders, a comedian or two and some who just did not want to be there.

With the constables settled in, Delta Company divided itself into three platoons. There were two inspectors to a platoon and they took turns in command. A platoon had four sections, each made up of a corporal and seven constables. Each section represented an increasing level of force. Number one section carried rattan shields and yard-long riot batons. Number two section carried a mix of Webley flare pistols and Federal riot guns. The Federal looks like a small rifle with a short length of 1½-inch diameter pipe where the barrel should be. The Webleys fired small teargas canisters; the Federals fired larger canisters. The men of number three section carried a mix of four Greener shotguns and four semi-automatic .30 caliber carbines. The Greener fired twelve-gauge buckshot and had a levered loading action that harked back to the Zulu wars. It weighed eight pounds and delivered a hefty kick. It took a strong man to carry a Greener, let alone fire one. The men with the carbines had a special role. It was their job to scan rooftops and windows for deadly threats. Bringing up the rear was number four section — the arrest section. They carried shields, handcuffs and standard-issue service revolvers.

The Platoon Commander's place was between the shields of number one section and the tear gas weapons of number 2 section. Flanking him was the platoon sergeant and the platoon orderly. The orderly had to manage his carbine and a collection of banners that warned of impending use of force. Some quipped that the orderly's talents lay more in juggling than anything else.

With the platoon in full riot gear and formed up on the drill square, the Platoon Commander raised a loudhailer to his lips. *'The crowd in front. Disperse peacefully.'*

His sergeant translated. *'Chin bin yan kwan, woh ping saan hoi.'*

Gleeful training staff replied with obscene defiance.

On the order, 'Fit respirators,' the platoon pulled rubber gas masks from their haversacks and fitted them in place. With the Commander's gas mask fitted, his next order was muffled and indistinct. *'Number two section – UP.'* With that, the teargas section marched past the Commander, through the number one section and halted in front of the platoon. The Commander and his aides followed and took position behind them. The loudhailer crackled again. *'Disperse peacefully or I use smoke.'* The orderly unfurled a banner and held it aloft. Written in English and Chinese were the words:

警告催淚煙
'WARNING – TEAR SMOKE.'

Again, derision from the training staff.

The Platoon Commander singled out the men carrying the Federal guns, *'One round – LOAD.'*

Four men simulated loading teargas canisters into the Federals' breeches.

The inspector tested the wind; it was blowing from his left.

HONG KONG POLICE: INSIDE THE LINES

'To the left of the crowd in front — PRESENT.'
Four breeches snapped shut. Four constables brought the Federals to their shoulders.
'FIRE.'
Four firing pins *clicked* onto four empty breeches.
In mock horror, the training staff retreated a few yards then continued their jibes.

And so, stage by stage, the level of force increased. Yard by yard, the platoon advanced as each section took its turn at the front. Teargas, buckshot, more teargas.

From the side of the drill square Wellburn watched the platoons. At first, they were slow and deliberate. Hour by hour, day by day, practice began to tell. Three weeks into full training, the drills were quick and seamless. The men were tanned, fit and sharp. When he thought no one was watching, even the company staff sergeant nodded his approval.

Yes, Wellburn thought, *I am well pleased.*

Since Victorian times, men from the Punjab and the North West Indian provinces have served in the Hong Kong Police. In 1947, those provinces formed part of newly-independent Pakistan. In the 1960s, the New Territories Emergency Unit had one platoon of Chinese officers and two of Pakistani officers. The Pakistanis were big men; big in body and big in heart.

On paper, the unit looked like a Police Training Contingent company: three platoons each commanded by an inspector and each skilled in riot control. Its armory held a stock of riot weapons that matched the armory at the PTC base. Kitted out in full riot gear, EU officers were indistinguishable from PTC officers with the exception of one piece of equipment. PTC officers wore helmets of navy blue. The EU helmets were snow white.

There was more to the Emergency Unit than riot control. Day to day, they manned the emergency response cars. Robbery in progress? Gang fight? Burglar alarm sounding? First to the scene was the Emergency Unit. For Zahid Khan, or for any young policeman looking for cops-and-robbers action, the unit was the only place to be. But for Khan, there was more to the unit than an exciting job. To him, it was a family. It had its base at Fanling Depot, not far from the Chinese border. There, the Pakistani officers and their families formed a self-contained community. They had their own married quarters and a canteen with cooks who specialized in *halal* food.

Zahid Khan was content. He had a good job and the company of men who were more brothers than colleagues. For him, two particular constables were dear and special. The first was the irrepressibly cheerful Khurshid Ahmed. The other was Khurshid Ahmed's best friend, Mohamed Malik. Malik played in goal with the police hockey team. He was something of a celebrity and a year earlier, had made the shortlist to represent Hong Kong in the Asian Games.

In that summer of 1967, Zahid Khan could imagine nothing that would shatter his contentment.

Straddling the border between Hong Kong and China, the village of Sha Tau Kok summed up Hong Kong's relationship with the mainland. The border ran through the village centre, along a narrow strip of concrete called Chung Ying Street, literally China-England Street. As far as borders with communist countries go, Chung Ying Street was an unassuming place. There was no electric fence, no probing searchlights, no watchtowers, no snarling dogs, no trigger-happy border guards. It was a cramped little street, about fifteen feet wide. On both sides, stone buildings squatted close together. Spaced every twenty yards or so, a knee-high stone marked the border. A casual observer would have found it hard to tell which side was in China, and which side was part of the British Empire. Overseeing the Chinese side was a lone soldier. He wore a loose-fitting, green tunic, buttoned to the throat and with crimson tabs at the collar. On his head was a soft Mao cap with a red star fixed above the peak. Strapped across his chest was a Kalashnikov AK-47 assault carbine. On the approach of a Hong Kong policeman, he sometimes made a show of cocking his Kalashnikov, but everyone had grown used to this and just ignored it.

On the British side, the police post was about ninety yards from Chung Ying Street. It was a sturdy looking building, two stories high. Surrounding it was a chain link fence with a rickety gate. The post had a flat roof on which stood a searchlight and an array of radio aerials. The doors and windows had steel shutters but they were always open. Spaced along the walls and rooftop buttress were small gun-ports from where defenders could observe, and if necessary, fire on any attackers. No one believed for a moment that the steel shutters and gun-ports were necessary. They were simply a hangover from a long gone, colonial way of thinking. At least they were until June 24, 1967.

On June 24, 1967, Mao Zedong's Cultural Revolution came to Sha Tau Kok.

Zahid Khan jammed on his riot helmet and held tight to his gas mask haversack as he ran across Fanling Depot's drill square. The platoon sergeant glared at him as he took his place in the platoon's number two section. Khan smoothed down the front of his bush shirt and half-smiled an apology to the sergeant.

'Platoon — draw *STORES*,' the sergeant bellowed and in a practiced drill sequence, the platoon filed into the armory to draw their riot weapons. Khan lifted his Federal riot gun from its rack and slung a haversack of teargas canisters over his shoulder. Then it was back onto the drill square where the platoon reformed: shields and batons in the first section, teargas weapons in the second section, Greener shotguns and carbines in the third and the lockup section with their shields, handcuffs and revolvers bringing up the rear. Behind them was their transport: a Land Roverand two Bedford trucks.

The sergeant called everyone to attention as their commander approached from the briefing room.

The commander's voice rang across the square. 'Bloody *jaw jais,*' — Bloody commies. 'They're causing trouble at Sha Tau Kok,' he said. 'And we're going to sort the buggers out. Any questions?'

The sergeant's eyes gleamed. 'No questions, *Sahib,*' he replied. 'We shall indeed sort the buggers out.'

The commander barked an order. The platoon executed an about-face then ran to their vehicles. Each man knew which vehicle was his and where he must sit. When the time came, the platoon would be out of the Bedfords and aligned in their four sections before the mob could react. Sha Tau Kok was just fifteen minutes' drive from the base. As the convoy rumbled along the Sha Tau Kok Road, no one spoke. For Khan, it seemed unreal. He had done the training but this was his first action. A hand fell on his shoulder and from the seat beside him came a musical baritone. It was Mohamed Malik, the force hockey player. 'Do not worry, young fellow,' he said. 'All will be well.'

'Indeed, all will be well,' echoed Malik's friend, the ever-cheerful Khurshid Ahmed.

Khan forced a smile and tried to relax.

The convoy passed the drop-arm barrier that marked the Frontier Closed Area. To the right, the waters of Starling Inlet were mirror smooth. The hills beyond the inlet were green and lush. To the left, traditional houses nestled among trees alongside vegetable plots and rice paddies. A water buffalo raised its head to watch them pass. *It is all so peaceful*, Zahid Khan thought. Then, as the convoy approached the village, it passed a burnt out police Land Rover, upside down by the roadside.

The Bedfords halted outside the police post, their tailgates banged open and the men piled out. The platoon formed up in front of the vehicles. The number one section men spread out until each could just touch the shoulder of the next man with the tip of his baton. That done, their eyes snapped forward. The rest of the platoon aligned themselves with the men at the front. The whole process was over in seconds.

About ninety yards ahead, hundreds of men milled behind a line of steel barriers blocking the junction with Chung Ying Street. They wore faded Mao jackets and baggy britches. Their faces were hard and leathery. Among them, stood a smooth-faced young man. He wore a soft Mao cap and around his upper sleeve was a red armband imprinted with the yellow characters, 红卫兵 — *Hongweibing* — Red Guard.

The Platoon Commander took his place behind the number one section. At the sight of a British officer the crowd chanted, '*Baak pei jue.*' — white skinned pig. '*Baak pei jue, baak pei jue.*' Then another chant. '*Mo lo cha.*' — Indian monkeys. '*Mo lo cha, mo lo cha.*' The crowd pressed against the barriers. There were raised fists and shouts of, '*Kong yi.*' — Protest. A man capered before the crowd. He took aim with a slingshot. A stone *thwacked* against a rattan shield. Another man brandished an iron bar and clambered over the barriers. His tunic was open, revealing lean muscle. '*Gam seung; gam gon,*' — Dare to think; dare to act, he shouted. Another man joined him. Then two more. The crowd surged over the barriers and moved towards the platoon, fists raised, voices clamoring, '*Saat baak pei jue.*' — kill the white skinned pig. '*Saat mo lo cha.*' — Kill the Indian monkeys. A stone clattered into the platoon. A constable used his shield to parry away another. Stones bounced off shields and helmets. There was a percussive '*CRACK*' and something punched at Zahid Khan's calf. Around him, men flinched, some ducked.

'*STAND STILL,*' the platoon sergeant roared. Then his voice became soothing. 'Stand firm, brothers. It is just a bomb for catching fish. They cause no serious injury.'

The sun was near its highest. Khan blinked sweat from his eyes. His bush shirt stuck damp to his back. His riot helmet felt a size too small.

'*Fit respirators.*' The platoon pushed back their helmets and dragged rubber gas masks from their haversacks.

'*Number 2 section* — *UP.*'

There was a single *crunch* as Zahid Khan and the rest of the teargas section stamped to attention. The section corporal gave the order, '*By the centre* — *quick MARCH.*' With their Federal riot guns at the high port, they brushed past the Platoon Commander and the men of number one section. They took position at the front of the platoon. Behind them, number three and four sections came to attention and stepped into the gap left by the teargas men.

'*Warning banner,*' the commander snapped. The orderly unfurled the teargas warning banner and held it aloft.

The commander raised his loudhailer. His gas mask muffled his words. '*Disperse or I fire smoke.*' He turned to his sergeant. 'We're supposed to repeat it in Chinese.'

Behind the gas mask eyepieces, the sergeant's eyes twinkled. 'Do not worry, *Sahib*. They will soon receive the message most clearly.'

The commander called the next order. '*Number two section federals. One round* — *LOAD.*' Khan reached into his haversack and pulled out a teargas canister. He unsnapped the breech of his Federal and the canister slid in with a satisfying '*tonk.*' The other Federal men did the same.

'*Low angle* — *PRESENT.*'

Khan brought the butt of his Federal to his shoulder, snapping shut the breech as he did so. He sighted down the barrel.

'*FIRE.*'

The Federals banged. The butt slammed into Khan's shoulder. Four teargas shells streaked across the open ground. They clattered against the tarmac and tumbled into the crowd. They spun like catherine wheels, hissing and pouring out clouds of white teargas. The effect was immediate. Blinded by tears, men ran in every direction. They clasped hands to their mouths and noses. They barged into one another. They elbowed, kicked and punched their way clear. Anything to escape the choking, stinging, blinding gas.

Khan snapped open his Federal, plucked out the smoking cartridge case and reloaded.

'Number one and number four sections .— UP.'

The number one section marched to the front and raised their shields. Seconds later, the men of number four section added their shields to the front rank.

'Remove respirators.'

Khan removed his gas mask and tucked it into its haversack. Traces of teargas lingered. It prickled his eyes, it burned his armpits, groin and exposed skin. Ahead, Chung Ying Street was deserted. The once neat line of barriers was crooked and in one place, lay flat. Iron bars, wooden staves and a few rubber sandals littered the ground. Spent teargas canisters lay scattered among the detritus left by the crowd. From one, there came a trickle of white gas.

Nothing moved. All was silent.

Along the border, people got on with daily life. Farmers crossed from China into Hong Kong and at the official crossing points of Lo Wu and Man Kam To, it was business as usual. All seemed normal, but to border veterans the peace had an undercurrent. A sullen silence hung over the workers making the morning crossing from China to Hong Kong. At the Lo Wu railway station, there was the occasional muttered obscenity. From time to time, someone spat at the feet of a border official.

Zahid Khan's platoon carried on with their regular patrol duties. Despite the troubles, there were still burglar alarms to investigate, drunks to pacify and suspicious characters to stop and question. All across the New Territories, the police canteens and officers' messes were awash with rumors. There had been secret meetings between mainland Red Guards and Hong Kong

leftists. Something big would happen, it was just a matter of time.
'It's true,' someone would claim.
'Who says?' another would scoff.
No one knew what was true and what was rumor. Then, in early July that year, the Sha Tau Kok duty corporal saw something that turned rumor into reality.

In a fit of revolutionary zeal, China's Peoples' Liberation Army abolished its rank structure. No longer would a bourgeois hierarchy oppress members of the world's largest standing army. Now, decisions on national defense, training and combat readiness would be in the hands of soldiers' revolutionary struggle committees. It was all nonsense of course, but ever the pragmatists, China's army played the political game. There were no badges of rank and all were supposed to wear the same soft caps, baggy trousers and Mao jackets. However, an experienced observer saw how soldiers squared their shoulders and straightened their tunics when an officer approached. In the People's Liberation Army, military courtesy was not dead, it was just in hiding.

If anyone needed proof of the army's hierarchy, they would have seen it on a summer's morning in the village of Sha Tau Kok. It was Saturday, July 1. The day started as normal. The little plaza in front of the police post was quiet. On the other side of Chung Ying Street, a bored Chinese soldier took advantage of the shade offered by a candy-striped awning outside a general store. Then, something further along Chung Ying Street caught his eye. He tugged straight his tunic, settled his Kalashnikov at a forty-five degree angle across his chest and came to rigid attention. A group of soldiers walked from Chung Ying Street and stepped up to the border. Their manner was brisk and at their centre was an older man whose uniform was of a finer cut. He spoke and the others stepped closer to catch his words. He pointed to features on the Hong Kong side of the border while an aide took frantic notes. After a few minutes, the older man strode back the way he had come and the others scurried after him. The sentry watched them go. He blinked, scratched his head then returned to the shade of the candy-striped awning.

Back in the village police post, the Duty Corporal reported the incident to Sha Tau Kok main station and the information made its tortuous way through the chain of command. Eventually, a headquarters staff officer tabled it to his boss.

'What's the source?' the senior officer asked.

'The... *um*... Sha Tau Kok Duty Corporal,' the staff officer answered, wondering if he should have mentioned it.

The senior officer raised an eyebrow. 'Hardly gilt-edged.'

The staff officer cleared his throat. No going back now. 'He's the man on the ground, sir. And there was trouble there just a week ago.'

The senior officer pinched the bridge of his nose. 'Very well,' he sighed. 'Tell the Commandant Police Training Contingent to prepare some kind of plan. Anything else?'

It had been a quiet day. The staff officer gathered his papers and went back to his office.

Saturday morning, July 8 1967. Mobile patrols cancelled. All three New Territories Emergency Unit platoons formed up in company strength. Each man wore his distinctive, white riot helmet. A gas mask hung at each waist. The men of number one and number four sections carried their rattan shields. 'Platoon Commanders to briefing,' the Company Commander ordered. His name was Duncan McNeil, an ex-soldier. Competent, steady, respected.

While the inspectors attended their briefing, the armory constable opened up the emergency arms store and the men filed in to collect their weapons. Federal riot guns, flare pistols, teargas canisters and grenades, shotguns, carbines. The transport sergeant chivvied along the drivers. A convoy of a Land Rover and two Bedford trucks formed behind each platoon. Wire mesh covered their windscreens and side windows. The drivers gunned their engines. Blue exhaust tendrils drifted across the drill square. Oily fumes hung in the air.

Briefing done, Zahid Khan' Platoon's Commander spoke to his men.

'Mainland Red Guards and local leftists are planning another border incident at Sha Tau Kok,' he said. 'This time, we're in reserve. Police Training Contingent will deal with any trouble. Any questions?' There were none. 'We and the other Pakistani platoon will standby in the village police post; the Chinese lads will be in the rural committee building, about four-hundred yards back from Chung Ying Street.' He smiled. 'We can relax. PTC will do the heavy work.'

Zahid Khan clambered into the back of the Bedford. 'Did you bring something to read?' Mohamed Malik asked him.

'This young one prefers books with pictures,' Khurshid Ahmed quipped.

Malik feigned a yawn. 'Indeed, PTC will have the fun and we will have a quiet time of it.'

Zahid Khan watched the faces around him. They were relaxed and why not? On that Saturday morning, the combined force of Emergency Unit and Police Training Contingent numbered nearly two-hundred and fifty men. More than enough to cover all the bases.

None of them knew it, but on that Saturday morning, there would be an extra base on the field.

And that base was not covered.

Duncan McNeil's Land Rover led the Emergency Unit convoy into the Frontier Closed Area. For a few minutes, they drove along the Sha Tau Kok Road, past rice paddies and lush greenery. The convoy stopped outside the village rural committee building. The unit's Chinese platoon disembarked, offloaded their weapons and took up their standby position inside the building. The convoy continued past the fire station and the village clinic before stopping outside the police post. A chain link fence surrounded the post. The gate was open and from there it was just a few paces to the front door.

The village was quiet, quieter than McNeil had ever seen it. Shop doors were closed, shutters barred the windows. The lanes and alleys were deserted. In the spot where a Chinese soldier normally stood, an effigy hung from a makeshift gibbet. It had a pig's head and slung around its neck, a scrawled placard read: 白皮膚的豬 — White-skinned pig.

Standing beside McNeil, a Pakistani sergeant scanned the village. He was a tall man with a broad face adorned with a military moustache. He frowned. 'It is very quiet, *Sahib*,' he growled. 'Perhaps there will be no trouble today.' He did not sound convinced.

McNeil spoke in a half-whisper. 'Get the men inside,' he said. 'Tell them to keep their weapons close.'

The two platoons, eighty men in all, shoehorned themselves into the little post. They spread themselves among the offices, storerooms, barracks, corridors and anywhere else they could find space. Zahid Khan's platoon sergeant pointed to an iron ladder leading to a hatch in the report room's ceiling. 'Number two and three section, go up to the observation post,' he ordered.

The observation post was little more than an enclosed platform. A low wall surrounded the structure and from the waist up, the observation post was open to the elements. Cut into the walls were gun-ports, measuring about nine inches square. The men manhandled their weapons and equipment through the hatch and each found himself a space.

From the observation post, there were broad views towards Chung Ying Street and across the village rooftops. 'We will have the best seats for the floorshow,' Khurshid Ahmed said.

Zahid Khan leaned his Federal against the wall, removed his

helmet and wiped sweat from his brow. He checked his watch, ten o'clock. 'I hope we can return to base in time for our lunch,' he said.

No one answered.

Ken Wellburn's Delta Company piled out of their vehicles outside the rural committee building but found the Emergency Unit's Chinese platoon had already staked their place inside. The building was about four hundred yards back from Chung Ying Street. It was a neat, stone-built structure with a flat roof and smooth, rendered walls. Wellburn raised his binoculars and checked out the village. All was still. Shop doors were closed, their windows shuttered. On the Chinese side of Chung Ying Street, a general store faced onto a small plaza. There, a crude effigy swung from a wooden gibbet. It had a pig's head and there was a sign around its neck but it was too far away for Wellburn to read. To Wellburn, the silence was unnatural. Something was wrong.

Wellburn sent Inspector Martin Cowley up to the rural committee building's roof for a clearer view. When Cowley returned, Wellburn did not like what he had to say. There were sandbags heaped on the general store's rooftop, Cowley told him, and men wearing Chinese army uniform were setting up a belt-fed machine gun. The report troubled Wellburn. Recently, the Chinese had become increasingly provocative but so far, nothing had come of it.

Wellburn's second-in-command was off sick. Replacing him was Gilberto Jorge, a young inspector who was a member of the Police Training Contingent's permanent staff. He was a one-pip, *bongban jai*, Cantonese slang for a 'boy inspector.' It would be his job to man the command radio and keep Frontier Control abreast of events. Wellburn was not too concerned about Jorge's junior rank. The young man knew his stuff.

Delta Company's staff sergeant joined Wellburn at the

roadside. As usual, his uniform was freshly starched, his red sash was brilliant, his leatherwork gleamed and it seemed to Wellburn he had even polished his riot helmet. 'Do you have any instructions, sir,' he asked.

'Instructions, Major? No, not yet,' Wellburn mused. 'But I will. Soon, I think. Yes, very soon.'

Zahid Khan leaned out over the observation post's parapet and strained to hear. From further along Chung Ying Street, there was a distant murmur. The sound drew closer. As it did, it grew louder until it became a roar. On the Chinese side, a metallic loudspeaker squawked to life. '*Mao Chu Jik maan sui!*' − Long live Chairman Mao!

'They're coming brothers,' Khan called. 'They're coming.'

A throng of men streamed from Chung Ying Street. Their faces were hard and sun-darkened. Their clothes were patched and work-soiled. They pressed against the post's perimeter fence. '*Mao Chu Jik maan sui! Mao Chu Jik maan sui!*' Their voices hammered across the village. They punched the air in time to the chant. Khan ducked as a stone *whickered* past him.

'Put down your head, my friend,' Mohamed Malik urged. 'We may not be as safe as we thought.'

More stones clattered against the wall. The chant became, '*Wong gau.*' − Yellow running dog. '*Mo lo cha.*' − Indian monkeys. '*Saat, saat wong gau.*' − Kill, kill yellow running dogs. '*Saat, saat mo lo cha.*' − Kill, kill Indian monkeys.'

There was the CRACK of a fish bomb.

From the report room, came the clamor of a gong.

'Attack on post alarm,' Khurshid Ahmed said. 'They're attacking the post.'

McNeil's head appeared in the hatch. 'Message from Frontier Control,' he said. 'Chinese troops are moving along their side of the border. Anyone know how to use a Bren gun?'

The Bren was a World War Two vintage, light machine gun. It

had a folding bipod support stand and a curved, high-capacity magazine that sat on top of the breech. It fired a .303 caliber rifle bullet and despite its age, was a fearsome weapon. Every border police post held a Bren but never had one been fired in anger.

'Bren gun, Sahib?' Mohamed Malik, the hockey player gasped. 'Are you sure?'

'Of course I'm bloody sure,' McNeil snapped back. 'Does anyone here know how to use the damned thing?'

Malik spoke up. 'I am fully competent with the Bren gun, Sahib.'

'Good,' McNeil said. His head disappeared back through the hatch.

Minutes later, the post constable struggled up the ladder hefting the station Bren behind him. He dumped it on the floor then clambered back down to the report room. Moments later, he reappeared with a muscular looking box of .303 ammunition.

Malik picked up the Bren and flipped down its bipod support. He carried it to a gun-port that sat just a foot above floor level. He peered through the port but it was less than nine inches square and he could not see much. He slid the barrel through the gun-port and slotted a curved magazine into its housing. He steadied the stock against his shoulder and squinted down the sight. He traversed left and right, checking the field of fire. Finally, he worked the cocking mechanism and snapped the change lever to '*safe*.'

Khurshid Ahmed flashed him a smile. 'I will help with the loading,' he said.

'Pray that is not necessary,' Malik answered.

'It will not be necessary,' Ahmed said. He paused for a moment then added, '*Inshallah*.' — God willing.

'Indeed, my friend,' Malik said. '*Inshallah*.'

From his place at the rural committee building, Delta Company's Inspector Adam Keen heard the crowd before he saw it. It started as a murmur then grew to a roar that moved unseen behind the houses lining Chung Ying Street. A crowd of about one hundred crossed the border and pressed against the post's chain link fence. The roar became a rhythmic chant.

Ken Wellburn heard it too, 'Fall in. FALL IN,' he bellowed.

There was a scramble to obey. Within seconds, the three platoons formed up on the road, one behind the other, each in parade ground formation. Keen's platoon was at the front, as it should be. Martin Cowley's platoon should have been in the number two spot but Mark Freedall had jumped in and snatched it. *No matter*, Keen thought. *We're first up*. Their training time had been short, just long enough to learn the basics but now, there was an eager purpose about them. *They've never looked sharper*, Keen thought. He sensed their tension but it was not a tension of fear, it was the tension of an athlete settling into the starting blocks.

Corporals bustled among the platoons, chivvying their sections into line, checking equipment, repositioning a helmet or two.

From Chung Ying Street, the chanting became louder and more rhythmic. There was the CRACK of a fish-bomb. The mob cheered.

Wellburn was speaking. 'Pay attention,' he called. 'I have just received a radio message from Assistant Commissioner, New Territories. The village post commander requests immediate assistance. Mister Keen's platoon will advance on the crowd. Remainder, standby and prepare to move up in support.' He turned to Keen. 'Ready?'

'Ready, sir.'

'The major and I will tag along, if that's all right,' Wellburn said.

'You're most welcome, sir,' Keen answered.

From behind, Mark Freedall shouted, 'See 'em off, Adam.'

'Meet you later for a beer,' Keen called back. He snapped to attention. His voice rose to a bellow. *'Platoon. Atten — SHUN.'*

There was a single *thump* and the platoon stamped to parade ground attention.

'Right — DRESS.'

Number one section spread out until each man could just touch the shoulder of the next with the tip of his baton. That done, their eyes snapped forward. They stood to rigid attention; shields up, baton tips resting on their shoulders. The other three sections aligned themselves with the front rank.

'Platoon. By the centre, quick — MARCH.'

As the platoon stepped forward, pride surged in Keen's chest. *This is it,* he thought. *This is bloody it.* Never had his men's shoulders been so square; never had their tread been so steady. Their boots were a rhythmic, *crunch, crunch, crunch* on the tarmac. His sergeant was to his right. To his left was the orderly and to the orderly's left were Wellburn and the staff sergeant.

Crunch, crunch, crunch.

The rural committee building fell away behind them. To their left, dense scrub gave way to mud-sodden rice paddies. To their right, a strip of rough ground lay between the road and the flat waters of Starling Inlet.

Crunch, crunch, crunch.

Not far to go. Ahead, was the village fire station. Beyond that, the village clinic and the police post.

Crunch, crunch, crunch.

Now, Keen could see and hear the mob clearly. He could see faces twisted with rage, hear chants of, *'Mao Chu Jik maan sui!'* and *'Saat, saat, mo lo cha!'* The mob pressed against the post's chain-link fence. The fence swayed and looked ready to collapse.

'Mao Chu Jik maan sui! Saat, saat, mo lo cha!'

A staccato line of firecrackers exploded. The platoon did not falter. They had heard it all before.

Crunch, crunch, crunch.

They neared the fire station. Distance from fire station to

mob, one hundred yards. He needed to be a little closer for the Federals to be effective.

Crunch, crunch, crunch.

There was movement on the roof of the Chung Ying Street general store. No time for distractions. He focused on the mob.

Crunch, crunch, crunch.

In his mind, Keen rehearsed the orders. *Halt − Fit respirators − Number two section UP − Federal guns, one round LOAD − Low angle PRESENT − FIRE.*

They were almost at the fire station.

Crunch, crunch, crunch.

There was another burst of firecrackers. The mob melted away. Some ran back to Chung Ying Street, some ran to a lane that led to Sha Tau Kok's jetty. Others ran to the border road heading west, out of Sha Tau Kok.

There was silence. No rhythmic chanting, no hate filled shouts, just the *crunch, crunch, crunch* of boots marching in time. The rest of Delta Company was far behind. His platoon was alone.

Something's wrong. What is it?

Back at the rural committee building, Martin Cowley took his place behind his number one section. For the umpteenth time that day, he checked his Sterling sub-machinegun. Magazine fitted and secure − check. Safety catch on − check. *Bloody stupid weapon.* He could think of no circumstance that would justify using it. Cowley was not in the best of moods. It rankled that Mark Freedall's platoon had jumped in and snatched his number two spot. Okay, so Freedall wanted some action. Who didn't? Cowley took consolation from the size of the mob. Just one hundred, maybe a dozen more. Adam Keen was almost there. He would see them off with a volley or two of teargas. Then it would be back to base for a shower, a couple of beers and a tall story or two. Cowley watched as more men ran from Chung Ying Street and joined the mob. Soon the plaza was full of them.

The chanting became louder. The mob punched the air in time with the chants. Even at this distance, Cowley sensed their rage. There might be a chance for some action after all.

'*Cowley, Sir.*' An Emergency Unit corporal stood by the roadside. At first, Cowley did not recognize him. Then he remembered — a police veteran from his last posting. As a young man, the corporal had served with Chiang Kai-shek's nationalist army in the fight against Mao Zedong's communists. He had a bottomless capacity for brandy and given half a chance, would take off his shirt and show off his battle scars. Yes, Cowley thought, Corporal 229, a real character. He grinned and waved back.

Cowley turned to look at Keen's platoon. Soon they would halt, show their warning banner and fire off a volley of teargas. He checked his watch. Eleven o'clock. 'Give it half an hour,' he mused. 'Maybe an hour to be on the safe side.' He needed something from his Land Rover. He would be gone for just a few seconds so he had a quick word with his platoon sergeant and slipped away. After all, what could happen in a few seconds?

Adam Keen's mind raced. His platoon had reached the fire station but the crowd had gone. Disappeared. Decamped. Gone. What should he do? Halt? Turn about? Go back? And why had the mob...

BAM-BAM-BAM. Waterspouts stitched a line in the rice paddy. *BAM-BAM-BAM-BAM.* Something *zipped* overhead. *BAM-BAM-BAM.* Bullets struck the road, the streetlights, the fire station wall. Each hit was like a jackhammer strike. *BAM-BAM-BAM-BAM.* The platoon's formation disintegrated. Everyone crouched and ran to the cover of the fire station. Someone banged on the fire station door. No answer.

'Break it open,' Keen ordered.

The door would not give. Men pressed themselves against the wall, eyes wide, breath rasping. Keen shook his head, dazed and uncomprehending. *What the fuck just happened?* Realization was like a slap.

'Stay put,' he shouted. 'We're safe here.'

Safe. His own words mocked him. *Safe for how long?* He moved to the side of the building furthest from the road. A few yards beyond the wall's protection, lay one of his constables. He had run further than the others and had shown himself. Now, he lay still, his head lying in a pool of blood. Choices tumbled around in Keen's mind. If he was fast enough, he might drag the constable to safety. He looked again at the head wound, looked again at how still the man lay. He pictured a skilled sniper nearby, pictured him with a high-powered rifle waiting for another policeman to show himself. The dead constable was Wong Loi-hing. He was twenty-seven years old and for now, he must wait.

Zahid Khan ducked behind the parapet as stones careered through the observation posts' open frontage and rattled along the floor. Men pressed their backs to the wall, knees drawn up, arms covering their heads. Outside, the mob shook the post's chain link fence, trying to wrench it down. Their chants filled the observation post. *'Saat, saat mo lo cha.'* – Kill, kill Indian monkeys. McNeil reappeared at the hatch.

'Stay calm,' he called. 'PTC Delta Company will be with us in a minute or two. Prepare to fit respirators.'

From his place behind the Bren gun, Mohamed Malik's voice was a musical chuckle. 'It is just as I said, my impetuous friend. PTC will have all the fun and we...'

BAM-BAM-BAM. The post wall shuddered. The sound was like a road drill hammering at concrete. Something zipped past Zahid Khan. It smacked against the wall, kicking out a shower of stinging concrete. Khan flattened himself against the floor. Mohamed Malik lay slumped over the Bren gun. The back of his head was a shattered mess. Khan shook him.

'Mohamed?' he whispered. Then louder, *'Mohamed.'*

Malik rolled away from the Bren. A line of blood seeped from a hole in his forehead. Beside Malik, lay Khurshid Ahmed. Blood soaked his bush shirt and spread about him in a growing puddle. Khan snatched a field dressing from his pocket, ripped it open and pressed it against Ahmed's wound. The blood just seeped through. Never had Khan seen so much blood. 'My God, they're shooting,' he cried. 'They're shooting at us through the gun-ports.' There was more gunfire. More hammer blows to the outer wall. More stinging chips of concrete. A constable drew his revolver, snaked his hand through a gun-port and fired blind. The machinegun fire came in short bursts, three or four at a time. *There is discipline in those shots,* Khan thought. *Discipline and training.* 'Stay away from the gun-ports, brothers,' he called. 'Stay away.'

BAM-BAM-BAM. Martin Cowley ducked as something *zipped* overhead. *Gunfire? Yes – gunfire. Jesus!* It came from beyond the rice paddies, off to Cowley's left. Eighty PTC officers dropped to a crouch then dashed for the rural committee building. Cowley sprinted after them. Two of Mark Freedall's men lay sprawled on road. Blood puddled about them. *BAM-BAM-BAM-BAM.* Bullets gouged lumps out of the building's wall. *BAM-BAM-BAM.* The windows of the Company Commander's Land Rover shattered. Cowley had a brief impression of Gilberto Jorge ducking down onto the Land Rover's floor. The two PTC platoons took shelter behind the building.

'*Ah Sir!*' Cowley's platoon sergeant beckoned urgently. Two men were down. Constable Chau Yuk-kui's face was pale and twisted in pain. His knee was a bloodied pulp. The other injured constable was Cheung Lam-mun. A bullet had passed through his neck. Blood soaked his collar. His breath was slow and shallow. He was slipping in and out of consciousness. A corporal called Lau Hing-wing knelt beside them.

HONG KONG POLICE: INSIDE THE LINES

'We must stop bleeding,' he said. 'Emergency Unit has first aid kit.'

He stepped away from the building and cupped his hands to his mouth. *'Wei, tung si,'* — Hey, colleagues.

No one answered. The corporal scooped up a handful of gravel and hurled it against a window. Nothing happened.

'I go to Land Rover. Get first aid satchel,' he said. Before anyone could speak, he took a breath then he was away, head down and sprinting to the platoon Land Rover.

BAM-BAM-BAM-BAM.

'Down. *Keep down,*' someone shouted.

The corporal seemed not to hear. He wrenched open the Land Rover's rear door.

BAM-BAM.

For a moment, Corporal Lau took shelter behind the Land Rover then, with the first aid satchel clutched to his chest, he scurried back to the rural affairs building. His face was red, his breathing harsh. He skidded to a halt beside the injured men and rummaged through the satchel. There were field dressings, antiseptic iodine and cotton wool. For pain, there was only aspirin. Corporal Lau tore away some wads of cotton wool, soaked them in iodine and used them to plug Cheung Lam-mun's neck wound. Still, blood oozed from the cotton wool dressings.

The platoon sergeant knelt beside them. 'He must go to hospital, *Ah Sir,*' he said. 'He must go to hospital or he will die.'

The sergeant was right. But it was not only the wounded that needed to get out. How long before the gunmen moved around the flanks? How long could any of them survive?

Gilberto Jorge lay on the floor of the commander's Land Rover, sandwiched between the front and rear seats. He still held the Land Rover's radio microphone. He pressed the transmit button. 'Frontier Control, this is Delta Company second-in-command. Over.'

No answer.

'Frontier Control. Delta Company 2 i/c. Urgent message. Repeat — *urgent message*. Over.'

The radio crackled back. '*Delta 2 i/c. Send. Over.*'

'Delta Company is receiving automatic gunfire. There are casualties. Over.'

There was a pause, then. '*Did you say, automatic gunfire? Over.*'

'Affirmative,' Jorge answered. 'Automatic gunfire. There are casualties. Over.'

'Roger. Wait one.'

The silence seemed to last and age.

'*Delta 2 i/c. Over.*'

'Send.'

'*We're in touch with the army. Roger so far.*'

'So far.'

'*For now, keep your head down and keep us informed. Over.*'

'Roger,' Jorge replied. 'I'll keep you informed.'

BAM-BAM-BAM. Jorge pressed himself against the Land Rover's floor as bullets, *clunk-clunk-clunked* through the Land Rover's aluminum skin.

Zahid Khan and another constable lowered Khurshid Ahmed to the ground floor. McNeil was on the telephone. He was shouting into the mouthpiece. 'Radio's buggered. They've shot out the aerials.' He listened for a moment then slammed down the receiver. 'PTC's taken casualties. We've taken casualties. And the bloody army needs the bloody Prime Minister's personal bloody permission to enter the Frontier bloody Closed Area.'

'*Sahib, Sahib*, come quickly.' The constable was from number three section. His weapon was a twelve-gauge Greener shotgun. Outside, two men ran in a half crouch towards the post. One carried a rucksack. The man with the rucksack paused then darted right. McNeil had to lean out from the window to watch him. The man's face was drawn. His lips were a thin line. He crouched by the fence and reached into the rucksack.

'It is a bomb *Sahib*. A bloody bomb.'

The man glanced from his satchel to the police post then back to the satchel. He was working on something inside it.

'Shoot the bastard,' McNeil ordered. 'Shoot him before he arms the bloody thing.'

McNeil took the constable's Greener and nudged the constable aside. He flipped the safety catch to *off* and sighted along the barrel. He squeezed the trigger. The Greener slammed against his shoulder. In the confines of the post, a hard *'BAM,'* numbed his ears. All twelve buckshot pellets slammed into the bomber. He pitched forward without a sound and lay still.

Adam Keen considered their situation, which was not good. Constable Wong's body was on a strip of waste ground that lay between the fire station and a low-rise apartment block that looked out over Starling Inlet. The apartment windows were dark and empty. *Where's the sniper?* Keen had deployed his men so there was a spread of firepower covering the rear and both flanks. It was good enough to repulse a mob but what if there was another sniper? The thought chilled Keen. The fire station was good cover but the road was a kill zone. Could he get his men out along the seafront?

The shooting stopped. Silence should have brought relief but it was a heavy silence, like the silence following a thunderclap. Keen set two corporals to watch the seaward side of the fire station. One of them, Corporal Chan Wan-kwong, had transferred in from the Emergency Unit and he still wore his white helmet. 'Watch yourself,' Keen warned. 'You make a good target.'

Corporal Chan peeked around the corner then ducked back. He pointed with his thumb. His voice was an exaggerated whisper. 'Rooftop. Chung Ying Street. *Leung goh Kai Fong Kwan* — two PLA soldiers.' He used his hands to mimic someone looking through binoculars. He pressed his back against the wall. Keen stood alongside him. Again, the corporal peeked around the corner.

BAM.

It felt like a mule kick. It punched the wind from Keen. Scorching pain burned his chest. There was no blood, but his bush shirt's left breast pocket was in tatters. A crimson welt scored a line across his chest. What was left of his pen lay shattered on the ground. Corporal Chan gasped. His eyes stared wide. The same bullet had carved a two-inch gash across his cheek. The wound showed pink and white against his sun-darkened face. Keen cursed himself. He had assumed the danger was the Chinese soldiers in Chung Ying Street. Instead, the shot had come from another building, one on the Starling Inlet side of the fire station. *Damn.* No escape along the shore. Both flanks of the fire station were kill zones.

Ken Wellburn stood beside him. His lips were pale, his face drawn. 'Bad do,' he growled. 'How are the lads taking it?'

'They're good men,' Keen answered. 'They'll hold up fine.'

'I must get back to the company,' Wellburn said. 'Have to tell the Assistant Commissioner what's happening. Have to organize some kind of relief.'

'It's too dangerous,' Keen warned.

'I'll keep my head down,' Wellburn answered. He turned to the staff sergeant. 'Major!'

'Sir.'

'Get rid of that red sash, it's too good a target.'

The staff sergeant slipped the sash over his head and handed it to Keen's platoon sergeant.

'Sit tight,' Wellburn said to Keen. 'I'll get you and your lads out as soon as I can.' He stepped up to the corner of the building and dropped to a half-crouch.

With the staff sergeant close behind, he began to run.

Corporal 229, the Chinese civil war veteran, was a busy man.

HONG KONG POLICE: INSIDE THE LINES

Earlier, there was movement beyond the rice paddies on the left flank. Someone was trying to work their way to a better shooting position. The corporal had snapped off a shot with his .30 caliber carbine. He was not sure if he had hit anyone but for now, all was still. Now, Corporal 229 was bustling around Delta's two platoons, dragooning the carbine men into service.

'What are you up to?' Cowley demanded.

The corporal's manner was brisk. 'Two platoons — ten carbines,' he said. 'My EU platoon has five carbines.' He allowed himself a smile. 'That is fifteen carbines. With fifteen carbines, I can stop ratbags from getting behind us. One ratbag; one hundred ratbags. No matter. I stop them.'

Throughout the day, Corporal 229 drew on his military experience. He took his fifteen carbines up to the rural committee building's first floor and set up a three-sixty degree arc of fire. During the day, armed men tried to take positions to the building's rear and left flank. With well-placed shots, Corporal 229's carbine men held them off. Later, he would receive no official recognition for what he did, but if not for him, the two platoons behind the rural committee building may have suffered dreadful casualties. Martin Cowley remains convinced that PTC Delta Company owes Corporal 229 a huge debt.

Nowhere was safe. Cowley's eyes were everywhere: the road, the bushes, the paddies, the seafront. Every wind-blown rustle of leaves was a sniper. The Sterling submachine gun was no longer a burden. Close by, there was movement in the bushes. Cowley dropped to one knee. Had he imagined it? His mouth dried; his heart thumped. Where the bush met the open ground, something moved. It was too sudden to be a trick of the breeze. Someone was there. Cowley slid back the Sterling's cocking lever. It *shlocked* home. He clicked the change lever to *'auto.'* He raised the Sterling and sighted on the bushes. His finger curled around the trigger. The bush parted. A woman stepped into the open. With her, were two children. She stooped and spread her arms to shelter them. Her face was pale, her eyes wide. Cowley lowered the Sterling and clicked the change lever back to *'safe.'* His breath escaped in a hard sigh. The tension was getting to him. It was getting to them all.

How quickly the abnormal becomes normal. For Delta Company's two reserve platoons, normal was sheltering behind Sha Tau Kok's rural committee building as gunfire pounded the walls. The sun passed its peak and moved into the west. Two lifeless bodies lay out on the road. *They're Mark's men,* Cowley thought. *They should have been mine. Poor lads.*

Poor Mark.

Ken Wellburn sprinted across the Sha Tau Kok Road and splashed into the rice paddy. Another splash told him his staff sergeant had followed. The water was warm. Clinging ooze tugged at his feet. He had to half-wade, half-swim to make progress. Why had they not fired? He felt a shiver between his shoulder blades. He sank lower in the water and moved close to the paddy's bank.

BAM.

Something slammed into the bank then ricocheted against his head. Stinging shards of stone raked his face. Never had anything hit him so hard. He tasted blood. His face was numb. He slipped sideways and the water closed over him. Strong hands pulled him back up. The staff sergeant's face floated before him. The staff sergeant was speaking but the words sounded muffled and indistinct. 'Sir, SIR. We must move *now.'*

Something warm and sticky clouded Wellburn's vision. He wiped it away. He saw his hand covered in blood. 'I'm shot,' he gasped. 'I'm bloody shot.'

'Just ricochet,' the staff sergeant said. 'You will be fine. Now, we move.' He grabbed the cross-strap of Wellburn's Sam Browne belt and dragged him forward. 'There is cover ahead. Hurry.'

With the staff sergeant lending his strength, Wellburn dragged himself up the paddy's far bank and into the cover of thick scrub. Five minutes later, they joined the rest of Delta Company behind the rural committee building. While the orderly sponged blood from Wellburn's face, the staff sergeant spoke to the platoon inspectors. The news was not good. The staff sergeant briefed Wellburn about the casualties.

'Two dead; two serious injuries,' he said. 'No pain relief. The wounded are suffering.'

'Where's the second-in-command?' Wellburn asked.

'In the Land Rover, sir.'

'What the hell's he doing there?' Wellburn demanded. 'He'll get his head blown off.'

'He is on radio watch,' the staff sergeant answered. 'He came under fire but kept sending reports to frontier control.'

Wellburn's head throbbed. Even with the blood swabbed away, his left eye was blind. *It's a mess,* he thought. *A God-almighty mess.* He had promised young Keen he would get him out.

But how was he to get them all out?

For two hours, Gilberto Jorge lay flat in the Land Rover's floor-well. Machinegun fire punched through the Land Rover's aluminum bodywork and *pinged* around inside its cabin. Finally, Jorge clambered from the Land Rover and took cover behind the rear wheel. Those watching from the rural committee building had never seen anyone look so vulnerable. For two more hours, Jorge continued to send back messages. All the time, bullets drilled into the Land Rover and took chunks out of the building's frontage. At last, with the situation becoming too fraught, Jorge ran for the cover of the building.

With that, all contact between Delta Company and Frontier Control ended.

The shooting eased. Delta Company's number eleven and twelve platoons gathered their weapons and equipment and moved into the rural committee building. Eighty-seven PTC officers joined the forty-one Emergency Unit men inside a building not much bigger than a village schoolhouse. Even with windows and doors swung open, the building became muggy and airless. The men consoled themselves that now, they were safe. Relief was on the way. But when would it arrive? The radio link was gone. There was nothing to do but wait.

So they waited.

At the fire station, Adam Keen also waited. At noon, the sun moved into the west and the shade provided by the fire station shrank away to nothing. Now, they sweltered under the July sun. They sat with their backs against the wall, shoulders bowed, heads lolling. Their bush shirts were crumpled and sweat-stained. Most had removed their helmets but Keen had no mind to chastise them. The composite-plastic helmets were no protection against a bullet.

Keen's tongue felt too big for his mouth. His throat felt as though it were full of sand. He slumped forward and rested his head in both hands. It should have been simple: fire a few teargas canisters then back to the mess for beer and sandwiches. He had been eager for action but instead, he had spent the day sheltering behind a wall in some village no one had ever heard of. One man injured and one dead. Bloody *dead*. Keen shook his head. The bastards had suckered him in like a hunter with a tethered goat. It was a fuck up. A shit-laden, ball-aching, ass-kicking, total fuck up. Immediate prospects? Poor. So long as the machine gunner covered the road and the sniper covered the seaward side, there was no escape. He had a spread of riot weapons to hold off a mob but he could not stay put. He made a decision. After nightfall, the platoon would crawl down to Starling Inlet then make their way along the seafront to safety.

From time to time, someone risked a glance towards Chung Ying Street. There were uniformed men on the Chinese side but no way to tell if they were Chinese army, People's Militia or Red Guards.

The afternoon dragged on. The concrete sucked in the heat and turned their refuge into an open kiln. Thirst clawed at Keen's throat. He went from man to man, forcing himself to speak words of cheer. The eyes that met his were glazed and empty. Once, a lookout reported armed men crawling through bushes beyond the rice paddies. Keen gauged the distance. Too far to pose a danger, but *what if...?* He conferred with his corporals. If needed, they had teargas, shotguns, pistols and carbines.

'Sunset,' Keen whispered to no one in particular. *'How much longer 'til sunset?'*

Zahid Khan stayed at Khurshid Ahmed's side. He spoke reassuring words and lay damp cloths on his friend's brow. In the afternoon, Ahmed slipped away. One moment his breath rasped slow and painful, the next he fell silent and was gone.

At the fire station, all was quiet. Then, the sound of an engine. It was distant and faint but it came from the direction of Sha Tau Kok's main police station. Keen stood and shielded his eyes against the afternoon sun. There was a vehicle approaching. It was grey and had the boxy profile of a police armored personnel carrier. It was small and ungainly with a round turret mounted on the top. It stopped outside the rural committee building just long enough to turn around. Then it was reversing along the Sha Tau Kok Road towards them.

Keen's platoon sergeant joined him. More platoon members gathered round. In the movies, men laugh, wave and slap the backs of their comrades. But here, in the shelter of the fire station, there were only blank stares from men too traumatized to speak.

The personnel carrier reversed off the road and into the cover of the fire station. The rear doors swung open. From the driver's seat, a grim-faced British police inspector asked, 'Any injured?'

Keen helped his injured corporal aboard then crammed in as many men as the vehicle could take.

'Back soon,' the inspector said. 'Stay safe.'

He crunched the personnel carrier into gear and it trundled away. Over the next half-hour, it made several trips. Keen was the last man aboard. The air inside the personnel carrier smelled of sweat and burnt petrol. No matter, they were out. Keen waited for euphoria to wash through him but none came.

They were out alright, but he wished to God they had never gone in.

Martin Cowley moved to a window and squinted at a low ridge a few hundred yards from his left flank. Was there movement? Yes. *Soldiers.* The soldiers wore camouflage fatigues of olive green and dark brown. *British soldiers. Gurkhas.* Joy leapt in Cowley's breast. *God bless the bloody Gurkhas.*

The Gurkhas were in no hurry. They advanced at a walk then stopped and hunkered down, disappearing into the landscape. There was the grumble of an engine and a six-wheeled, Saracen armored car rolled past the rural committee building. Its paintwork was a jumble of olive green and brown. The crest of the Lifeguards Regiment adorned its front armor. The barrel of a Sterling submachine gun protruded from a square turret on its roof.

BAM-BAM-BAM.

Bullets *pinged* off the Saracen's armored front, chipping the paintwork. The Saracen grumbled to a halt but did not return the fire. Gurkhas on the ridge rose from the landscape and advanced towards the border.

BAM-BAM-BAM-BAM.

In an instant, there was a crackle of gunfire from the Gurkhas' position. *They're shooting back,* Cowley thought. *They're giving it back to the bastards.* He dropped to the floor. *Bugger this,* he thought. *The ratbags missed me. I'll not have the Gurkhas get me.*

HONG KONG POLICE: INSIDE THE LINES

The Gurkhas hunkered down and the Saracen moved forward, taking more ground. And so it went. As one advanced, the other paused. As one paused, the other advanced. The Gurkhas took charge of the ridge then moved into the flat ground bordering the village.

The village police post telephone jangled. McNeil took the call and a grin split his face. He gave a thumbs-up. The Gurkhas were on their way. McNeil appointed carers for each of the wounded. Outside, there was another flurry of machinegun fire. The post's main entrance was off limits, the only safe way out was through the rear. This was a problem, there was no back door. Zahid Khan joined a group of constables to raid the post's emergency equipment store. With shovels and crowbars, they punched a hole through the rear wall. For a while, they stared at it, waiting for some miraculous salvation. The hole just stared back at them.

The gunfire eased. It stopped. There were footsteps on the other side of the hole. A head appeared. It wore a dark green beret adorned with a crossed kukris cap badge. A soldier stepped through the hole and slapped dust from his shirt. His shoulders bore the insignia of a lieutenant colonel. He looked around and raised an eyebrow. He spoke with a cultured English accent. 'Good afternoon chaps. Gurkhas. Any chance of tea?'

Zahid Khan stepped through the post's front door and took a moment to enjoy the silence. A Saracen armored car dominated the little plaza. The paintwork around the turret and the driver's hatch was chipped and scarred. Gurkha soldiers took up positions facing Chung Ying Street. They were watchful and unsmiling. These men knew they had the situation under control. The mob had gone. All was quiet. In Chung Ying Street, only the hanging effigy remained.

Police vehicles arrived. First aboard were the wounded. Next,

Khan's comrades brought out the remains of Mohamed Malik and Khurshid Ahmed. They carried them with all the tenderness afforded the wounded. No one spoke. Everywhere, faces were blank, uncomprehending.

The casualty evacuation vehicles headed off to Fanling and safety. The Emergency Unit inspectors chivvied their platoons together and called up their company transport. The platoon sergeant called Zahid Khan to follow him. Together, they went from room to room checking for stragglers and forgotten equipment. The post was silent. It felt dead and empty.

Back at Fanling Depot, they offloaded the weapons and equipment. On the order to dismiss, Khan headed back to the barracks. On the first floor landing was a mirror where constables checked their appearance before parades. Khan gasped as he caught sight of himself. Dried blood caked his bush shirt and shorts. There were splashes of blood on his forearms, legs and face. He checked himself for injuries. There were none. The blood belonged to Mohamed Malik and Khurshid Ahmed.

That evening, a great weariness swept over Zahid Khan but sleep would not come. As he lay on his bunk, gunfire hammered inside his head. He saw men flattened against walls, bullets ricocheting around them. Mohamed Malik's eyes stared blankly at him as blood trickled from a hole in his forehead. He saw blood; more blood than he thought possible. He screwed shut his eyes and pressed his flattened palms against his ears but still he heard the gunfire.

Still, he saw blood.

CHAPTER 5
AFTERMATH

KEN WELLBURN recovered his sight but needed three weeks sick leave. In his absence, Gilberto Jorge, the young inspector who had filled in as company second-in-command, took over as Company Commander. Never before or since, has a one-pip, probationary inspector taken day-to-day command of a riot company. For Jorge, it was worth it just to see divisional superintendents' faces when he introduced himself as the Company Commander. For his courage in remaining at his post and continuing to send vital situation reports whilst under fire, Jorge received the governor's gallantry commendation, which entitled him to wear a red lanyard on his left shoulder.

After a few days off, Corporal Chan Wan-kwong, sporting a neat dressing on his cheek, rejoined Adam Keen's platoon.

Constable Chau Yuk-kui's knee took a long time to heal. He endured much pain and a long period of sick leave. He did not return to Martin Cowley's platoon but in time, he went back to normal police duties.

Constable Cheung Lam-mun recovered quickly from his neck wound and was soon back at work. His doctor was not sure if he was lucky or unlucky. Had the bullet's path been a fraction of an inch different, he would have died or suffered permanent disability. The flip side was that the bullet had nearly missed him completely.

Corporal Lau Hing-wing, who had braved gunfire to retrieve

the platoon first aid satchel, also received the governor's gallantry commendation and the right to wear the red lanyard. Tragically, some years later, Corporal Lau took his own life.

After the Gurkhas secured the village, Martin Cowley spoke to one of his constables, a man named Wu Shing-hing. Constable Wu showed Cowley burn marks on his arm and leg, both the result of grazing bullets. They had come close to causing life-changing injuries but throughout that day, Wu never mentioned them.

With the passage of time, the Sha Tau Kok story grew, as do all good stories. A favorite was that the gunmen fled when the Gurkhas drew their broad-bladed kukris, screamed their age-old battle cry, *'Ayo Gorkhali,'* and charged into the village. For many years, the story did the rounds of army officers' messes. Sorry, as much as we love it, it isn't true.

Officially, the Gurkhas did not open fire during their advance. However, according to Martin Cowley, as they advanced along the ridge the Gurkhas came under fire and returned fire without hesitation.

The records show five Hong Kong police officers died and eleven more were injured. The records give the casualty figures but say nothing about the real people behind the statistics. Men with friends and loved ones. Men with favorite songs and pet hates. Men of humor and men of purpose. Who killed Corporal Fung Ying-ping, Constable Khurhshid Ahmed, Constable Kong Shing-kay, and Constable Mohamed Malik? Who was the sniper that killed Constable Wong Loi-hing, temporarily blinded Superintendent Ken Wellburn and came so close to killing Inspector Adam Keen and Corporal Chan Wan-kwong? Who shot Constable Cheung Lam-mun through the neck? Who pulled the trigger and shattered Constable Chau Yuk-kui's knee and so nearly crippled Constable Wu Shing-hing?

Martin Cowley fulfilled his ambition to become a detective

and spent most of his thirty-year career investigating serious crimes. He cannot name those who fired the shots but he has forensically dissected the incident and come to some logical conclusions. There are two main suspects. China's Peoples' Liberation Army was, and still is, a disciplined and well-trained fighting force. The People's Militia was an assortment of workers, farmers and spare hands. They received some military training but lacked the army's discipline. Compared to the PLA, they were a second-rate force. The gunmen's marksmanship was not consistent. Whoever fired at the police post showed high levels of training and skill. They shot away the post radio aerials then fired through the post's small gun ports, killing two police officers. Bullet scarring close to the gun ports showed that the fatal shots were not a fluke. The sniper who killed Constable Kong Shing-kay at the fire station reacted quickly and fired with great accuracy.

The rural committee building was more than four hundred yards from Chung Ying Street, which is beyond the effective range of a Kalashnikov AK47 or a Simonov rifle. Whoever shot at Martin Cowley and the two standby platoons, most likely fired from within Hong Kong territory. Cowley has considered the injuries to his two constables. Cheung Lam-mun recovered relatively quickly from his neck wound, which was small and well-defined. Chau Yuk-kui's knee injury, while serious, did not leave him permanently disabled. From this, Cowley concludes that the gunman used a hand-held weapon like a Kalashnikov or a Simonov. Powerful though these weapons are, a heavier, belt-fed machinegun would have caused injuries that were more serious.

Seven days before the shooting, a senior People's Liberation Army officer appeared in Chung Ying Street and seemed to give instructions to a group of staff officers. Later, the gunmen's' firing positions showed expert pre-planning. From a strategic standpoint, we would expect a senior PLA officer to rely only on well-trained and disciplined soldiers, even if that meant sending them into Hong Kong territory. However, in 1967, things were not that simple. China was in turmoil. The army was a patchwork of political factions, all with different agenda and allegiances. Civil and military policies changed by the day, sometimes by the hour. Senior officials and army officers found themselves purged, then reinstated, then purged again. Allegiances shifted; imperatives changed. Had the police killed or captured a Chinese soldier in British territory, could our senior PLA officer count on his commander's support? Probably not.

So, who fired on Martin Cowley and the men at the rural committee building? Whoever he was, he could not have had a better target. Firing an automatic weapon, he shot at more than eighty men, standing stock-still, in parade ground formation. That he managed to hit only four suggests he was not a professional soldier. Similarly, the first burst of machinegun fire aimed at Adam Keen's platoon did not hit anyone.

Returning to our senior People's Liberation Army officer. Would he have baulked at deploying poorly-equipped and undisciplined local militia into British territory? Militarily, not the best choice but politically, the more astute one. If things went wrong, he could claim that poorly-trained and undisciplined civilians had acted alone. This looks an attractive option, but the PLA does not get off the hook so easily. The Chinese soldiers present in Sha Tau Kok must have known that armed militia were active in the village. That they did nothing to control them indicates at best, passive support. But might the PLA have played a more active role? On the day of the shooting, several police officers saw men in army uniform on the roof of the Chung Ying Street general store. The disciplined and accurate shots fired at the police post came from this rooftop.

The official version does not help. According to the Hong Kong Police website:

'... The true identity of the gunmen could not be established and there were different versions of them ranging from (1) 'communist militia'; (2) 'Chinese militia'; (3) 'villagers in the border area'; (4) 'villagers in the immediate vicinity'; to (5) 'unknown gun-men in the Mainland'.'

Where does that leave us? Incidences of undisciplined and inaccurate fire point to the People's Militia. There was also disciplined fire, which implicates the better-trained People's Liberation Army.

The jury is still out.

PART 4
BOAT PEOPLE

HONG KONG POLICE: INSIDE THE LINES

CHAPTER 6
INFLUX

IN THE SPRING of 1975, Saigon's street markets were as busy as ever. Throughout the city, there were tree-lined boulevards and *al fresco* cafés. Glaze-tiled pagodas with hooked eaves, rose seven stories or more. Leafy parks offered shaded respite from the year-round heat. Bicycles, motor scooters, pedal taxis, and gleaming limousines jostled for road space. There were pretty girls in conical hats and silky, ankle length tunics. In the bars, the beer was cheap and for a few Yankee dollars, women would provide comfort to a lonely visitor. The war had not touched the city since the Vietcong's Tet offensive in 1968. For the ever-optimistic Saigoners, the Vietnam War was just a grainy snatch of newsreel.

But the North Vietnamese was pushing south. On March 25, they captured Vietnam's ancient capital, Hue. They rounded up government officials, journalists, intellectuals, and any others they considered a threat. Some were shipped north for re-education, others they executed on the spot. Three days later, Da Nang fell. On April 9, the Northerners attacked Xuan Loc, just fifty miles from Saigon. Thirteen days later, Xuan Loc's defenders staggered back to Saigon. By late April, northern troops encircled Saigon. As rockets landed in Saigon's suburbs, American ambassador Graham Martin went on local television, insisting that he and his embassy staff were going nowhere. The following day, the North Vietnamese shelled Saigon's Tan Son Nhut Airport. That was the signal for nearly three thousand people to gather in the US embassy grounds. There were generals, senators and senior officials, all with their families. Thousands more surrounded the embassy. They clamored at the gate, pleading for help.

Inside the embassy, there were orders and counter orders. Assignments given; assignments cancelled. The embassy's secure file room held the identities of thousands of Vietnamese who had served the Americans. Too late, ambassador Martin ordered his intelligence officers to shred everything. With the airport closed, Martin prepared to evacuate everyone by helicopter. Marines and army engineers cleared the embassy compound of trees and shrubs. Diplomatic staff rolled up their sleeves and joined them.

Offshore, the US Navy's Seventh Fleet Commander, Admiral Donald Whitmire, ordered his Sea Knight and heavy lift Sea King helicopters into the air. Their marine pilots flew in low and settled on the embassy's newly-cleared landing spaces. Marines piled out of the helicopters and reinforced the embassy guard. All day and into the night, a steady relay of overloaded helicopters made the one hour round trip to the fleet and back. Pilots worked beyond their safety hours.

The South Vietnamese military collapsed. Army and air force pilots commandeered helicopters and saved as many family and friends as they could. The fleeing helicopters swarmed towards the American fleet and landed where they could: aboard Whitmore's command ship and on the tiny flight decks of escort destroyers. One destroyer, the *USS Kirk* took on board two hundred refugees. When flight decks became crowded, sailors heaved the helicopters into the South China Sea.

As North Vietnamese tanks crashed through the presidential palace gates, what was left of South Vietnam's navy put to sea. With them was a ragtag collection of coastal steamers, pleasure craft, fishing boats, and sailing dinghies. Most were short on fuel, many were unseaworthy. People crammed themselves into cargo holds and clung to every inch of deck space. For two days,

US Navy engineers repaired failed engines and made leaky ships safe. Then, under US Navy escort, an evacuation fleet of forty vessels, carrying more than thirty thousand people set out for the Philippines.

But one ship did not head for the Philippines, instead, she set out on her own. As she chugged slowly to the southwest, everything that could go wrong, went wrong.

Underway on the South China Sea, bound for Hong Kong, the container ship, *Clara Mærsk* received a distress call. It was in the early hours of May 2, just two days after Saigon's fall. The Motor Vessel *Truong Xuan* had lost power and was taking on water. Aboard were more than three thousand refugees, including women and children. The *Clara Mærsk's* Captain Anton M. Olsen ordered a change of course. Three hours later, the *Clara* pulled alongside the *Truong Xuan*. From the containership's bridge, the *Truong Xuan* must have seemed tiny. Built in Japan during the 1950s, she was just ninety-three meters long. The ship had spent her life beating back and forth between Thailand, Malaysia and Vietnam, and the years had not been kind to the little ship. With a full load, she could barely manage six knots and her pumps just about kept the sea out of her engine room.

As the *Clara Mærsk* towered above the *Truong Xuan*, people jammed the little ship's decks. Others straddled her derrick engines. Some stood atop the bridge house. Still more filled cargo holds that were sloshing with seawater. The sight must have worried Captain Olson: how would he transfer so many in safety? There was another worry: if he managed to get them all aboard, would the Hong Kong authorities let them ashore? Most Asian countries demanded that a ship's home nation take in refugees picked up at sea. Lawyers spent months wrangling the legalities while the rescue ship languished in port, under impound. The cost to a container ship's owners could run to millions of dollars.

HONG KONG POLICE: INSIDE THE LINES

It took six hours to transfer everyone from the stricken ship. After two days spent on open decks, the passengers were a raggedy-looking crowd. They were unwashed, their clothes sweat-stained. Short of water and food, their faces were gaunt and pained. Last man off the *Truong Xuan* was her captain, a China Seas veteran called Pham Ngoc Luy. He presented himself to the bridge and thanked Captain Olson for his rescue. Among the refugees, he explained, were some ex-soldiers and a few policemen but most were from Saigon's middle classes. They were educated people and had elected a representative committee to make collective decisions. Above everything, they feared a return to Vietnam. They wanted a written assurance they would be safe.

Captain Olsen weighed his options. Among the lawyers, teachers, and businessmen, were soldiers, policeman and no doubt, a few criminals. How many were armed? How desperate might they be? Was his ship and crew safe? He radioed his new passengers' concerns ahead then set course for Hong Kong.

On May 4, the *Clara* nosed into Hong Kong waters. The Marine Department controller directed her to an offshore mooring and soon, a pilot came aboard to guide her in. A helicopter landed on the *Clara's* rear deck. A Hong Kong official stepped from the helicopter and asked to speak to the refugees' representative committee. It was a nervous group that answered the summons. The *Clara's* bridge was spacious and air-conditioned. Her officers were well-scrubbed and wore starched summer uniforms. The Hong Kong official looked calm and impassive in neat slacks, a crisp cotton shirt and gleaming shoes. The committee members glanced at each other, feeling shabby and out of place. Their leader cleared his throat. He spoke English with a trace of an American accent.

'Have you received our request?' he asked.

The official said nothing, instead he handed over a note. The committee leader read it aloud:

CHRIS EMMETT

'The Governor and the Government of Hong Kong on behalf of her Majesty, Queen Elizabeth, have, in response to your call for help, granted you a temporary stay in Hong Kong while awaiting to be settled in countries of the free world.'

'Will you return us to Vietnam or transfer us to another communist country?' a committee member asked.

The official's reply was short and clear. 'No,' he said. 'We will never return you to Vietnam or send you to any communist country.'

Aboard the *Clara Mærsk*, there was joy. Back in Vietnam, there was joy of a different kind. For the traffickers in human cargo, and corrupt officials of the new regime, Hong Kong's promise meant great opportunity.

Vietnam's new rulers found much to keep them busy. When they abandoned their embassy, the Americans left behind cabinets full of secret files. Among them were the identities of thousands of Vietnamese who had served the Americans during the war. There were informants, double agents and members of shadowy units that had targeted the Vietcong militia. The regime set about rounding them up. Many simply disappeared.

With known undesirables out of the way, the regime turned on anyone whose background made them suspect. They detained ex-soldiers, government officials, politicians, intellectuals, schoolteachers, religious leaders, judges, in fact anyone who might question party diktat. The watchword was, *'re-education.'* On the face of it, this meant unlearning the bourgeois past and embracing the progressive future. Re-education would last just a few weeks, the party promised, maybe a few months for stubborn cases. The regime took foreign visitors to camps where contented, well-fed inmates spoke of seeing everything afresh. But in other camps, foreign visitors were not welcome. Writing in the Indochina Newsletter, award-winning human rights activist Ginetta Sagan, reported that as many as 300,000 inmates spent their working days at heavy labor that included digging wells and latrines, cutting back jungle and, without proper equipment, clearing landmines. Food was inadequate and medical treatment was rudimentary. Inmates lacked the strength to ward off malaria, beriberi, dysentery and tuberculosis. Failure to meet work quotas meant beatings, extra work and reductions in already inadequate food rations. Repeat offenders suffered solitary confinement in unventilated, metal shipping containers or in dark underground cellars.

Many died.

And many left. They trekked overland through Laos and Cambodia, seeking sanctuary in Thailand and Burma, now officially named Myanmar. Others sold their homes for a fraction of their value. They converted their possessions into gold or American dollars then bribed their way past Vietnamese officials. US$3,000 bought the promise of a sea passage to safety. A promise is one thing; reality another. The boats were mostly inshore fishing vessels, unseaworthy and underpowered. Many were open to the elements, without even a tarpaulin for shelter. Boat owners jammed as many aboard as there was space to take them. Beyond sight of land, sea thieves waited. They took the American dollars, they took the jewelry, they took the gold, they even took gold-filled teeth. Often, they took the food and water. And when there was no more to take, they used the women and girls. They spared the lives of those who did not resist. Spared them for the hunger, the raging thirst and the China Seas storms that come up from nowhere. How many of the little craft did not survive? No one knows. The survivors sought sanctuary in Malaysia, Singapore, Indonesia and the Philippines. But Southeast Asia was in no mind to give sanctuary. Whichever shore the refugees found, the authorities gave them food, water

and fuel then towed them back out to sea. They criss-crossed the South China Sea, thirsty, hungry and fearful. In time, word filtered back to Vietnam about the *Clara Mærsk* and Hong Kong's promise: 'We will never return you to Vietnam...'
Now, the human traffickers had a promise they could sell.

Hong Kong Police Launch 54 rounded Fan Lau Point and turned north, towards Tai O. As it passed beyond Lantau Island's leeward coast, the launch dipped into the swell rolling in from the South China Sea. Inspector Harry Evans steadied himself against the compass binnacle and ordered the helmsman to steer closer to the shore where the sea was flat. Below deck, the engine grumbled, driving the launch at its top speed of ten knots. The sun dazzled off the launch's brass fittings, the water chuckled along her hull and the tang of sea salt drifted into the wheelhouse. It was the kind of day when all was right with the world. *With luck, I might get in a bit of shore patrol,* Evans thought.

'Ah Sir. Tai jue.' – Sir. Look. Evan's sergeant pointed southwest and handed him the binoculars.

'M'yeh lei ga?' – What is it? Evans asked.

'M'ching choh,' – Not sure, the sergeant answered. 'Nei tai jue.' – You take a look.

Evans raised the binoculars and scanned left and right. Nothing. No – something. It looked like a log, probably poorly secured deck cargo lost overboard. Was it a hazard to shipping? He ordered the helmsman to steer towards it. Again, he raised the binoculars. Something moved. People? Yes, people. It was not a log, it was a boat. It was low in the water, just a few feet of freeboard. Evans cursed under his breath. Bloody townie picnickers caught out by the tide and currents. Silly sods would need a tow. He would give them a royal bollocking then tow them into Tai O. They could sort out any mooring fees and figure out how to get themselves home.

The helmsman reduced power as the police launch neared

the boat.

'My God,' Evans muttered. 'How many are aboard?'

From bow to stern, the boat was a mass of people. They were smiling and waving. One stood, making the boat rock. The others pulled him down as water sloshed over the gunnels. Evans ordered his engines cut as the launch drew alongside. The boat was little more than an open dinghy. In its belly, people squatted among bundles of belongings. An outboard motor puttered at the stern. Evan's stepped out of the wheelhouse and looked down into the boat. Dozens of sun-blackened faces gazed back up at him. Sea salt caked their clothes and matted their hair. A woman sat slumped in the bow, her face vacant. As she felt Evans' eyes on her, she hunched her shoulders and turned away.

Evan's sergeant followed him onto the deck.

'Illegal immigrants?' Evans asked.

The sergeant frowned. 'Not IIs,' he said and gave a snorting half-laugh. 'Looks like people from shipwreck.'

'Ask where they're from,' Evan ordered.

His sergeant spoke in rapid Cantonese. No one answered. The sergeant spoke again, his voice louder and harsher.

On the boat, a man stood and steadied himself against the launch's hull. His voice was a rasping croak. 'I speak English,' he said. 'We come from Saigon.'

'Sai Kung?' Evans asked, unconvinced. Sai Kung was a long haul from west Lantau. It was a pleasant little harbor on the eastern side of the New Territories, favored by Hong Kong's yachting crowd.

'No,' the man croaked. '*Saigon*. Saigon, Vietnam.'

Evans blinked at him. *Saigon*? That could not be right. There was a thousand miles of ocean between Saigon and Hong Kong. He looked again at the crowded little boat and the salt-crusted faces. *Bloody hell*, he thought. *It's true. Saigon.*

'Any instructions, *Ah Sir*?' the sergeant asked.

Evans thought for a moment. 'Get the women and children

onto the launch,' he said. 'They'll need water but don't give them too much or they'll puke it back up.' He moved to the radio set, picked up the microphone and pressed the transmit button.

'Marine control, this is Police Launch 54, over.'

'*PL 54, send, over.*'

'PL 54 is returning to Aberdeen base. So far?'

'*Roger so far.*'

'We have picked up approximately thirty people. So far?'

'*Roger so far.*'

'We have men, women, children, elderly,' Evans said. 'All are in distressed condition. They need food, water, clothes and medical attention. So far?'

'*Roger so far.*'

'They claim to have come from Vietnam. Over.'

'*Vietnam?*' Marine police control sounded dubious. '*Is this an illegal immigration case? Over.*'

Buggered if I know, Evans thought. 'Will advise you later,' he said and closed the transmission. He made his way back out of the wheelhouse and watched as his crew pulled the first child aboard.

In the following days and weeks, more boats arrived. Day by day, week by week, their numbers grew. Each ramshackle, overcrowded, underpowered little craft was a miracle of survival. For some, Hong Kong was their second or third attempt at landfall. The old army barracks in Chatham Road became the refugees' temporary home while the Hong Kong government held urgent talks with the United Nations High Commission for Refugees. Within a year, many of those early arrivals started new lives in the United States, France, Germany and Australia. For the human traffickers, the news could not have been better. The price of a passage went up. For Inspector Harry Evans and other police launch commanders, shore patrol would become a luxury. Within hours of putting to sea, police launches came across at

HONG KONG POLICE: INSIDE THE LINES

least one refugee boat. With survivors picked up and boats under tow, the launches returned to bases that were fast becoming clearinghouses for the Chatham Road refugee camp. As pressure on police launches and crews grew, the marine police found it more difficult to meet their day-to-day commitments.

It was hard to imagine how things could get worse.

There has been a Chinese community in Vietnam for as long as anyone can remember. Collectively, they are the Hua people and as with all Chinese communities, they are hard working and entrepreneurial. Before the Vietnam War, the Hua ran businesses ranging from corner shops to major corporations. It was only a matter of time before Vietnam's communist regime clamped down on them. First came a decree outlawing all wholesale trade. Next, there was a ban on large corporations. Thousands of businesses closed, which hit the Hua community hard. Then history took one of its unexpected turns and for the Hua, life got even harder.

It started when Cambodian soldiers moved onto a Vietnamese island called Phu Quoc. Nine days later, they did the same at Tho Chu. Battle-hardened Vietnamese troops soon recovered the islands but just to hammer the point home, they took tit-for-tat control of some Cambodian islands. China watched in alarm. Was this the start of something bigger? Did Vietnam mean to take over all Indochina? As tensions racked up, China moved troops closer to the Vietnam border. Vietnam's new rulers did not receive this news well and the first to feel their displeasure were Vietnam's ethnic Chinese, the Hua. Word spread to the villages, towns and countryside: the Hua were spies and Chinese collaborators. As rumor took hold, the Vietnamese government seized Hua property and banished Hua people to labor camps. They drafted the Hua's young men into the army and sent them to fight in Cambodia. In their tens of thousands, the Hua fled their homes. Some travelled overland into China, others took to the boats. Before the communist victory, the Hua had dominated Vietnam's business class. Many had hoarded gold and American dollars. Now, they were on the move. The Hua had the gold and the people traffickers had the contacts. The people traffickers were quick to spot new consumer demand and they knew just how to satisfy it.

It was December 23, 1978, just two days before Christmas. To make things worse, it was a Saturday, which is a bad day for a major flap. The flap was no one's fault, well, no one in Hong Kong, that is. A day earlier, authorities in the Taiwan port of Kaoshung had refused entry to a Panama-registered cargo ship. The refusal was unexpected. Kaoshung was the ship's designated destination and maritime law required the port authorities to let her in, particularly given the nature of her cargo. But regardless of maritime law, the ship's master knew he was on the receiving end of an argument he could not win. He put back to sea and the next day, arrived at Waglan Island, just outside Hong Kong waters. There, he dropped anchor and asked for a berth. It sounds simple enough, but Hong Kong's Director of Marine and Port Control was quick to react. Under no circumstances was the ship to enter Hong Kong waters, he ordered. It must return immediately to its designated port of call, Kaoshung.

The ship's master, tired of that particular game, played his trump card. He had more than 3,300 people aboard, he said. There were men, women and children. Not only children but also babies, some born in the last day or two. The people were in bad shape, he reported. They were suffering from thirst, hunger and the cold. Worst affected were the children. The ship's name was the *Huey Fong* and she was the latest tool in the people traffickers' kit box.

And so, there was a flap. The port control room called the police control room. The police duty controller called the Marine Police duty controller and he called the Assistant Commissioner

in charge of the Marine Police. The Assistant Commissioner in charge of the Marine Police did what all police officers do when there's a flap.
He sorted things out.

Compared to the regular police launches, *Sea Lion* was big. She was 110 feet long by twenty-five feet wide. She carried a crew of twenty-seven, who were no doubt a bit nervous as they pulled alongside Kowloon Public Pier. Waiting for them was Chief Superintendent John Turner, the marine police's second-in-command. He was in uniform but instead of his gold-braided cap, he wore a police riot helmet. Standing at *Sea Lion's* gangway, was her commander, Chief Inspector Yau Siu-fan. He grinned and snapped Turner a salute. Turner was glad to see him. Chief Inspector Yau was a marine veteran. He had joined as a constable and worked his way up the ranks. Hong Kong's waters were his backyard. He had seen typhoons, shipwrecks, fires at sea and all manner of crises. He knew every community leader in every village on every outlying island. He was the complete operations man. He was a man who got things done.

Turner stepped aboard *Sea Lion* and ordered Yau to head east, past Junk Bay then south to Waglan Island. Low cloud darkened the sky and once they left the harbor, a chill wind spattered the wheelhouse with salt spray. The launch turned south and shouldered its way through surging seas. Turner mulled over his orders — they sounded easy: board the *Huey Fong* and assess the situation. But nothing is ever easy. What if some or, God help us, all the three thousand-plus passengers were hostile? Were they armed? Who was in charge? Was the master still in command? With *Sea Lion's* full complement, Turner had just over two dozen men. Each carried a .38 caliber service revolver and there were two Sterling submachine guns in the arms locker. Turner peered forward and his eyes fell on the deck gun, a 0.5 caliber Browning. A two-second burst could unleash more than fifteen, half-inch diameter rounds. For now, he lay that thought aside. Waglan Island was just one mile ahead.

Waglan Island is not a welcoming place. It is two rocky outcrops and on a map, they look like a scrawled exclamation mark. Breakers burst white against low cliffs as *Sea Lion* rounded Waglan's southern tip. And there was the *Huey Fong*. She was old, built in 1948 for a Danish shipping line. Rust streaked her hull and superstructure. She looked ready for the breakers yard but crowding her decks, there were people. They pressed against the ship's railing. They jammed the forecastle, poop and weather decks. They clambered onto her cargo hatches, straining to see over the heads of others.

Turner took Chief Inspector Yau aside and gathered a small team around him. 'Take no chances,' he said. 'As soon as we board, we go straight to the bridge and secure it.'

They nodded, grim-faced.

'We detain the ship's master,' Turner continued. 'After that, we'll work out some way of speaking to the passengers.'

Again, nodded acknowledgement.

Hanging against the *Huey Fong's* hull, was the ship's pilot gangway, a rickety metal staircase leading to the deck. *Sea Lion* drew alongside. The helmsman threw the engine into reverse then cut power as the big launch scraped against the gangway landing. Turner was first off. As he stepped onto the *Huey Fong's* deck, a wall of humanity met him. They were wide-eyed and unkempt, their clothes were grimy and crumpled, their faces mournful and afraid. Turner looked to the bridge. The people moved back, clearing a path for him. Turner went up to the bridge where a man stepped forward to meet him. A grin split his face. 'You Royal Navy?' he asked.

'Police,' Turner replied. 'Are you the ship's master?'

'Master?' the man replied. 'Yes. Ship's master.' He indicated another man. 'Mister Dinh,' he said. 'Mister Dinh is passenger spokesman. You want anything, you speak Mister Dinh.'

Later, Mister Dinh would prove a huge help, but for now, Turner had a ship to secure. He left men to hold the bridge, then he moved back to the deck. Evening was drawing in and a chill wind came off the sea. People huddled together, gaunt and hollow-eyed. Some cast pleading looks and made motions of bringing food to their mouths. Others squatted alone on the deck, their eyes cast down. Never had Turner seen so much distress in one place. He ordered the cargo hold opened. As the hatch slid back, the stench of unwashed bodies, human waste and stale vomit drifted onto the deck. In silence, hundreds of faces stared up at him. Young, old, babies. There was desperation and there was sickness. It was like a fog that clung to the very young and the very old. Just a short time ago, Turner had left a city reveling in joyous excess. Stylish people walked streets ablaze with Christmas lights. Revelers filled the city's bars and restaurants. They drank, ate, chatted, laughed, boasted and argued. Turner looked into the stinking dark of the ship's hold. *No joy here,* he thought. He cast his eyes around the decks. *No joy anywhere here.*

Turner went back aboard *Sea Lion* and radioed marine police control. He confirmed that *Huey Fong's* passengers were all Vietnamese. They needed urgent medical aid, food, water and blankets. *Fat chance,* he thought. *Saturday afternoon, two days before Christmas. What's the chance of contacting anyone with enough clout to get things moving?*

As it turned out, the chances were good. An emergency body called the Governor's Committee had convened in Police Headquarters. The Police Commissioner was there, so were members of key government departments. There were senior army, navy and air force officers. Chairing it all was an aide to Hong Kong's governor. Within two hours, launches carrying fully equipped medical teams arrived. Helicopters airlifted the seriously ill to hospital. There was food, water and blankets. Later, under police escort, the *Huey Fong* came into Hong Kong harbor.

With all emergency needs filled, immigration officers started the slow job of checking the passengers. Not until the end of January, did the last of them receive clearance as genuine refugees. The ship's master had his story ready and he reeled it off like a practiced sales pitch. He had been underway to Kaoshung, he said. Off the Vietnam coast, he stumbled across a flotilla of small boats and, like the master of the *Clara Mærsk,* had taken them aboard.

As far as cover stories go, it was a good one and the ship's officers backed their captain in every tiny detail. The marine police detectives were not convinced. People are imperfect creatures and memory is an imprecise thing. Had there been small differences in their accounts, the detectives might have believed them but the stories were too good; too well learned. Experts looked at the *Huey Fong*'s log. Someone had altered it. Cracks appeared in the crew's story. A search team came aboard. For three days, they opened hatches, lifted deck plates and dismantled fittings. Water cisterns, wiring conduits, bilges, safety gear, they stripped down everything. On the third day, they entered the engine room. After three hours, they unbolted the propeller shaft casing and there, they struck gold. To be precise, they struck gold leaf. It was as thin as baking foil. Layer by layer, the team stripped it away. When the final tally came in, they had recovered more than 130 kilos of gold, worth a little over one-million American dollars.

The ship's passengers, now classified as refugees, had nothing to lose. All told the same story. After paying off officials in Saigon, now renamed Ho Chi Minh City, they boarded buses that took them to the port of Vung Tau. There, moored to the wharf, was the *Huey Fong*. They checked in like regular passengers and paid their fares in gold leaf.

Piece by piece, the evidence clicked into place. Marine police arrested the ship's master, seven of his crew and four Hong Kong businessmen. They went on trial for conspiracy to defraud and received prison sentences ranging from fifteen months to seven years.

As he settled back to normal duties, Chief Superintendent John Turner might have thought the *Huey Fong* was a one-off; something no one would see again. He was wrong. On February 7, just fifteen days after the last *Huey Fong* passenger left the ship, Turner received a late night telephone call. The freighter *Skyluck*, unannounced and unwelcome, had steamed right into Hong Kong harbor. Aboard were 2,700 Vietnamese men, women and children. Turner grabbed his gear, called marine control and asked for a driver to collect him from his quarters.

The small boats kept coming. Refugees arrived in their dozens, then in their hundreds, then in their thousands. They were Vietnam's best and brightest: intellectuals, doctors, engineers, lawyers, entrepreneurs, teachers. They came and Hong Kong gave them shelter. Elsewhere in Asia, there was no such welcome. Newscasts showed patrol craft towing battered little boats out to sea. There were close-up shots of frightened children and tearful mothers. The United Nations applied pressure and Southeast Asian countries finally agreed to provide temporary asylum. Vietnam eased exit restrictions and Western countries increased the rate of resettlement. The result: Southeast Asia's asylum camps soon became full and again, the Vietnamese found themselves towed back out to sea. After shuttling from one shoreline to the next, the boats found their way to Hong Kong.

The Vietnamese were not the only ones with their hopes set on Hong Kong. Every day, people slipped in from China. They wormed their way through the border fence. Some swam, braving the Mirs Bay and Deep Bay sharks. Others stowed aboard fishing boats, trains and lorries. Once arrived, they could apply to stay, but for newcomers, wages were low. Shantytowns of plywood and corrugated iron covered Hong Kong's hillsides. The government built new and affordable housing projects but construction could not keep up with demand. For every person who moved away from the hillside shanties, another moved in. For the first time ever, the government decided to treat undocumented entry from China as illegal immigration. In short order, newly-classified illegal immigrants found themselves on buses that took them to the border and from there, back to China.

Some border crossers were Vietnamese. In their flight from Vietnam, they had trekked north into China's Guangxi province where they found life tougher than expected. But how should Hong Kong treat them? Were they illegal immigrants or refugees? The legal experts *hummed* and *hahhed* but eventually came to a decision. The Chinese border crossers must return to China; the Vietnamese border crossers could stay. This did not sit well with Hong Kong's citizens. It rankled that the authorities expelled their Chinese compatriots but gave shelter to Vietnamese who arrived by the same route.

In Hong Kong, the strain on living space and government coffers began to show. The refugee camp at Chatham Road was no longer enough. The government moved more than two thousand Vietnamese to a new camp in west Kowloon. Shortly afterwards, another disused army barracks became home to twenty thousand. As soon as the new camp opened, it became instantly overcrowded. Ten thousand moved into accommodation next to the airport. A factory building in the New Territories housed sixteen thousand more. There was food, shelter and medical care but conditions were basic. Families lived on three-tiered bunks measuring four-feet wide by six-feet long. There was only a curtain for privacy. The noise was unrelenting. Rats foraged in the garbage. Drains were inadequate.

Back in Vietnam, things were changing. There were economic reforms and greater freedoms. The days of the boat people should have been over but small boats continued to arrive. It struck the police launch crews that many of the boats looked in remarkably good condition. Their passengers seemed unruffled by the hardships of long sea crossings in open boats. Rumors spread that some Vietnamese travelled overland to Guangdong, the province bordering Hong Kong. There, they purchased boats and sailed into Hong Kong waters masquerading as refugees. It was not only the boats that had changed, the new boat people were no longer Vietnam's middle class elite. Many seemed rough and uneducated. Some instinctively turned away their faces when they saw a police officer.

In the camps, hostility seethed between North and South Vietnamese. There were fights and night ambushes. Gangs called Bear Heads, preyed on weaker camp residents. Food, money, valuables, cigarettes, women, the Bear Heads took what they wanted. Outside the camps, shops reported petty thefts. In nearby lanes and alleys, street robberies increased. More and more, the culprits were young toughs with strange accents. A drug trade blossomed. In Kowloon, police vice squads found young Vietnamese women working in brothels and massage parlors. There were whispers of forced prostitution. The camps' young toughs sported gold chains, designer casuals and mobile phones. Police stepped up action but this posed another problem: Western countries would not resettle anyone with a criminal record.

Hong Kong people started to ask, were the new arrivals really refugees or just opportunists looking to leapfrog the queue for a new life in the West? As suspicion grew, the United States set stricter immigration conditions and the number of Vietnamese moving to the USA halved. Resettlement slowed and Hong Kong's Vietnamese population mushroomed. Then, something happened that hardened attitudes even further.

The authorities should have seen it coming but, as ever, hindsight is a wonderful faculty. Next door to the airport was Kai Tak camp. It housed about ten thousand Vietnamese, half from the north, the other half from the south. Inside the camp, the mood was dark. Hostility between north and south had grown into hatred. The Bear Head gangs crystallized into north-south groups. Something had to give and on May 1, 1982, it did just that. A North Vietnamese gang raised the flag of communist Vietnam and held a noisy party to celebrate the fall of Saigon. As word spread, furious South Vietnamese converged on the northerners. Rival gangs took makeshift weapons from pre-prepared hiding places. There were running fights. People were injured, property smashed. Police in riot gear moved in to separate the two sides. Gangs of young men wielding homemade spears and machetes, charged police lines. Yard by yard, the police retook control but as soon as they quashed trouble in one area, it flared up somewhere else. It was dawn before there was any semblance of order.

Among the wider community, there was a sense that little Hong Kong had already done enough. Government introduced what it called a *humane deterrence policy*. Starting in July 1982, any Vietnamese entering Hong Kong must live in closed camps. No more freedom to venture outside, no factory work, no getting away from the overcrowded, rat-infested living space. Instead, there was barbed wire and security guards. Each resident had an identification number. There were daily head counts.

Some believed the policy was inhumane and it deterred no one. As the closed camps filled, the boats kept coming. In 1989, 34,000 people arrived and claimed asylum. There was rigorous screening to separate real from bogus refugees. For a while at least, the number of arrivals fell, but by the end of 1989, the camps still held more than sixty thousand people. Most had no chance of resettlement. The United Kingdom held talks with the Vietnamese government and with the United Nations High Commission for Refugees. A Vietnamese delegation visited Hong Kong and promised camp residents there would be no reprisals against anyone who went home. The United Nations offered US$360 to everyone, including children, who went back. Camp residents could apply for overseas resettlement but only if they first returned to Vietnam. There would be no resettlement for those who stayed. A month later, eighty-one people voluntarily boarded a flight back to Vietnam. It was a low-key affair, no speeches, no press, no well-wishers. Shortly after dawn, the eighty-one climbed the loading ramp of a privately chartered, Hercules cargo aircraft. The Hercules is principally a military aircraft and apart from a few canvas seats, it offers no comfort. Once aboard, the passengers simply laid out their possessions and settled on the cargo bay floor. At the appointed hour, the crew raised the loading ramp, gunned the engines and they were away.

In the coming years, more would volunteer to return home but many thousands decided to sit tight. As chances for resettlement waned, frustrations grew. In the camps, the violence grew worse. There were mass escapes, riots, injuries and deaths. At Whitehead camp, inmates set fire to the administration offices and beat down the main gate. The police came under pressure from all sides: the public demanded tougher action; the United Nations High Commission for Refugees demanded restraint. The Bear Heads found they could apply pressure wherever and whenever they wanted. The gangs' power grew. Public attitudes hardened even further.

Of course, it had to end, and end it did. The end came in stages. Stage one: the government promised true refugees they could remain until resettled overseas; stage two: non-refugees must return to Vietnam. The torrent slowed but still they came, some genuinely escaping oppression but most looking for a free ride to a better life. But who was genuine and who was not? And, once identified, what to do with the bogus asylum seekers? The answer to that question was in stage three.

Stage three was Operation Drumbeat.

CHAPTER 7
DRUMBEAT

DURING THE FIRST half of the twelfth century, in the reign of China's Southern Soong emperors, a soldier born of tenant farmers rose to prominence. He became renowned not only for his military prowess but also for his righteous treatment of his soldiers and of the ordinary people. His name was Yue Fei and even today, his name is a byword for courage and loyalty. It seems only right that a hard-hitting columnist for the Chinese language newspaper *Ming Pao* should use the *nom de plume*, Yue Fei. In his daily life, the columnist's name was Jim Elms. He was Eurasian, a man grounded in Hong Kong's multi-cultural community. Born and educated in Hong Kong, Elms was fluent in spoken and written Chinese. He knew the city and her people; knew how they worked, how they played and what drove them. This was a big asset to Elms' main employer. When not writing his column for the *Ming Pao*, Jim Elms was a police officer and he worked in East Kowloon's Regional Police Headquarters.

The Hong Kong Police management structure looks much like that of any major corporation. There is a head office, known as Police Headquarters. Below that are the regional offices, or the Regional Headquarters. Under the Regional Headquarters are the local outlets, called districts and divisions. From there, the police deliver day-to-day services, like beat patrols and criminal investigation.

The Regional Headquarters are pretty much mirror images

of each other. There is an Administration Wing, taking care of logistics and human resources. There is a Crime Wing, made up of experienced detectives. Traffic Wing does its best to bring antisocial drivers to book and keep the traffic moving. Finally, there is the Operations Wing, known to everyone as Regional Ops. Regional Ops is a great place to work. It has the first response cars of the Emergency Unit, it has the Regional Missing Persons Unit and the region's paramilitary, Police Tactical Unit, better known as the 'Blue Berets.' The trickiest part of Ops Wing's job is contingency planning. If there is a major problem, it is no good the Ops Wing Commander giving a shrug and saying, 'Gee, we didn't see that one coming.' The Ops Wing Commander is supposed to see problems coming and have plans ready to deal with them. As a result, Ops Wing holds and updates contingency plans for major problems like typhoons, fires, floods and public disorder, not to mention crowd management at festivals like Chinese New Year, Ching Ming and all the other special celebrations. The Ops Wing Commander needs the skills, experience and foresight to handle any curve ball that Hong Kong's supercharged way of life can pitch. It takes someone special to run a Regional Ops Wing and in the early 1990s, the man in charge of East Kowloon's Ops Wing was Senior Superintendent Jim Elms.

To say the Regional Headquarters are mirror images of each other is true only in part. The management structure looks the same but each region has a distinct character that calls for a bit of flexibility. For example, the day-to-day problems facing a rural region are very different from those facing a densely populated urban region. East Kowloon was special because it had a bit of everything. It had factories, public housing projects, important temples and a large country park. It looked after Hong Kong's Mass Transit Railway system. Before Hong Kong's airport relocated to Lantau Island, the region also policed the old Kai Tak airport in Kowloon Bay. On top of that, there was a Vietnamese detention centre at High Island, in rural Saikung. For Jim Elms, the camp was a headache but to be fair, it had not always been so. During the early days, the Vietnamese were honest-to-goodness fugitives from oppression. They were middle class, cultured and well-educated. But by the time Jim Elms took over East Kowloon's Operations Wing, things had changed. The lawyers, the teachers, the writers, the artists, the thinkers and the entrepreneurs were gone; gone to America, Australia, New Zealand and Europe. The only ones left were the no-hopers. They had nothing to fear from Vietnam's new government but they hankered after a better life in the West and saw the camps as a way to bypass the immigration queues. Yes, the closed camps were a headache. Operation Drumbeat was the plan to cure the headache and on one muggy day in late spring, it was Jim Elms' job to make sure that Operation Drumbeat worked.

Elms stood before the gates of High Island camp knowing that inside, he would find nothing but sullen resentment. *Sullen*, the word summed up the day perfectly. It was late spring. The summer temperatures had started to show themselves but still, a lingering northern airstream brought low cloud that pressed down from a sullen sky. There was no rain but the air felt damp. You could smell it on the trees, bushes and undergrowth. Beyond the gate, the buildings were grey, the perimeter and internal fences were grey, the access roads and pedestrian pathways were grey. Yes, the mood in the camp was sullen. Sullen because tomorrow, one hundred camp inmates would return to Vietnam and they were not volunteers.

This was stage three. This was Operation Drumbeat.

High Island camp was a community of three thousand people. It sat on a plot of flat ground measuring nearly half a mile square. Surrounding it, were two parallel fences, separated by a narrow walkway. Coils of razor wire topped both the inner and outer fences. The camp had three entrances, the main one at the front and one on each flank. Each entrance had two gates. The first opened into a quarantine compound, large enough to take a couple of ten-ton trucks. Only when guards closed and locked the first gate would they open the second, allowing access to the compound proper. Inside, there were five large accommodation blocks, each within its own fenced compound. Set apart from the accommodation blocks, were smaller huts: the canteen, laundry, storerooms, classrooms, an administration block and staff quarters.

The camp's manager and guards were members of Hong Kong's Correctional Services Department. In short, they were prison officers. The inmates were mostly South Vietnamese, many of whom had been there for years. As hopes for resettlement waned, frustrations grew. Weeks earlier, camp staff had tried to enforce a minor camp rule. It was something and nothing but in an instant, it became the focus for all the camp's bottled frustrations. Hundreds surrounded the administration building, imprisoning the camp manager and his staff. By the time the trouble kicked off, everyone had forgotten what had started it. There were no demands, nothing to negotiate, only a mob venting their fury. Eventually, police in riot gear restored order. Yes, Elms thought, High Island camp is a drab and troubled place. He felt a twinge of sympathy for the inmates but pushed it to the back of his mind. Today, there was a job to do. A man standing beside Elms was speaking.

'It's complete overkill,' the man sniffed. He fluttered his hand towards the row of police trucks. 'So many police,' he said. 'And why are they wearing berets? They look like soldiers. No wonder these good people are afraid.' He was tall and slim, probably in his early thirties. He had a mass of blonde hair that tended to flop forward. To Elms it seemed he was forever tossing back his head to keep his hair out of his eyes. He had puffy cheeks and a small mouth that gave his face a look of permanent petulance. Pinned to his shirt was a laminated card that bore the words:

CHRIS EMMETT

Piers Thorne
United Nations High Commission for Refugees.

There was a third man in their group. He was a middle-aged Asian with a sharp, intelligent face.

'Perhaps we won't need you today, Mister Nguyen,' Elms said.

The Asian grinned back. 'But then I would not get my interpreter's fee,' he chuckled. 'Perhaps I stay.'

A police superintendent stepped close and snapped a salute. He wore a khaki bush jacket and slacks tucked into calf-high boots. Instead of a peaked cap, he wore a beret that marked him as a member of the Police Tactical Unit. Around his waist was a thick, Sam Browne belt. A leather cross-strap passed across his body and over his right shoulder. At his hip, the grip of a Smith and Wesson revolver peeked from a leather holster. Next to him, stood a bereted constable who was the superintendent's orderly. In a pouch at the orderly's belt, was a portable radio.

'All ready to go, sir,' the superintendent said.

'Good,' Elms answered. 'Orders clear enough?'

'Crystal,' the superintendent answered. 'Secure all entrances. Move into the camp and isolate the accommodation blocks. Search for weapons, drugs, and other contraband. When we've done that, we're to search the public areas.'

'How about the women police?' Elms asked.

'We have forty women from Tango Company,' the superintendent said. He half-turned and nodded towards a group of women police, aligned in four ranks. They wore the same uniform as the men: khaki bush shirts, slacks, boots and berets. 'They're ready,' he said. 'First-rate bunch of officers.'

'Right,' Elms said. 'Give the order to move in. You and your orderly, stick with us.'

The orderly raised the radio to his lips. 'Start op,' he said. 'Repeat, start op.'

HONG KONG POLICE: INSIDE THE LINES

There was a shouted order. The male and female Tactical Unit officers came to attention. In four rank formation, they jogged towards the front gate. Elms and his party followed. They stepped into the quarantine area and with a ringing *ker-lonk*, the outer gate swung shut behind them. The inner gate opened and the police fanned out into the main compound.

The superintendent was listening to a radio message. 'Side gates secure,' he said. 'The platoons are moving to their target locations now.'

'Any resistance?' Elms asked.

The superintendent shook his head. 'Some shouting,' he said. 'A few pushes and shoves. Nothing major.'

Police surrounded the nearest accommodation block. A sergeant led a group of male and female officers inside. Moments later, the occupants filed out. The accommodation blocks were large, and soon the crowd numbered in the hundreds: men, women, children. In what looked like a rehearsed move, the men stood at the back, close to the block's walls. The women and children stood at the front, shielding the men from the police. From the rear of the crowd, a man shouted, *'Di an cut.'* He raised a clenched fist and pumped the air. *'Di an cut. Canh sat, di an cut.'* Others took up the shout. It grew into a rhythmic chant. Hundreds added their voices. *'Canh sat, di an cut...Canh sat, di an cut...'* It rolled across the compound, growing louder and louder.

Piers Thorne leaned close to the interpreter. He had to shout to make himself heard. 'What are they chanting, Mister Nguyen?'

'They're telling the police to eat shit,' Elms snapped. He took a breath and leveled his voice. 'We'll hear worse before we leave.'

A woman stepped from the crowd. She jiggled a child on her hip. She wore a faded T-shirt and loose fitting shorts. Her hair was piled high, fastened with what looked like a jade pin. Care-lines etched her face. Her eyes and mouth had a hard set. She was probably in her early twenties but life in the camp had aged her. The child screwed up its eyes and began to cry. She pointed to Elms and called out, *'Si quan cao cap.'* Her voice was loud and shrill. *'Toi muon noi chuyen voi ban.'*

'She wants to speak to the senior officer,' Nguyen said.

The Tactical Unit orderly grinned and adopted a falsetto voice. *'Canh sat an cap tien.'* He gave a humorless laugh. 'Police steal money.'

'Bloody fucking police steal money,' the woman shouted in English.

The interpreter raised an eyebrow. 'Seems the English lessons are working,' he said.

Thorne's eyes gleamed. 'What was that?' he demanded. 'The police have stolen money?' For the first time that day, he smiled. 'We'll have to stop the operation,' he crowed. 'Stop it right now. I want every police officer searched.'

'Radio message from number one platoon,' the orderly announced.

The superintendent took the radio and held it close to his ear. He nodded and pressed the transmit button. 'Understood,' he said. 'We'll join you there. Out.' To Elms he said, 'Weapons cache in accommodation block number two. No arrests.'

'Where did they find it?' Elms asked.

The superintendent frowned. 'In the bunks,' he answered. 'Obviously ready for use.'

'Let's see,' Elms said. He moved towards the accommodation block and signaled the others to follow. The chanting faded away. By the accommodation block door, a group of men balled their fists and thrust out their chests. Gold glinted at their necks, wrists and fingers. The men moved to block the way but the Tactical Unit constables pushed them back. For long moments, the two sides stood their ground, glaring at each other. Then, a man turned away. Another followed. In seconds, the way was clear.

Inside the accommodation block, neon strip lighting threw hard white light. Rows of tiered bunks lined the walls. Hanging limp from each bunk were flimsy drapes. Once bright with color and patterns, they were now grimed and patched. Torn newspapers, plastic bowls and plywood sheeting littered the floor. There was a smell of tobacco smoke, sweat and stale food. Somewhere, a radio played tinny music.

Thorne shook his head. 'I see your officers are as heavy-handed as ever,' he said.

Elms ignored him. 'Where are they?' he asked.

The superintendent pointed towards the block's far wall. 'My officers have them.'

Elms walked to where a group of police officers stood guarding something on the floor. There, laid out on the concrete, was what he had come to see. There were lengths of pipe, sharpened at one end to form a spear-point. There were crude machetes with handles fashioned from sawn-up chair legs. A club, spiked with nails and as long as a man's arm. Elms picked up a knife. Like the other weapons, it was homemade. He tested the blade with his thumb. He turned to Thorne and held the knife close to his face. 'See that?' he snapped. 'You could shave with that.'

Thorne shuffled his feet. 'Well... I mean... people need protection from the gangs,' he said. He smiled, finding his confidence. 'Gangs, I would add, the police seem powerless to control.'

'Gangs?' Elms snapped. *'Gangs?'* He swept his arm to encompass the cache of weapons. 'These aren't for protection from the *gangs*, my friend. They're to use against the police.'

Thorne opened his mouth to speak but Elms cut him off. 'Why do you think they're in here and not hidden away outside?' He gave Thorne no chance to answer. 'They've been brought in, ready for tomorrow's operation.'

Thorne's mouth worked and for a moment, it seemed he would argue but as his eyes fell on the pile of weapons, he was silent.

Elms turned to the superintendent. 'Bag this lot up and book it in at Wong Tai Sin main station,' he said. 'And pass my thanks to your men and women.'

The superintendent smiled. 'Certainly, sir. Any further instructions?'

'No,' Elms answered. 'Tomorrow, have your company at Wong Tai Sin station by oh-five-hundred hours. Normal working uniform but have your riot gear in transport boxes, loaded onto your vehicles.'

'Will do,' superintendent answered.

'Good,' Elms said. 'At the airport, Tactical Unit's Oscar Company will take over and escort the people onto the aircraft.'

The superintendent saluted, turned and strode away.

Elms made his way back to the main gate. The first half of the operation had gone well but tomorrow would see the real test. The High Island detainees had rejected Vietnam's promised amnesty and the United Nations offer of cash. Instead, they were holding out for resettlement that in their hearts, they knew would never come. Tomorrow, one-hundred would return home. Home to Vietnam.

And Jim Elms would go with them.

The airport duty constable raised the barrier and waved the convoy through. Ten trucks: one hundred Vietnamese; eighty-five uniformed police officers. The gate opened onto the eastern sector of the airport apron, a flat expanse of concrete. Jim Elms stood beneath the wing of an Airbus A300. On the fuselage, above the line of port windows, a legend read, *'CHINA SEAS AIR.'* Set on idle, the A300's engines whined. The oily smell of burnt aviation fuel drifted in the morning air. The sun had been up for less than an hour but already, sweat stung Jim Elms' eyes. His shirt clung to his back, damp and uncomfortable. Standing beside Elms was Chief Superintendent Paul Jakes, the commander of today's operation. Like Elms, he wore civilian clothes. Elms frowned. People volunteering to go back to Vietnam spent the journey on the floor of a cargo aircraft; those forcibly deported had the comfort of a modern airliner.

Behind the cockpit windows, the flight crew relaxed, pre-flight checks done. The passenger doors were open. A half hour earlier, mobile stairs had maneuvered into place. Gathered at the foot of the stairs were groups of young men and women. They wore casual clothes but their neat hair and straight bearing identified them as members of Hong Kong's Police Tactical Unit. The men were from the unit's Oscar Company, the women were with Tango Company. Earlier, they had chatted and joked but as the time grew near, they fixed their eyes on the airport's eastern gate. Were they enough to handle any trouble? For the tenth time that morning, Elms did a mental head count. Forty officers on the apron, more aboard the aircraft. There would be another eighty-five on board the trucks. Enough for now at least.

As the trucks eased to a halt beside the airplane, the jokey banter fell silent. The trucks' tailgates banged open. Uniformed police vaulted from the back and formed two aisles leading to the stairs. Others stayed to help women and children down onto the apron. The children kept close to their mothers, their eyes wide, uncomprehending. The women fussed among a growing pile of cloth bundles and candy-striped, zip-up bags. Most of the men stayed by their families. Six men stood apart from the others, silent and hard-faced.

'We'll have trouble with them,' Jakes muttered, nodding at the group.

'We'll board them last,' Elms answered. 'I'll make sure they're not sat together.'

A camp official made his way among the Vietnamese. He held a clipboard and checked off names from a list. The hard-faced men ignored him.

'The checks look a bit hit and miss,' Jakes commented.

'He wants to get away,' Elms answered. 'Can't say I blame him.'

Checks complete, the boarding started. The adults busied themselves safeguarding their luggage. There was lively chatter. The children seemed less fretful, some were smiling, excited by the prospect of travelling on an airplane. Boarding took just a few minutes. The uniformed officers clambered back aboard the trucks and the convoy snaked its way back to the eastern gate. The only Vietnamese left on the apron were the hard-faced men. Elms signaled to a group of plain-clothed officers then moved towards the men. Mister Nguyen, the interpreter followed. The men watched him, chests thrust out, fists resting on their hips. One was taller than the others. He had an angular face, a half-moon scar sat below his right eye. Pectoral muscles bulged under his T-shirt. Elms looked him square in the face but directed his words to the interpreter. 'Tell this one he's to board now,' he snapped. 'The others can wait.'

The man smirked. 'I speak English,' he crowed. 'We don't go on airplane.' He jabbed his finger at the ground. 'We stay Hong Kong. We stay Hong Kong until we go America.' He turned his head and spat.

'Name?' Elms demanded.

'I am Giap,' the man said.

'I want you on that plane now,' Elms ordered.

Giap's lips formed a slow smile. He lowered his voice. 'You have American dollars? You have cigarettes?' He leaned close to Elms. 'I make sure everyone cooperate. You help me; I help you.'

Elms took a step back and nodded to the escort constables. Two of them grabbed Giap's arms and bundled him up the stairs. Within seconds, he was aboard. Elms scowled at the others. Without a word, they lowered their gaze and followed their leader up the stairs.

'He could cause problems at the other end,' Paul Jakes said. 'According to the rules, they have to disembark with dignity. No pushing and shoving when we get to Hanoi.'

'We'll deal with them if we must,' Elms said. 'There's always one or two like our friend Giap.'

Elms and Jakes were the last to board. A middle-aged westerner met them at the door. He had iron-grey hair and wore dark slacks and a white cotton shirt. On his shoulders were black epaulettes bearing four gold stripes. He spoke with an Australian drawl. 'You must be Messrs Jakes and Elms,' he said. 'Chips O'Malley. I'm your captain today. We have a full complement of cabin crew. All male. We'll help out if needed.'

'Excellent,' Elms said. 'Ready to go?'

'All ready,' O'Malley answered. 'Air traffic control will give us priority. Just say the word.'

In the main cabin, constables walked both aisles, counting the number of people. Count complete, they reported to their sergeant. The sergeant approached Elms. 'Final count complete, *Ah Sir,*' he said. 'All correct.'

Elms nodded his satisfaction. The ratio of police to passengers was just short of one to one. To O'Malley he said. 'Okay. Let's go.'

O'Malley nodded. He turned and walked into the first class cabin. Jim Elms and Paul Jakes followed. 'First class cabin,' O'Malley said. 'Your command post for the flight. I'll be in radio contact with my Hanoi station manager. I'll relay any problems or requests through him.'

A slim Chinese stood and came to greet them. Jakes introduced him as John Au-Yeung, a member of the Civil Service Branch Diplomatic Section.

'After we land, John will deal with the Vietnamese authorities,' Jakes said. He smiled. 'Rather you than me, John,' he added.

John Au-Yeung replied in unaccented English. 'The Vietnamese are fine,' he said 'So long as we stick to the rules.' His voice was quiet but there was calm authority in the way he spoke. He had smooth features and neat hair. He moved with unstudied grace and wore casual clothes that were all the more stylish for their lack of designer logos. He glanced at his wristwatch. 'If all is well, gentlemen, perhaps we should depart.'

O'Malley nodded, stepped into the flight deck and shut the door behind him. Elms took a window seat and fastened his seatbelt. The engine whine grew louder and with a small jolt, the A300 began to roll towards the runway.

At thirty thousand feet, the seatbelt sign *bonged* and the A300 leveled off. Elms unclipped his seatbelt and stood. The first class cabin was now a command centre. In addition to Paul Jakes and John Au-Yeung, there was the Vietnamese interpreter and an English-speaking constable who would maintain the operational log. Two inspectors from the Tactical Unit's Oscar Company stood by. Jakes sat with his spectacles perched on the end of his nose. There was a wad of papers on his lap and on the seat next to him lay a folder marked, 'OPERATION DRUMBEAT — CONFIDENTIAL.' At Elms' approach, he removed his spectacles and looked up. 'Ever had a problem on these ops, Jim?' he asked.

'Like what?'

'Like people causing trouble at the other end?'

'Sometimes a bit of *argy-bargy*,' Elms replied. 'But the Vietnamese officials always have the army behind them. One sight of that lot calms things down.'

Jakes tapped the folder beside him. 'Says here *'..all returnees will leave the plane in a dignified manner of their own free will, like normal passengers...'* We can't have any frigging about at Hanoi.'

'I'll check on the troublemakers,' Elms said. 'I'll warn them to behave.' He moved into the main cabin and took a slow walk down the left hand aisle. Halfway, he caught the tang of tobacco smoke. Near the aircraft's rear, lounging in his seat was the man, Giap. He drew lazily on a cigarette. Beside him, one of the escort constables pretended not to notice.

'No smoking!' Elms barked. He glared at the constable. 'Where did he get the cigarette?'

'Ah Sir,' the constable wheedled. 'He says he make trouble unless I give cigarette...' His voice tailed off.

'Okay,' Elms answered. 'No more cigarettes. No more nothing. Understood?'

'Yes, *Ah Sir*,' the constable answered. 'Understood.'

Elms reached across and snatched the cigarette from Giap's fingers. 'No smoking. You understand?' he said.

Giap gave a hard laugh. 'If I want smoke, I smoke,' he said. A muscle on his cheek twitched. 'At Hanoi, if I want cause trouble, I cause trouble.' His eyes gleamed. '*You* understand?'

Elms turned and made his way to the galley. He doused the cigarette in a cup of water and dropped it into the trash. He checked the galley clock. Nearly eight o'clock; two more hours to Hanoi.

Nine o'clock. Some of the passengers dozed, others handed round snacks brought along for the trip. Some were chatting with the escort police officers. Children pressed their faces against the aircraft windows. They laughed and pointed at clouds scudding past below. Elms reported back to Paul Jakes.

'Looks like it's going smoothly,' Jakes commented.

Ten minutes past ten, less than one hour to Hanoi. The cabin suddenly went quiet. It was an expectant silence; tense and resentful. When Elms' eyes fell on anyone, they looked away. *Something isn't right,* he thought.

Then, from the rear of the aircraft a man shouted, '*CHI SONG CHO TU DO.*' Another voice joined in. Within seconds, men and women were shouting. '*CHI SONG CHO TU DO.CHI SONG CHO TU DO.*'

Elms called the interpreter and the escort team sergeant to him.

'They say, "*Live only for freedom,*"' the interpreter said, raising his voice above the din.

The sergeant checked his watch. 'Nearly landing time. Always near Hanoi, someone starts. Not usually so many.' He shook his head. 'Don't worry, *Ah Sir*. As soon as we land, they become quiet.'

'Try to calm things down,' Elms said. 'Use women officers only. Calm the women and children first. They're the key.'

Women police officers moved among the passengers. They smiled and joked with the children. They spoke to the women, touching them, reassuring them. Within minutes, all was quiet but for one familiar voice. *'Cai chet tot hon so voi cong san.* Death better than communism.' The voice grew louder. *'CAI CHET...'* It cracked with emotion. *'CAI CHET TOT HON SO VOI CONG SAN.'*

Elms moved to the rear of the cabin. The lead troublemaker, Giap was trying to stand. He strained against the grip of two male police officers. *'CHI SONG CHO TU DO,'* he shouted. His eyes were wide, his cheeks flushed. He saw Elms and the anger fell from him like a carnival mask. He smiled and lowered his voice. 'Ah, it is the big shot. I ask again, you have American dollars? You have cigarettes?'

There was a musical *bong* and the fasten seatbelt sign came on.

'Well, Mister *big shot,*' Giap hissed, 'you want trouble or you want everything peaceful?'

'No dollars. No cigarettes,' Elms growled. 'Fasten your seatbelt. You're going home.' He turned and made his way back to the first class section.

At eleven-fifteen, the A300 floated above Hanoi Airport's main runway. There was a thump, a bounce then the engines roared into reverse thrust. The aircraft slowed then turned off the runway. It travelled along a taxiway before lurching to a standstill on the airport apron. In the distance, the terminal building shimmered in the morning heat. The engine note died. A battered truck drew alongside and soldiers clambered from the back. They wore olive green uniforms with crimson tabs at the collars. On their heads were solar helmets embellished with a gold star set on a crimson background. They carried Kalashnikov assault rifles, each fitted with a curved magazine. Someone barked an order and they fanned out, surrounding the aircraft. A convoy of empty trucks arrived. Mobile staircases eased up to the aircraft doors.

Then it started.

'CHI SONG CHO TU DO. – LIVE ONLY FOR FREEDOM.'

'CAI CHET TOT HON SO VOI CONG SAN. – DEATH BETTER THAN COMMUNISM.'

Row by row, people took up the call. Someone stood and punched the air in time with the chant. Others did the same. Their voices filled the cabin. Men banged on the windows and gesticulated at the Vietnamese soldiers.

The sergeant rushed to Elms. The chanting drowned his voice. He put his head close to Elms'. *'Ah Sir, dim suen ho ah?'* – Sir, what do we do?

'Keep them in their seats,' Elms replied. 'Let them shout themselves out.'

Paul Jakes came into the main cabin. 'What the hell's going on?' he demanded, shouting over the noise. 'You said they'd calm down when they saw the army.'

'The ringleaders are stronger on this flight,' Elms answered. 'It's my bet they're asking our people for money.'

'I can't hear myself think,' Jakes said. He nodded to the first class section. 'We need an operations review, now.'

The curtain separating first class from the main cabin did little to stifle the noise. 'We are in something of a dilemma,' John Au-Yeung said. 'The repatriation agreement is fragile to say the least. We must avoid doing anything the Vietnamese might want to use as leverage.'

'Leverage for what?' Jakes asked.

Au-Yeung shrugged. 'Who knows?' he replied. 'But they'll likely threaten to suspend the agreement unless they get... what we shall say... a financial aid package of some kind.'

The sergeant poked his head through the curtain and beckoned Elms to him. There was a hurried conversation.

'I knew it,' Elms said. 'I just bloody knew it.'

'Knew what, Jim?'

'They're demanding money and cigarettes. One of the buggers wants the sergeant's wristwatch.'

The shouts and catcalls from the main cabin grew louder.

Enough! Elms thought. He called the sergeant to him. 'Get your biggest, toughest, ugliest men and make that lot pipe down. Tell them, if they keep up that racket, there'll be trouble.'

Elms had no idea what kind of trouble he could deliver but as his men worked their way down the aisles, they left behind a wake of silence.

Elms returned to the first class cabin. 'Now, where were we?' he said.

Au-Yeung nodded his gratitude. 'My opposite number should be somewhere in the airport,' he suggested. 'I'll ask the control tower to dig him out.' He went forward to the flight deck. Moments later, he returned, shaking his head. 'No luck,' he said. 'It's lunchtime.'

'Can't stay here all day,' O'Malley said. 'Much longer and they'll have to fly out a fresh aircrew.' He gave an apologetic shrug. 'Sorry, air safety regulations.'

'Let them play their games,' Au-Yeung said. 'We'll give it an hour.'

An hour later, Au-Yeung emerged from the fight deck. He shook his head. 'Now he's in a meeting.'

Paul Jakes called everyone together. 'We've not many choices, he said. 'Choice number one: We wait. God knows how long. An hour? A day? Longer? Choice number two: We take everyone back to Hong Kong. Choice number three?' He looked at each man in turn, letting the question hang between them.

'First two choices are out,' Elms growled. 'I suggest we grab the main troublemakers and carry the bastards off. The others will follow as meek as lambs.'

John Au-Yeung raised an eyebrow. 'Interesting thought,'

he said. 'I'm sure it would attract the attention of my opposite number. It might even drag him from his meeting.'

'I'll get it organized,' Elms said, turning towards the main cabin.

Au-Yeung raised his hand. 'Hold up,' he said. 'If it were only us facing the consequences, I'd agree. But it isn't. The Vietnamese might suspend future flights or even cancel them.' He chewed his lip. After a few seconds, he nodded to himself. 'Right,' he said. 'I'll contact the British Embassy through the airline's Hanoi office. They can seek instructions from Hong Kong.'

'And how long will that take?' Paul Jakes sighed.

'It will take as long as it takes,' Au-Yeung answered. He turned and disappeared into the flight deck.

With the engines shut down, the ventilation and air-conditioning no longer worked. Faces glistened with sweat. Damp patches formed on shirts. In the main cabin, people used the safety instructions sheet to fan themselves. Elms ordered the A300's doors opened and relief drifted into the cabin on a cooling breeze. The breeze did nothing to calm the mood. As he walked the main cabin, men watched him though narrow eyes. Everywhere, people were whispering. They fell silent when he turned to confront them. Everything in Elms' guts told him that in another hour, he could have a riot on his hands.

Then it got worse.

The sergeant met Elms midway along the aisle. Lines furrowed his forehead. *'Ah Sir,'* he said. 'Galley out of water. Half the toilets are blocked.'

Elms groaned. 'I'll see what I can do,' he said, knowing he could do nothing. 'For now, assign two constables to each of the six ringleaders.' He pointed to Giap. 'Particularly that one.'

'Sir?'

'Soon, all will be clear,' Elms said. *At least I hope it'll be clear,* he thought. He returned to the first class cabin. Jakes, O'Malley and Au-Yeung were in hushed conversation. As Elms entered the cabin, Jakes grinned at him.

'Word from Hong Kong is "*go.*"' he said.

'*Jesus!*' Elms said. 'That must have come from the top.'

'Who bloody cares,' Jakes said. 'Let's get to it.'

Elms stepped into the main cabin and called to his sergeant. 'Are the men in place?'

'Ready, *Ah Sir.*'

Elms led the sergeant to where Giap sat. Two constables hovered in the aisle. 'I'm going to give you a choice, my friend,' Elms said. 'You can walk off this airplane with dignity or my men will carry you. I give you five seconds to make up your mind.'

Giap feigned a yawn. 'I think I stay here,' he drawled.

Elms nodded to the two constables. One grabbed Giap's arm and dragged him into the aisle. The two of them held him firm. Giap's jaw dropped, his eyes widened. His voice was a croak. 'What you doing?' The constables hoisted Giap up onto his toes and pushed him towards the front of the aircraft. His voice rose. ' STOP. NOT PERMITTED.'

Elsewhere in the cabin, constables dragged the other five troublemakers from their seats. Cries of surprise became shouts of protest. The five tried to shake themselves free. They kicked at the constables and lunged with the heads, snapping their teeth. They tried to dig their heels into the floor. The constables held them fast. Within seconds, they were at the aircraft door, blinking in the sunlight. The cabin was behind them, the mobile steps in front. Elms nodded to the constables and they bundled all six men down the stairs.

Drawn by the commotion, the soldiers moved closer to the stairs. One carried a pistol at his belt and on his shoulders were gold epaulettes, decorated with a single star. He put his hand on his pistol, pointed at the policemen and began to shout. There was an oily *ka-shlock* as a soldier cocked his Kalashnikov. Others did the same. *Ka-shlock, ka-shlock, ka-shlock.* They were shouting, their words jumbled and unintelligible. The constables shoved the six troublemakers onto the airport apron then turned and retreated up the stairs, taking the steps two at a time. The soldiers followed, shouting and brandishing their Kalashnikovs. Elms grabbed the last constable up the stairs, dragged him into the cabin and shut the door. Through the door's small window, Elms could see the soldiers' faces: wide-eyed, faces a mask of outrage.

'I didn't expect that,' Paul Jakes said. 'But our six friends saw sense pretty quick. They boarded the lorries nice and obliging like.'

From the flight deck, O'Malley called. 'Mister Au-Yeung. The control tower is sending transport for you. They didn't sound too happy.'

Minutes later, an olive green, jeep-style vehicle halted by the stairs. The soldiers stepped away as Elms opened the aircraft door. Au-Yeung moved past him and without a backward glance, descended the stairs and boarded the vehicle. The driver knocked it into gear and it sped away. Au-Yeung was gone for nearly an hour. When he returned, it was in the company of a uniformed official. There was news. As Elms listened, he felt all his plans begin to unravel. The Vietnamese were not pleased, Au-Yeung said. Pushing people out of the aircraft went against the agreement. There was a *situation*, the Vietnamese insisted. A situation that required a solution.

'How much do they want?' Elms snorted.

A smile played on Au-Yeung's lips. 'They'll let us sweat a bit before they come up with a figure,' he answered. He gestured towards the uniformed Vietnamese. 'In the meantime, my colleague from the People's Diplomatic Bureau will conduct his compatriots safely off the aircraft.'

'Vietnamese diplomats wear uniform?' Elms asked.

Au-Yeung shrugged. 'It's Hanoi. Doesn't everyone?'

The uniformed Vietnamese passed along the body of the aircraft. By the time he had finished, all passengers had stood, collected their belongings and were waiting to disembark. The official called an order and everyone moved towards the door. On the airport apron, there was no sign of the soldiers' earlier hostility. They lifted the bags onto the transport and helped the women and children to board. When every passenger had left the aircraft, Elms turned to Au-Yeung. 'That's the last one,' he said. 'Time to go.'

'Not quite,' Au-Yeung said. 'I failed to mention that now, I must go with them. There is still the...*er*... situation to resolve.'

Paul Jakes checked his wristwatch. It was five in the evening. 'Two hours' flight time to Hong Kong,' he said. 'Hong Kong airport has a midnight curfew. If we're still here after ten o'clock, we'll miss the deadline.'

'I'll try to hurry things along,' Au-Yeung said. 'But...' He left the rest unsaid.

With Au-Yeung gone, the police escort team settled down with their packed meals. A wave of fatigue washed over Elms. He laid aside his food and went into the main cabin. The escort team sat silent, slumped in their seats.

It was another two hours before Au-Yeung contacted them. Elms and Paul Jakes crowded into the flight deck. 'Be careful what you say,' O'Malley warned them. 'Every word will be on their loudspeaker.' He pressed his transmit button. 'Hanoi tower. China Seas 001. Over.'

'*Hanoi tower. Wait one. Over.*'

'Standing by.'

Au-Yeung's voice crackled over the radio. '*Mister O'Malley, this is John Au-Yeung. Are Mister Jakes and Mister Elms with you?*'

'They are. Go ahead. Over.'

'*Our hosts are being very reasonable,*' Au-Yeung said. '*They are with me now. Understood?*'

'We understand,' O'Malley answered. 'We understand perfectly. Over.'

'*Excellent. There will have to be an indemnity paid for our... our misconduct,*' Au-Yeung continued. '*But you may depart as soon as the tower clears you for takeoff, over.*'

'Roger,' O'Malley said. 'We're ready to go as soon as you return.'

'*I will not be returning with you,*' Au-Yeung said. '*Our hosts have invited me to stay a little longer.*'

'*Indemnity!*' Elms spat. 'Ransom, more like. Bastards are holding him hostage.'

O'Malley spoke into the radio microphone. 'Would you like us to contact the British embassy?'

'*No, no, no,*' Au-Yeung answered, for once sounding alarmed. '*That is not necessary. In fact, it would be most unhelpful. Everything is in hand. All will be well. Do you understand?*'

'I bloody understand, alright,' Elms growled. 'There will be a payout to local officials. What's the betting it's in cash and there'll be no receipt?'

O'Malley made a shushing motion with his hand. 'Roger,' he said. 'Please pass me back to air traffic control.'

Five minutes later, the engines began to whine. The mood on the aircraft became buoyant but Elms could not share it. Operational police officers did not have a high opinion of central government bureaucrats. They were the implacable voices on the end of a telephone, quoting policy, questioning budgets, denying resources. But this quietly-spoken, dapper man from Civil Service Branch had surprised Elms, he had surprised everyone. Without question or hesitation, he had surrendered himself as a virtual hostage so that Jim Elms and the rest of the escort team could return home. It was an unselfish act of courage and Elms promised never to forget it.

The seatbelt sign *bonged*. The engine pitch grew louder and the A300 began to trundle towards the main runway. The cabin intercom crackled.

'*Captain O'Malley here. There will be a small delay while a military aircraft lands. Relax, we'll be away in a few minutes.*'

The A300 lurched to a halt and through his window, Elms watched a MiG 19 fighter jet touchdown and barrel along the runway. It came to a halt then moved onto the taxiway.

'Just waiting for clearance,' O'Malley announced. There was a pause, then, 'Sorry, another military aircraft has priority for takeoff.'

A second MiG crept onto the runway. The fuselage and wings were a patchwork of olive green and grey. Emblazoned on the wings and fuselage was the Vietnamese gold star. Stenciled on the nose, in bold red, was the number 37. The MiG was Korean War vintage. It hunkered low to the ground and looked deadly. The MiG pilot gunned the engine. Even inside the soundproofed cabin, the noise was thunderous. It made the A300's cabin trim buzz. The MiG accelerated down the runway. Its nose came up and a jet of flame shot from its tail. As soon as it left the ground, the fighter nosed up until it was nearly vertical. In an instant, it was gone. Elms settled in his seat but the A300 did not move. O'Malley's voice came back on the intercom. He sighed.

'More military movements, I'm afraid. Sit tight, we'll be away soon.'

But they were not away soon. As one MiG landed, another prepared to take off. The landings and takeoffs continued for more than an hour.

'It must be the whole Vietnamese bloody air force,' Paul Jakes muttered.

'Not quite,' Elms answered. 'There's just two of them. Next one you see, check the number. It's either 37 or 153.'

Jakes' breath escaped in a hiss. 'So, they're stuffing us about. What's the bloody point?'

'They're pressuring John to speed up payment,' Elms answered. 'Either that or they want us to miss Hong Kong's midnight curfew.'

'Jesus wept,' Jakes groaned. 'We could be here all night.'

'If we are, we'll need a fresh aircrew,' Elms shot back at him. 'Air safety regs.'

An hour passed, then another. The same two fighter aircraft took turns to dominate the runway.

'How much fuel do they carry?' Jakes sighed. 'Perhaps they'll run out.'

Night fell. Ten o'clock came and went. *Too late to beat Hong Kong's no-fly curfew,* Elms thought.

Then the intercom squawked to life.

'Right boys and girls, air traffic control says we can depart. Fasten your seatbelts and cross your fingers.'

The A300 moved onto the runway. The engine pitch grew from a whine to a roar. The cabin started to vibrate. The A300 rolled forward, picking up speed. Elms felt himself pressed into the seat as the A300 accelerated down the runway. The nose came up. The cabin floor tilted. There was a *thump* as the landing gear left the runway.

Too late, Elms thought. *We're too bloody late.*

O'Malley's voice came back on the intercom.

'Sorry folks, forgot to mention. I've just received a curfew waiver from Hong Kong air traffic control. The Hong Police want me to tell you that the weather's fine and the beer's cold.'

In the main cabin, there was applause and cheers. In-flight movie projectors dropped into place. The film was new, only just released into general circulation but no one paid it much attention.

They were going home.

They arrived back at one in the morning. As predicted, the weather was fine and the beer was indeed cold. John Au-Yeung returned the following evening. He was as unruffled and dapper as ever. Asked about the indemnity, he just smiled and changed the subject.

The Hong Kong government put the episode behind it. Officially, there was no armed confrontation between the Hong Kong Police and the Vietnamese People's Army. Neither was there a Hong Kong civil servant held hostage in Hanoi. This means, of course, there was never any money paid to Vietnamese officials. The episode was to be one of Hong Kong's secrets. Of course, within days, everyone knew about it. Word filtered back to Jim Elms that to secure John Au-Yeung's release, the Hong Kong government had apologized for insulting the Vietnamese people, promised there would be no repetition of the incident and paid a US$100,000 indemnity.

There is no record to show if the payment was in cash or who received it. No one has seen a receipt.

Nearly four million Vietnamese died during the war with the United States. No one knows how many fled the country but conservative estimates put it at 1.5 million. Of these, more than 200,000 arrived in Hong Kong. It is likely that many thousands died during the perilous sea crossing. Some say the United Kingdom ordered Hong Kong to offer itself as a port of first asylum. Not true. When the *Clara Mærsk* steamed into Hong Kong on May 4, 1975, Hong Kong needed no prompting to give sanctuary to the Vietnamese refugees who were aboard. For the next twenty-five years, Hong Kong never refused a single Vietnamese request for sanctuary.

These were hard times for Hong Kong. Every year, the little territory absorbed thousands of people who illegally crossed the border from China. The United Nations High Commission for Refugees offered to pay for the Vietnamese refugee camps but the payment never arrived. Hong Kong ended up footing a bill of HK$1.61 billion, which is more than US$205 million.

At midnight on May 31, 2000, Hong Kong's last Vietnamese camp closed. Fourteen hundred Vietnamese remained in Hong Kong. They were not eligible for resettlement overseas and the Vietnamese government refused to take back any with criminal records or health problems. So Hong Kong let them stay. They received official identity cards and government help in applying for permanent residence.

Today, more than five thousand Vietnamese live in Hong Kong. There are businesspeople, restaurateurs, lawyers, linguists and health professionals. But there are also drug addicts, petty criminals and impoverished homeless who sleep on the streets or in makeshift shelters. Charities and outreach groups have had some success but there is still a long way to go.

True to its word, Vietnam's government never persecuted anyone who returned home. Today, Vietnam's borders are open and the little boats are redundant. The country has a vibrant and growing economy. Forbes business magazine heralds Vietnam as, '...the next Asian tiger...'

Jim Elms is proud to be part of a community that, without hesitation, offered safe haven for genuine refugees. But he reserves his greatest praise for the men and women of the Hong Kong Police with whom he shared the repatriation escort duty. They suffered abuse and physical assault. The hours were long and arduous. There was no overtime pay, no hard duty allowance but no officer ever complained.

The last words belong to Jim Elms:

'We, true to "The Hong Kong spirit of Can Do" showed the world we could do it and we did. Now, so many years later, we can hold our heads up high and tell the world we did what we did without reward or return. Which is why it is a part of our history that is worth retelling.'

PART 5
FLYING TIGERS

HONG KONG POLICE: INSIDE THE LINES

CHAPTER 8
HING DAI

BARRY JOHN SMITH was an affable sort but he was not one to suffer any nonsense. He was Barry to his friends and Mister Smith to everyone else. To anyone close, he was just plain BJ. As soon as he arrived at the Police Training School, Smith was a round peg in a very round hole. The meeting of Chinese and western cultures fascinated him. The academic side of police law was stimulating and to be frank, he found the physical training a breeze. Smith's squad mates were in two camps. There was the studious, ever-so-focused camp that had academic grades in the stratosphere and there was the smoking, drinking and having-a-good-time camp who managed to cram in just enough study to manage a decent passing grade. Between the studying and the partying, neither camp had much time for the temple that was the human body. And so it was that Smith gained himself a reputation as an ironman.

'You're very fit,' a Chinese squad mate remarked. 'I'd say you're SDU fit.'

'SDU?' Smith asked, at a bit of a loss.

The Chinese inspector looked around then put his head close to Smith's. 'Special Duties Unit — Flying Tigers.' He nodded earnestly as though he had made himself perfectly clear.

'Is it a circus act?' Smith asked.

The Chinese inspector sighed. 'No, no, no,' he said. 'Counter terrorism. Trained by British Special Air Services — SAS.' His voice dropped to a whisper. 'Very secret.'

'How come you know about it?'

'Everyone knows about it.'

'So, it's not a secret.'

The Chinese inspector made shushing signs with both hands. 'It is secret,' he hissed. 'Very *very* secret. Say nothing.'

And that was it, Smith was hooked. The Flying Tigers sounded like something out of an Ian Fleming novel: elite, secretive, tough. How would Fleming have written it? 'So 007, how do we handle these international, super-bad guys?'

'Out of my league, I'm afraid, M. We'll have to send in the Flying Tigers.'

For most people, the lure would have passed but Smith could not get the unit out of his mind. Over a beer in the mess, he mentioned it to a chief inspector on the training staff.

'How do you know about the Special Duties Unit?' the chief inspector demanded.

'Everyone knows about it,' Smith replied.

'No they don't,' the chief inspector sniffed. 'It's secret.' He drew Smith aside. 'Forget it, my lad,' he cautioned. 'They're all crazy. The selection process is crazy. They make the candidates fight each other just to see who's the craziest.' He lowered his voice. 'Some mad bastard tried to beat out the other guy's brains with a rock. And *he* was the one they chose.' He shook his head. 'Forget the SDU. A bright young chap like you should find a cozy headquarters job. Get close to the bosses. You'll be a chief inspector in no time.'

For the duration of basic training, Smith put thoughts of the SDU behind him. In time, there was an officers' mess dinner and a graduation parade. Shortly afterwards, Smith moved to Kowloon City police district. Sometimes, he reflected on the chief inspector's advice, which was indeed excellent.

In future years, Smith often wondered how things might have been had he taken it.

In Kowloon City, Smith took command of a beat patrol sub-unit then moved to the district's anti prostitution squad. Later, he received orders to swap his peaked cap for a navy-blue beret, brush up on his riot drill and become a member of the paramilitary Police Tactical Unit.

At the heart of the Tactical Unit is the internal security company. Smith's Company Commander was a stocky Welshman with a ready wit and a wealth of common sense. The riot drills and physical training were easy enough but come the practical exercises, things got more difficult. Training staff set up simulated situations with other Tactical Unit officers playing the role of enemy. They delighted at confounding the trainees. 'He's deploying in full riot gear,' a staff member would chortle into his radio. 'Passive demonstrators only.' Alternatively, 'Silly bugger's not taking his riot gear...'

Well, you get the picture.

The officers' mess was a retreat from all this. There was cold beer on tap and the kitchen provided enough food to satisfy a Viking's stag party. Smith got on well with the company's inspectors. In particular, he found himself much in tune with Inspector Andy Churton, a man with a quick smile and a hearty love of life. Within days, Smith and Churton became known as *hing dai* — the brothers.

Sometimes, members of the Special Duties Unit, dubbed The Flying Tigers, visited from their base at Fanling Police Depot. They wore army-style camouflage fatigues but their hair was stylishly long. They sat together, chatting quietly over soft drinks. Smith watched them from his seat at the mess bar. 'Do they look crazy?' he asked Andy Churton.

Churton furrowed his brows. 'Not particularly,' he answered. 'But the real crazies never do.'

On a morning run, Smith's route took him near the SDU base. Running towards him were a group of men. They wore no shirts and despite the humid heat, each wore a police issue gas mask. They were tanned and muscular. To Smith, they looked darned near bulletproof.

As Smith's Tactical Unit training neared its end, a circular arrived from Police Headquarters. As Smith read it, his heart raced:

'Applications are invited for selection to a specialist unit within Operations Wing. Applicants must be physically fit and will be required to display exceptional levels of leadership and initiative. Applications must be approved by the applicant's commanding officer.'

The circular screamed, 'The Flying Tigers are recruiting.' That evening, Smith drafted and redrafted his application. The next morning, the sun seemed brighter; the birdsong more melodious. He gathered up his carefully crafted application and made his way to the Company Commanders' office. There, his mood evaporated. Three of the company's inspectors had got there before him. One was a second-generation Hong Kong policeman, another was an ex-Royal Marine who had seen service in the Falklands war. The third was Andy Churton.

'Oh...hello,' Smith said, trying not to seem over concerned. 'Here to see the Company Commander?'

Yes they were.

'Anything...er...special?'

'Nothing *especially* special,' Churton replied, raising an eyebrow. 'You?'

Behind them, footsteps announced the Company Commander's arrival. 'My God,' he chuckled. 'It's a bloody delegation. What is it? Confessions or complaints? ' He caught sight of Smith's application and held out his hand. 'Come on my lad, let's see what it's about.' He squinted at the paper then moved into his office and signaled all four inspectors to follow.

He sat down and laid the application on the desk. He held up his hand for silence. 'SD bloody U,' he growled. 'Is this all four of you?'

Four heads nodded.

'Well, you can forget it.'

Four jaws dropped.

The Company Commander gave a placatory smile. 'Sorry lads, but it's not on,' he said. He leaned back and regarded all four of them.

Four pairs of eyes looked implacably back.

'What if we're needed for a major incident?' the Company Commander demanded. 'This isn't the Boy's Brigade, it's the bloody Police Tactical Unit.'

Smith thought through his pre-planned speech, searching for a killer argument. There was nothing.

The Company Commander's voice softened. 'There's always next time,' he said. 'With a Tactical Unit tour under your belts, you'll be better candidates.' He looked from one to the other. 'Anything else? Good. Now bugger off, I want my breakfast.'

Smith left the administration block in fog of gloom. As he adjusted his beret, Andy Churton fell in step beside him. 'He's right, BJ,' Churton said. 'Too soon for us, my old mate, too soon. We'll show 'em. You and me together. The *hing dai,* the brothers. We'll be back.'

And back they were, but not right away. First, they had to finish their Tactical Unit attachment, then there was that most wonderful of colonial perks — the long home leave, with two-way passage paid by government. Hong Kong travel agents built a nice little earner around this. Civil servants could swap their travel vouchers for budget travel plans that took them round the world. Smith and three other Hong Kong policemen travelled the globe before touching back down in Hong Kong four months later.

Smith found himself in a temporary posting to the Police-Military control room. Barring a major flap, there was nothing to do except monitor what was happening in the police regions. It was dull fare but the job had two positives. First, the regular work hours gave Smith time to get back into physical shape. Second, he was part of the Police Headquarters Operations Wing, which meant he was first to get routine circulars.

The circular came in one evening, just after five o'clock: Applications are invited for selection to a specialist unit within Operations Wing...'

You know the rest.

Smith put in his application but his mates thought he was mad.

'Are you serious? Thumper James dropped out after two days.'

'But he's a karate black belt.'

'Left in tears, I heard.'

The one voice of encouragement was Smith's old friend, Andy Churton. Churton had signed on for the same selection course and in the coming months, they trained together, pushing each other harder and harder. They ran winding paths in the hills overlooking Kowloon. They worked with weights then ran some more. They tried to second-guess the psychological tests.

'I hear there's sleep deprivation.'

'They work you to physical breaking point.'

'There's a flooded pit.'

'Forget that,' a mutual friend told them. 'They want you to give up. *That's* the test.'

Then came bad news. The SDU wanted just one inspector. Smith and Churton would be up against each other. Now, Smith saw his best friend through new eyes. Churton was strong and focused. Perhaps too strong; too focused. Doubts gnawed at Smith, could Andy Churton be the better man for the job? Smith's mood darkened further as news drifted in of the other candidates. All were tough and single-minded. Doubts and more doubts drove Smith into ever-harder training. He drank a final beer a month before the start date. Under normal circumstances, there might have been tension between Smith and Churton but their friendship overrode it. But would they feel the same when they were slugging it out in the fabled SDU free-for-all?

On Monday September 1, Smith ate a decent breakfast, climbed onto the pillion of Andy Churton's motorbike and an hour later, they rolled through the Fanling Police Depot's gate. Including Churton and Smith, there were twelve candidates waiting on the depot's drill square. All were chasing the one inspector post. The mood seemed light but beneath the banter, each was sizing up the others, searching for weakness.

At exactly 08.45 hours, a member of the Special Duties Unit Training Team joined them on the square. He wore a beret and army-style camouflage fatigues. He did a quick head count and checked his clipboard. 'One missing,' he said. 'Not a great start. Did everyone bring their running kit?'

They all nodded.

'Good. Get changed and join me in hut twelve.

Hut twelve was a pre-fabricated structure. Inside were a dozen desks, laid out like a classroom. In the corner was a pile of numbered bibs. With everyone changed and seated, the SDU inspector rejoined them. 'I am Inspector John Sader of the Special Duties Unit,' he announced. 'Shout out when I call your name. Mister James?'

'*Here.*'

'Mister Smith?'

'*Here.*'

With each acknowledgement, he ticked a name off his list.

'Mister Duncan.'

Silence.

'*Mister* Duncan.'

More silence.

The door opened and a musical Irish voice spoke. 'That would be me. Fergus to my friends,' he said. 'I suppose you'll be wondering where I've been.'

Sader glared at the newcomer.

'It's just that I'm recently back from the Philippines and I'm feeling a little frail, if you get my drift.'

Sader shot Fergus Duncan a look that should have left him pinned to the far wall.

'Ooookay,' Duncan crooned. 'I'll just be taking a seat then.'

Sader scowled and made a note on his clipboard. 'As you know,' he said. 'This is a two-week trial for selection to the most elite unit in the Royal Hong Kong Police.' He paused to let his words sink in. 'We will test not only your physical strength but also the strength of your character.' He looked square at Duncan. 'Anyone may give up at any time. Questions?'

No questions.

Sader lifted the bibs from the floor and dumped them on the nearest desk. 'Everyone take one then gather outside on the drill square.'

Smith picked up a bib marked A3 and slipped it over his head.

Duncan took one and regarded it at arm's length. 'Will we be getting cake and jelly?' he asked of no one in particular.

'Maybe you'd prefer champagne and oysters,' Sader growled. 'Now get yourself out on that square.'

The drill square shimmered under the morning sun. Waiting for them was another SDU inspector. He wore running kit and his singlet stretched tight over bulging pectorals. He flashed a wolfish smile. 'Peter Trammel's the name,' he chirped. 'We'll just take a wee jog to set us up for the day.' He led the candidates across the square, through the depot's gate and out onto the road. The pace was not too hard and forty minutes later, they were back in the depot.

'Well, done,' Trammel called. 'You can take a well-earned rest in the gym.'

Inside the gym, SDU men descended on them like a pack of terriers. They bullied the candidates to a line of gleaming multi-gyms. A multi-gym looks like a child's climbing frame. It is a perfect cube of steel tubing, about eight feet tall. Set into the frame is a collection of stations. Each station has a set of weights and pulleys. There is a station to work the upper arms, another for the thighs, others for the chest, the abdomen and every other muscle group. Smith took a moment to consider the long game. If he spent all his energy too soon, he would not last the full course.

Peter Trammel read his mind. *'NO SLACKING,'* he bellowed. 'Any slackers will be off the selection.'

Smith moved from station to station. Chest, abdomen, legs, shoulders, repeat. His heart thudded against his ribs. He stopped just long enough to suck in a deep breath.

'Smith. Slacking. Twenty push-ups.'

Smith risked a glance at the other candidates. Sweat streamed down their faces. Their torsos gleamed.

'Rest.'

Weights clattered back into place. Candidates sank to the floor. Some sat, others kneeled. One lay on his back, a forearm thrown across his eyes.

Seconds later, another order. *'Outside!'*

Outside, the sun hammered at the drill square. Smith felt the heat burn through the soles of his running shoes. Now, it was sprints. This meant running flat out between two points just a dozen yards apart. Sprint, turn, sprint back to the start, repeat until told to stop. After a few laps, Smith was light-headed. Sweat blinded him. His breath came in gasps.

'Faster!'

There was a brief rest then it was back to the sprints. This time, the candidates had to run doubled over, using their hands and feet. Within seconds, Smith was running last.

'Fifty push-ups for the last man home. Faster. *Go, go, go.*'

Smith drove himself faster. Nearly home. He lunged for the finish. He skidded over the line. Tarmac and loose grit ground into both palms. Pain bit into his hands. He stared at them in horror. The skin on his palms had curled up like roller blinds. They were a bloody mess. Trammel sent him off to the orderly office where a station sergeant applied a stinging antiseptic and dressed both hands with a sterile bandage.

'For you, selection over,' the station sergeant said. 'Not your fault. Injury too serious. Best you go home.'

Smith looked at his hands, wishing the injury away. An earlier conversation drifted back to him: 'They want you to give up. *That's* the test.'

He thanked the station sergeant and walked back to the square.

'Who's a silly bugger?' Peter Trammel chuckled. 'That's you done. No shame in giving up,' he added.

Smith squared his shoulders. 'I'll manage,' he said.

'Will you now?' Trammel snorted. 'You missed a drill,' he said. 'That'll cost you twenty sit-ups.'

As Smith counted his nineteenth sit-up, the other candidates started another round of sprints.

'Move it *Mister* Smith. You're falling behind.'

By lunchtime, everyone was too tired to eat. Smith forced the food down, not knowing when he would eat again.

In the afternoon, there was another distance run, then volleyball and football, each with punishment exercises for the losing side. There was a session with the SDU's primary weapons: the Heckler and Koch MP5 sub-machine gun and the Browning semi-automatic pistol. 'You will know these weapons better than you know your girlfriends,' John Sader said. 'You will break them down to their component parts. You will then reassemble them. You will then break them down again. After that, you will reassemble them. Do you get my drift?'

They worked in silence, stripping and reassembling the weapons. As the afternoon wore into evening, their actions became as well-oiled as the weapons themselves. Smith tried to ignore the pain in his hands. He fumbled the Browning and a component clattered onto the workbench.

'Problems, Mister Smith?'

'No problem,' Smith said.

After the weapon training, the mind games started. 'Ten mile run,' Sader announced. 'No penalty for tail-end Charlie. Call it a fun run.'

Everyone lined up. Gone was the cocky optimism of the morning. There were bowed heads and faces blank with fatigue. Three miles into the run, a Ford Transit collected them and took them back to Fanling. In the back of the Transit, Churton groaned and doubled over. He waved away Smith's help. 'Stomach cramps,' he said. 'Just cramps. I'll be fine.'

Back at the depot, Smith's hands were on fire, his mind was like cold porridge. It was only day one and already, two inspectors had dropped out. Smith should have shown them some sympathy but in his heart, he rejoiced. The competition was falling away. That night, he barely remembered getting to bed. The next morning, he felt like he had spent the night on a torturer's rack. He held his hands before his face. Blood had seeped through the dressings, staining them black. He dragged himself to his shower, ate a light breakfast then went downstairs. In the car park, he met Churton. His friend's eyes were blank; his face expressionless.

'You look like shit,' Smith said.

'That makes two of us,' Churton replied. 'From now on, we're the look-like-shit brothers.'

'How's the stomach cramp?' Smith asked.

Churton waved away the question. 'I'll be fine,' he said. He fired up his motorbike and an hour later, they were back at Fanling. First up: a trip to a firing range. At lunchtime, the station sergeant changed Smith's dressing. The old dressings had stuck to Smith's hands. As soon as the station sergeant peeled them away, the wounds began to bleed.

'You should go to hospital,' the station sergeant chided.

Smith shrugged off the suggestion and rejoined the others.

'How're the hands?' Sader asked.

'Your station sergeant says I'm okay to continue,' Smith lied.

After lunch there was rope climbing. Next, they raced around the assault course. There were walls to climb, tunnels to clamber through, netting to scale. All the time, the call was, *'Faster. Go, go, go. No slacking.'* Smith's dressings fell away. His hands oozed blood. He tried to bury the pain and somehow kept going.

Another inspector called it a day. He was a member of the force rugby team: tough and competitive.

In the mid afternoon, Trammel grabbed Smith's wrists and examined his hands. 'Not good,' he muttered and pointed to the unit's Ford Transit. 'Have the driver take you to Fanling Clinic.'

The wait at the clinic was mercifully short. The doctor prescribed painkillers, a nurse changed his dressings then it was back to back to Fanling. The painkillers had little effect but inside Smith, a switch marked *automatic pilot*, clicked on. He heard the orders; he obeyed the orders. Trammel ordered another distance run. They ran until they arrived at a new high-rise housing project. Apartment blocks of gleaming concrete soared nearly forty floors. Trammel pointed to one of the blocks. 'Take the stairs to the thirty-sixth floor,' he ordered. 'Last man back does twenty push-ups.'

'C'mon BJ,' Churton called. He set off at a loping jog and signaled Smith to follow. 'You and me, mate,' he called over his shoulder.

Smith took a long breath and set off after him. The stairwell smelled of dust. The walls and ceiling were bare concrete that trapped the heat. Smith thought his chest would burst. *Sixth floor, seventh, eighth.* Smith put down his head and forced himself on.

On the ninth floor landing, one of the candidates sat in a corner, head cradled in his hands. The staircase went on forever. In his mind, Smith ticked off the floors. *Thirteen..fourteen...fifteen...* On the landing between the twenty-fourth and twenty-fifth floors, a candidate lay on his back, his breath rasping. *Twenty-five... twenty-six.* Smith's legs were like dead meat. *Thirty...thirty-one...* He cast down his eyes and willed himself on. Then, standing before him was an SDU constable carrying a clipboard.

'A3...A3,' the constable said to himself, running a finger down his list. 'Ah. A3. Mister Smith.' He ticked the name off his list then raised an eyebrow as if to ask, *what are you waiting for?*

As Smith stumbled back down towards the ground floor, he passed others, staggering up the stairs. He must have looked much like them. Eyes pained; face grimed with sweat and dust. Later, they assembled at the start point. Smith did a quick head count. One missing. Another inspector had dropped out.

'Well done lads,' Trammel chortled. 'Let's get back to the depot.' His eyes widened in mock horror. 'Oh dear,' he said. 'Looks like the transport's gone without us. Never mind, it's just a short run.'

On the run back, Smith saw an SDU first-aider kneeling beside an inspector who had collapsed by the road. It was Andy Churton. His friend's breath was short and shallow. His eyes stared. Smith slowed but behind him a voice growled, 'Move it, Mister Smith. *No slacking.*'

'Come on, Andy,' Smith shouted. 'You and me mate, you and me.'

Churton did not answer, nor did he move. For Smith, it was a kick in the guts. Andy Churton was a hard man, hard and stubborn.

Back at the depot, John Sader sent everyone home. Smith went to the Fanling Clinic to change his dressings. There, in the emergency room, he found Andy Churton lying motionless on a gurney. Smith touched Churton's shoulder. 'How's it going, mate?' he asked but Churton just lay still, eyes fixed on the ceiling. 'It's me, BJ,' Smith said. Churton's eyes flickered towards Smith's face but in them, there was no recognition. The nurse chivvied Smith into a cubicle. By the time he came out, an ambulance had taken Churton to a larger hospital.

Smith stepped out into the evening. His head throbbed and he could not catch his breath. For a moment, he did not know where he was. A taxi pulled up to the kerb and Smith clambered into the back. He sank into a form-fitting seat and luxuriated in the taxi's air-conditioning. He closed his eyes. Inside his head, Sader's voice taunted him. *Just walk away. No shame in giving up.*

Alone in his flat, Smith tried to drink some water. As he swallowed, his gorge rose and bitter bile filled is throat. What had the Tactical Unit's First Aid Instructor said? Nausea, breathlessness, dizziness, throbbing headache. *Heat stroke?* Smith sat on his bed. His head lolled. *Stop. Stay awake.* Now he remembered the advanced heatstroke symptoms: drowsiness, unconsciousness, *possible death*. He fumbled around on his bedside table and found his telephone. What was the emergency number? There was a nine in it. Yes. Nine-nine-something. He started to dial then paused. It was only day two. *Day bloody two.* He slammed down the phone. Fruit. Fruit has water, sugar and vitamin C. He nibbled an apple and the nausea subsided. He managed some water. He felt a little better, even euphoric. *Walk. Keep walking.* He took a step and staggered sideways. Fatigue washed through him. *Drowsiness, unconsciousness, possible death.* He must not sleep. He walked to the door, stepped outside and visited a friend in a neighboring flat. They chatted. Smith ate more fruit and drank more water.

At one-thirty in the morning, he slept.

Five hours later, he was out of bed. He caught the train to Fanling. The nausea and headaches were gone but pain racked his body to its core. He tried to clench his fists and pain stabbed through his hands and forearms.

The first run of the day cleared Smith's head. When they returned to the depot, John Sader was waiting on the square.
Now what?
Sader's face was somber. 'Gentlemen,' he said. 'I have some bad news.'
A knot tightened in Smith's stomach. 'Is it Andy?' he asked. 'Has he been ruled out?'
Sader's lips set in a hard line. 'It's worse than that, Barry,' he said. 'About one hour ago, Inspector Andy Churton passed away at Prince of Wales Hospital.'
Smith shook his head like a dazed boxer. 'Passed *what?*' he asked. 'Is he still on the selection or not?'
Sader laid a hand on his Smith's shoulder. 'Andy passed away Barry. He died. I know you were close. I'm so very sorry.'
Smith's eyes prickled. He backhanded something wet from his cheek and turned away so no one would see. *Dead? No. It must be someone else.* First denial, then realization. It was true. Andy, dead. *Dead!* For what? For a crack at joining the Special fucking Duties Unit? It should have been an adventure but it was absurd. The physical trials, the mind games. Senseless. *That's it*, Smith thought, *I'm done here.* Then, another voice, unheard but insistent. *You and me BJ. You and me mate.*
Sader's voice cut into Smith's thoughts. 'You were good friends,' he said. 'If you want to pull out, that's fine.' He raised a hand as if to ward off an argument. 'No bullshit,' he said. 'You'll need your head together for what's coming.'
Smith squared his shoulders. 'Right, no bullshit,' he snapped. 'There's nothing on this earth can make me give up. I'm in. I'm fucking staying in.'
'You'll get no favors,' Sader warned.
'Absolutely,' Smith said. 'No favors.'
'Right,' Sader said. 'Best get moving.' He nodded towards the others. 'They've started without you.'
The others were sat in a circle, discussing a terrorist scenario.

The imagined target was a cruise ship. An SDU station sergeant had deck plans laid out on the ground and was talking through the sniper options. Smith paid no attention. He watched as a couple of laborers loaded Andy Churton's motorcycle onto a lorry. They slammed shut the tailgate.

Then the lorry and its load was gone.

CHAPTER 9
LAST MAN STANDING

PEOPLE SAY THINGS like, 'I've been in meetings all day, I'm *exhausted*,' or, 'The kids drove me crazy today, I'm *exhausted*.' By day three, Smith felt like an old party balloon. His legs were like rubber. Pain bored into every muscle, sinew and tendon. He was exhausted.

On day three, the sleep deprivation started.

At dusk, a Royal Air Force helicopter dropped Smith and Fergus Duncan, on a hilltop in rural Saikung. Primary objective was a pier on an isolated stretch of coast. Smith and Duncan were to find the pier and watch for suspicious activity. Second objective was to meet John Sader at a Saikung telecoms building. To get to the telecoms building, they had to navigate ten miles of open countryside in the dark. As they settled down to watch the pier, it rained. Hard, relentless, tropical rain. It soaked their clothes, their boots, their hair. For hours, they watched the pier. Smith thumbed rainwater from his watch face and shone his torch on it. 'We should get to the secondary,' he said.

They moved off through a blackest night that Smith had ever known. They found a road and managed to beg a ride from a construction truck. A mile short of their objective, they left the truck and continued on foot. As they approached the telecoms building, there was a blaze of light and the rumble of a Land Rover engine. The Land Rover's headlights drew closer. The engine pitch grew higher. The Land Rover did not slow, it accelerated and came straight at them. Smith and Duncan turned and ran. Behind them, the engine's roar grew louder; the headlights brighter. Their shadows stretched ahead of them, bouncing like crazy marionettes. The Land Rover's roof mounted loudhailer boomed. 'Let's not play silly buggers, lads. Time to take your medicine.'

Smith jogged to a halt. Fergus Duncan was on one knee, massaging his side. The Land Rover's brakes squealed. The door opened and John Sader joined them in the headlight beams. 'All right, boys,' he chortled. 'It's time for your medicine.' There was a *pffzt* sound and Smith felt a cold can of beer shoved into his hand. He put the can to his lips and the cold beer hit his palate like all the ambrosia of heaven.

Sader jerked his head towards the Land Rover. 'Hop aboard,' he said. 'Lots of fun tomorrow.'

At 04.30 hours, they stumbled into the SDU barrack room. In an instant, they were asleep.

Three hours later, Peter Trammel inflicted a special torture on Smith — wheelbarrow races. Within minutes, Smith's dressings were tattered and bloody. His gorge rose and he vomited by the side of the square. He was light-headed and nauseous but more than anything, he was tired. Tired to the bones. Tired to the soul. That afternoon, orders came for another night exercise. The following night, there was another. During the next forty-four hours, Smith and the others managed just three hours sleep.

Friday morning started with the usual gym work. After lunch, they gathered on the drill square. 'Aggression,' John Sader announced. 'It pushes ordinary men to perform extraordinary acts.' He stepped aside and an SDU constable handed him two pairs of boxing gloves.

'Where's the gum shields and head guards?' Smith asked.

'They're in the champagne lounge with your private dancing girls,' Sader snapped back. 'Fergus Duncan and Steve James,' he said. 'Let's see what you're made of.'

There was no boxing ring, just a circle of candidates and SDU men. Duncan and James squared up to each other. Then they were at it, throwing punches like barroom rowdies. The SDU men crowded in. They were shouting like fight fans pumped up on adrenalin and whisky. *'Hit him.* Bloody, *HIT HIM!'*

Duncan and James' punches became faster, harder, more damaging. When one took a step back, the SDU men shoved him back into the fight. As his friends battered the daylights out of each other, Smith looked on, part in horror, part in sorrow.

It was Smith's turn. Sader paired him with Steve James. James came at fast and low, lips thin, eyes clear and determined. Smith was ready for him. He punched, ducked, punched, weaved and punched again. Straight left, right hook. He landed punch after punch. James just soaked it up and kept coming. Smith landed another blow and sensed he was on top of the fight. Then, from nowhere, James sliced in an arcing haymaker that split Smith's lip and dumped him backside first onto the tarmac.

Next, it was every candidate in for a free-for-all. Last man standing wins. No rules, no ring, no mat, just hard tarmac and a circle of jeering SDU men. Smith lowered his head and piled in like a rugby forward. He punched, elbowed, kicked, shoved, pulled, grabbed, tripped and punched again. Claw-like hands grabbed at his arms and legs. He reeled as an elbow slammed into his face. His head connected with a chin and a man went down. He grabbed someone in a bear hug and upended him onto the tarmac. Then all was still. Smith crouched and turned full circle. The SDU men were grinning, some even applauded. Smith was alone. He was the last man standing.

Afterwards, John Sader took Smith to the orderly office. He opened a first aid kit and produced an aerosol spray. 'Plastic skin,' he said. 'Seals the wound and stops infection.' He turned Smith's hands palm up and peeled away the crusted dressings. 'Might sting a little,' he added with some glee. As he played the spray over Smith's palms, needles of pain bored into Smith's hands. He clenched his teeth and could not hold back a cry of pain. Almost instantly, the pain was gone. He clenched and unclenched his fists. For the first time that week, he had full movement in his hands. 'A question,' Sader mused. 'Do you trust me?'

Trust? Smith thought. *I trust you to act like a bloody psycho.* 'Of course I trust you,' he said.

Sader raised an eyebrow. 'Are you sure? We'll see. But that's for tomorrow. For now, bugger off home.'

Smith felt better for a night at home. He arrived back at the Fanling Depot to find more candidates had dropped out. Now, there was just Smith and three others: Fergus Duncan, humorous and outgoing; Steve James, sociable but more thoughtful than the others; and Mike Groves, tall, competent and unflappable. Smith summed up the opposition. All were at their physical peak; inside each was an iron determination.

There was a new face on the drill square. He was an athletic-looking man who, like the other SDU inspectors, wore army-style camouflage fatigues.

'This is Tommy Tomlin of our Water Team,' Sader announced. 'Today you'll be messing around in boats.'

'We will shortly board a helicopter,' Tomlin announced. 'When we reach our destination, we will do a rapid rope descent to the ground.'

'Er... that's a specialist operation,' Smith said. 'Will we get any training?'

'Training? Of course there will be training,' Tomlin replied. 'When I say *follow me*, you will follow me. The training is now complete.'

A Wessex helicopter clattered onto the square, throwing up clouds of stinging grit. The seats were just strips of canvas slung across spindly aluminum frames. The smell of burnt aviation fuel filled the cabin, cloying and sickly. Coiled on the floor was a thick rope of green hemp. Smith fastened his lap strap. The engine pitch rose, the helicopter wobbled on its landing gear and was airborne. It made a sharp turn to the south and Smith found himself hanging by his lap strap. He grabbed his seat frame as the helicopter banked even more sharply. Twenty minutes later, G-forces crushed Smith into his seat as the pilot raised the nose and used the main rotor as a brake. Tommy Tomlin moved to the door and signaled everyone to unclip their lap straps. He made an impromptu megaphone of his cupped hands and shouted, *'Follow me.'* With that, he turned and jumped out of the open door. Smith gawked at the door then at the cabin floor where the rope remained untouched and neatly coiled. Smith, Fergus Duncan, Mike Groves and Steve James swapped open-mouthed stares. One thought filled four heads.

Mad bastard.

As a little boy, whenever an unruly friend led him into mischief, Smith's excuse was, 'But Jimmy did it first.' In reply, his mother would ask, 'If Jimmy jumped out of an upstairs window, would you follow him?' Now, for the first time, Smith could answer that question. He unclipped his lap strap and took a step towards the door. He sucked in a breath, put down his head, shouted, *'Oooh Shiiit,'* then bounded through the door. About twenty feet below him, the sea sparkled in the morning sun. For a second, Smith hung in space like some crazy cartoon character then he was tumbling down, arms and legs thrashing. He hit the water with a soggy *thump*. Water jetted into his nose and he came up spluttering.

Around him, the other three hit the water. An inflatable powerboat, called a Zodiac, buzzed in at high speed. Tomlin grabbed the side and the helmsman hauled him aboard. Once aboard, he turned to the four in the water. 'You'll want a lift, I suppose,' he called.

'A lift would be nice,' Fergus Duncan called back. 'But you have to promise there'll be no hanky-panky.'

Tomlin dragged them aboard. Once ashore, he ordered them back into the water for a one thousand meter swim. It was clear to everyone that Mike Groves was spent. His face was pale and despite the mid-morning heat, he was shivering. Minutes after entering the water, Groves rolled onto his back and raised his hands. In an instant, the Zodiac was there and the crew pulled him aboard. An ambulance rushed him to hospital where the duty doctor diagnosed pneumonia. For Groves to have carried on whilst so ill was testimony to his courage but there could be no question. He was out.

Now they were three.

They boarded a rigid-hulled boat, a constable cranked the outboard motor and they *puttered* away from the shore. A short distance out, the constable killed the engine and the boat rocked in a light swell. Tomlin stood at the prow. 'Trust, gentlemen,' he declared, 'is part of the Special Duties Unit ethos.'

A constable produced some twine and bound their hands and feet. Strong hands dragged Smith to his feet and from behind, someone blindfolded him. The bulwark banged against his knees. There was a hard shove in the small of Smith's back and he tumbled over the side. He went down then bobbed, wallowing, to the surface. He sucked in a breath and choked on water. He struggled against the rope but that made him wallow even more. Off to his left, Tomlin's voice mocked him. '*Trust*, Mister Smith, *trust.*'

Someone grabbed Smith's arms and a voice spoke close to his ear. 'On the count of three, take a deep breath. One...two...*three*...' The water closed over Smith and he felt himself dragged deeper and deeper. Pressure pain bored into his ears. How deep was he? The hands released him. He floated free but the blindfold blocked any reference points. Which way was up; which way down? His chest tightened. *Air*, he needed air. The pain in his ears eased. *Relief.* Soon he would be on the surface. Then his chest banged against the boat's keel. He tried to kick out but the bindings made it impossible. *Ohshitohshitohshit.* He was trapped under the boat. *Air,* he needed air. What had Tomlin said? *Trust, Mister Smith, trust.*

That was it, that was the test.

Smith forced himself to relax. Hands grasped his shoulders and pulled him clear. His face broke the surface. The sun was warm; the air was sweet. Someone tugged away the blindfold and he blinked away salt water. Next, they cut the bindings from his hands and feet. The boat crew helped him clamber over the bulwark and he collapsed against a bulkhead. Tomlin loomed over him. 'Where would we be without it?' he asked. 'Where would we be without *trust?'*

The next day, Smith hobbled to his bathroom on raw and blistered feet. He showered, bandaged his feet and made his way to the rail station. There, he met Fergus Duncan and Steve James. Both were haggard and limping. Later, they gathered at Fanling Depot. On day one, there had been twelve inspectors, laughing and swapping companionly insults. Now there were just three, each quietly assessing the staying power of the others. Smith looked over his competition and felt his confidence slip.

Smith was to plan an assault on a high-rise building and brief one of the regular assault teams. As he entered the briefing room, he stopped. The team was in full combat gear — black overalls and full-face hoods. Smith waited for them to snap to attention. Instead, they made a show of slouching back in their seats. Smith cleared his throat. 'Good morning, everyone,' he said, all bright and cheerful.

No answer.

'I said...'

A paper airplane drifted across the briefing room.

'Pay attention,' Smith snapped.

The room fell silent. At the back, someone snickered. There was the tang of tobacco smoke.

'No smoking,' Smith ordered.
'Must smoke,' the offender answered. 'Need it for my nerves.' Laughter filled the room.
'*Pay attention,*' Smith ordered.
The team went into a huddle. After a few moments one of them spoke. 'We agree to pay attention,' he said and the room fell silent.

Smith thought his briefing masterful. He covered every contingency. In addition to the strategic plan, he had arranged reinforcements and reserves of ammunition. There was a holding area for prisoners, there were plans to evacuate any wounded, there was even a rest area in case the operation went over its allotted time. 'Any questions?' he asked, confident there would be none.

The team sergeant stood. 'No questions,' he growled. 'If we follow your plan, assault team all dead.' They stood and filed out of the briefing room. Last man out threw Smith a mocking salute and closed the door behind him.

After lunch, the phobia tests started.

Have you noticed that a high place always seems much higher when you stand on top of it? The high place in question was an iron frame, about thirty feet tall. From the ground, it did not look too daunting. Heavy netting hung at the sides and at its top were two platforms joined by parallel bars, about two feet apart. As he stood on one of the platforms, Smith considered the frame's concrete base, thirty feet below. Slung across his back was a sniper rifle.

'Rifle above the head,' John Sader called.

Smith unslung the rifle and held it straight-armed above his head. It weighed nearly sixteen pounds, twice the weight of a World War Two infantry rifle.

'Good,' Sader said. 'Now step out onto the bars.'

Smith held his breath and stepped onto the bars. If he lost his footing, the concrete would not forgive him. He set his eyes on a fixed point in the distance.

'That'll do,' Sader called. 'Now, look up to the sky.'

Smith looked up. Adrenalin flashed through him as he felt himself begin to topple backwards.

'Now look down.'

Smith's head swam as he looked at the concrete below.

'Look up.'

Nausea rose in Smith's throat as again, he felt himself begin to topple backwards.

'What's the name of the Police Commissioner?' Sader asked.

For a moment, Smith struggled for the answer. 'It's...it's... Anning,' he said at last. 'Commissioner Ray Anning.'

'You're no good if you can't think under stress,' Sader chided. 'Next question, what's the capital of Paris?'

'France.'

'*Bollocks*,' Sader barked. 'Keep it together. Think.'

'Right,' Smith said. 'Paris. Paris is the capital of France,'

'Better. What's seven times eight?'

'Forty...no...fifty...fifty-six.'

'What's the gross national product of Uzbekistan?'

'Buggered if I know.'

'Me neither. You can come down.'

Next, came the pit. It was an open-topped concrete box, sunk into the ground and filled with scummy water. Smith was first in. The water was blood warm and chest deep. 'Now what?' he asked.

'Now you get out,' Sader answered.

Smith grabbed the pit's rim and prepared to lever himself out.

'No, no, Mister Smith,' Sader said. He pointed to the distance. 'The exit's about forty yards that way.'

Smith looked around the pit. The sides were smooth and unbroken.

'There *is* a way out,' Sader said. 'Seek and you will find.'

HONG KONG POLICE: INSIDE THE LINES

Smith squatted down and felt along the sides of the pit. There was an opening below the water's surface. 'How far does it go underwater?' he asked.

'For your sake, I hope not too far,' Sader answered.

Smith sucked in a breath, paused then ducked through the opening. Almost immediately, he was through. He surfaced. The darkness was complete. His head banged against concrete. The clearance was just a few inches. He tilted back his head and his nose brushed against the roof. He sucked in another breath and ducked down again, feeling for another tunnel. He ran his hands along slime covered concrete. Nothing. He resurfaced. Isolation crushed down on him. His breath came in gasping sobs. *Out*, he had to get *out*. There was light. A few yards from him, someone had opened a manhole cover. He saw he was in a short tunnel that ended just beyond the manhole opening.

'This way,' a voce called. 'This way Mister BJ.'

Relief flooded through Smith. He was getting out. An iron ladder led up to the opening. Smiling faces peered down at him. He put his foot on the first rung.

'Sorry. Only joking.' There was hard laughter and the manhole cover *tunked* shut.

In blackness, Smith held onto the ladder. He fought the urge to hammer at the manhole cover, to push it open and climb into the sunshine. He forced himself back into the water and searched for another opening. He ducked from one tunnel to the next. Sometimes there was a longer underwater swim. Each time he surfaced, there was another air pocket and the same crushing darkness. Occasionally, there was a flash of daylight and mocking calls but then the manhole cover would *tunk* shut. He lost sense of time. He had no way of knowing where he was or how far he had come. He ducked through another submerged passage and came up in a larger tunnel. This time, his head and shoulders were out of the water. His feet were on the bottom. There was daylight and again, taunting voices. 'Here, this way. Come on.'

Smith cursed them but still, he waded towards the daylight. The water was liquid ooze, holding him back. He blinked up at the sky. The same smiling faces peered back at him. 'Come on Mister BJ. This way.' Smith grabbed the ladder and paused on the bottom rung, waiting for the cover to slam him back into darkness. He took another step up, then another. His head emerged into the real world. He climbed up into the daylight then lay back on the grass and felt the sun warm on his face.

On Tuesday, a dark mood settled over them all as they wrote their statements for the inquest into Andy Churton's death. Smith's statement was concise and factual but in it, the funny, clever, steadfast friend that was Andy Churton became lost. There was so much more he wanted to write but the coroner's court is no place for a eulogy. Later, as he planned a simulated raid on barricaded stronghold, Smith's thoughts slipped into a bleak place. Overlaying it was the ever-present, mind-numbing fatigue. He could not think, could not act. He stared at his part-written plan, barely recognizing his own handwriting. *Why bother?* He laid his pen aside. Then, Andy Churton's face floated before him. Inside Smith's head, a familiar voice spoke. *Giving up BJ? Really? Not your style, my brother. Not your style at all.*

In that instant, it all became clear. It could have been any of them collapsed by the side of the road: Steve James, Fergus Duncan, it might even have been Barry Smith. For Andy Churton, getting into the unit had been his dream but he knew it would be his greatest ever challenge. If anything, he would be proud to see his friend, no his *brother*, finish that challenge.

Smith retrieved his pen, furrowed his brow and considered how best to finish the plan.

More forced marches, more weight training, more mental exercise. The three of them were like spectators to someone else's misery. During another night exercise, an assault team blasted them with stun grenades. By now, none of them cared. As the transport rattled along back roads leading back to the depot, Smith slumped in his seat and rested his head against the window. He remembered little about the trip back to the depot. He awoke with a jolt as the transport squealed to a halt on the drill square. As the three of them stepped from the transport, Smith thought them a sad sight. Mud spattered, unshaven, blank-faced, drained.

'Line up,' Trammel ordered.

Jesus. What next?

'That's it,' Trammel declared. 'Selection course is over. We'll have a decision in two weeks.' Without another word, he turned and walked towards the SDU offices.

No one moved; no one spoke. Smith, Duncan and James stared at each other.

'Bugger me,' said Steve James at last.

'Time for a beer,' said Fergus Duncan.

Smith laughed. Then they were all laughing. It was over. They made their way back to the changing room, chattering like schoolboys released from detention. Smith paused and let the other two walk ahead. He put his hands on his hips, threw back his head and drew in a long breath. It was really over. He made to follow the others but a touch on his shoulder stopped him. He turned but there was no one there. Smith was alone but he could not shake off the feeling that someone was near, someone strong and protective.

'*Andy?*'

A sudden breeze ruffled the trees and tugged at Smith's sleeve.

'We did it Andy,' Smith whispered. 'You and me, mate. We did it.'

Then the presence was gone and Smith was alone again. For a moment, he was still. Then he squared his shoulders and followed the others back to the changing room.

Two weeks later, orders arrived from Police Headquarters. They announced Smith's transfer to the Special Duties Unit.

Some thought Fanling a tranquil retreat from the bustle of town. For Smith, it had been a place of crushing fatigue, pain and personal loss. But now, he was aware of the sun on his face and the birds quarreling in the trees. He had done it. He was a member of the Special Duties Unit; an honest-to-goodness, real-deal, Flying bloody Tiger. He showed his warrant card to the gate guard and strolled across the square. He flexed his fingers as a remembered pain chewed at his hands. At the far end of the square, a group of athletic young men played football. They paused their game to watch him, their gaze a mix of curiosity and appraisal. Smith went direct to the hut that served as the SDU Commander's office. He knocked and entered. The Commander was Harry North, a superintendent in his early thirties. He wore an olive green T-shirt and military-style camouflage trousers tucked into calf-high boots. He offered a firm handshake and invited Smith to sit. On his desk was a report bearing the stamp, 'STAFF — IN CONFIDENCE.'

'You did well.' North said. His voice was quiet but had a firm edge. 'Sader and Trammel tell me you were...' He glanced at the report. '"...*exceptionally tenacious and committed...*"' He raised an eyebrow. 'How are the hands?'

'Completely healed, sir.'

North chuckled. '*Sir?*' he scoffed. 'There's none of that malarkey here. I'm Harry.' He leaned back and studied Smith. 'You'll find things very different here,' he said. 'None of that jumping to attention and saluting rubbish. In time, your men will give you a nickname. If you're lucky, it won't remind you of any bollocks you've dropped. You okay with that?'

'Yes, sir. Sorry, I mean, yes. That's fine.'

'How's your physical fitness?' North asked.

'Er... pretty good,' Smith replied. 'I've... I've had duty

commitments...' His voice tailed off.

'*Pretty good*, isn't good enough,' North said. There was no rancor in his voice. To Smith it seemed he was just stating a fact. 'Every year,' North continued, 'the British army's Special Air Service sends a team to make sure we're on top of things. They don't want us to be good. They don't want us to be excellent. They want us to be one of the world's top counter-terrorist units. Nothing less will do.' For a moment, he let the words hang between them. 'I'm sure you're up to it,' he said at last. 'If not...' He shrugged and left the rest unsaid.

The barrack sergeant issued Smith three sets of army-style camouflage fatigues, three olive green T-shirts, a black, one-piece combat overall, a black hood and a pair of calf-high boots. There was a state-of-the-art gas mask that was proof against nuclear, biological and chemical weapons. The sergeant piled the equipment on the counter and handed Smith a stores receipt to sign. Next, the armory sergeant assigned him a set of Kevlar body armor, a Heckler and Koch MP5 submachine gun and a Browning automatic pistol. 'Use same weapons for everything,' he said. 'Firing range, combat training, operations. Always same.' He flashed Smith a smile. 'Partners for everything.'

Twelve constables joined the unit with Smith and for the next six months, they trained together. Peter Trammel urged them on but his tone had changed. No longer were there calls of, '*No slacking.*' Now it was, 'Not bad. Well done. Next time, try to do it faster.' Every day, Smith and the constables took their MP5s and Brownings from the armory. They stripped and reassembled the weapons again and again until Smith was sure they could do it blindfold.

'Good,' Sader said. 'Now do it blindfold.'

They practiced with their Browning pistols and MP5 submachine guns. Standing, kneeling, prone, right-handed, left-handed. Then against the clock. So-many-shots in so-many-seconds. 'Every missed shot is a dead hostage,' Sader told them. 'Now, do it again. This time, faster.'

They fast roped down the sides of buildings. There were rapid rope descents from helicopters onto hillsides and high-rise rooftops. They practiced in daylight and in the dark. Always, the inspector went first. Never must he hesitate; never must he show fear.

Eventually, Smith took command of a nine-man assault team. Back in Kowloon City, the constables had always called him, *'sir.'* Now, his new team regarded him with the same cool curiosity he had seen on that first day on the drill square. The sergeant was *Fu Saang*, literally *Mister* Tiger. He had an open face and an air of understated competence.

'Here is our new *Dai Lo*,' Fu Saang announced. *Dai Lo* — Elder Brother. He introduced the men by their nicknames. As he called out each one, the men acknowledged with a cursory wave or a spoken, *'Dai Lo, nei ho.'* — Elder Brother, hi.

Smith gave a short speech, after which, *Fu Saang* drew him aside. 'All will be well, *Dai Lo*,' he said. He nodded towards the team. 'Good men; the best. We support you; you support us.' He gave a curt nod. *'Hai gam doh.'* — that's it.

Training, training, training. It never stopped. There were blank-firing exercises in darkened rooms. A flash of light showed a human form. Hostage or hostage taker? Shoot or no shoot? Just a second or two to decide. They practiced with non-lethal stun grenades, better known as *flash-bangs*. The grenades produced a huge bang and a flash of intense light designed to disorientate a barricaded enemy. Then it was the killing house. There, they practiced hostage rescue and room-to-room combat. The inside walls were moveable partitions and the layout changed for every exercise. The partitions were just plywood; the ammunition was live. In the killing house, everyone had to know exactly where their colleagues were. The house had a grim history: one dead and one seriously injured. In the killing house, SDU training got serious.

Day by day, week by week, a collective sixth sense developed between them. A look, a nod or a hand signal replaced spoken orders. They called Smith, *Dai Lo*. It was respectful yet friendly but in SDU parlance, it was standard fare.

This was the tough one: fast roping, at night, onto the deck of a moving cargo ship. Smith and his team boarded a Wessex helicopter at the Shek Kong Royal Air Force base. An air force corporal stood by the door. A thick rope lay coiled on cabin floor. The SDU team wore full combat gear, including body armor. Hoods covered their faces, only their eyes showed. There was an MP5 strapped to each chest and a gas mask haversack at each hip. It was a blustery night. The Wessex shuddered as it lifted off and banked to the south. It skirted western Hong Kong Island then headed southeast, over the South China Sea. The door was open but still, the air was thick with the smell of burnt fuel. The engine roar and the thump of rotors filled the cabin. Below them, they could just make out white-tops scudding across the water. Then, the lights of a cargo ship winked through the dark. The Wessex slowed, matching the ship's speed. The corporal gave the *'ready'* sign. Smith checked his MP5 was secure then put on his roping gloves. He yanked hard on the rope. The fastener held. He gave the corporal a thumbs-up and took a two-handed grip on the rope. The corporal peered down through the dark and showed Smith the flat of his hand, like a traffic policeman. Seconds later, with a sweep of his arm, he signaled, *'go.'* Smith stepped into the dark and plummeted down. The rope skidded through his hands. Even through the gloves, he felt its heat. He could see nothing. *Jesus, where's the deck?* If he landed in the water, there could be no rescue. Then, the helicopter's searchlight lanced through the dark. There was the gleam of iron decking. Smith tightened his grip, slowing his descent. His boots hit the deck.

He dropped to one knee and tugged the MP5 free. Beside him a *thud*, told him the next man had landed. In less than a minute, his whole team was on the deck and the helicopter was banking away. The men formed a circle, presenting a three-sixty degree arc of fire. *Fu Saang* identified himself with a raised fist. The ship's superstructure was a dark mass. Smith scanned the upper deck railings, looking for would-be ambushers silhouette against the sky. He raised his fist and pumped the air once. The team split into two. Smith's team scurried along the starboard deck. *Fu Saang* paralleled him along the port side. They moved in a half crouch, weapons ready. A series of ladders took them up three decks to the bridge where the water team leader, Tommy Tomlin waited.

Throughout the exercise, not one word had been spoken.

'Well done,' Tomlin said. '*Fu Saang, nei ho ma?*' — Fu Saang, are you well?

Fu Saang grinned. 'Very well,' he said. 'Me and *BJ Dai Lo*. Both very well.'

Tomlin flashed a smile. 'So, it's *BJ Dai Lo*, is it?'

Smith raised a puzzled eyebrow.

'*BJ Dai Lo*,' Tomlin said again. 'You've passed the final test,' he said. 'Your men have named you.' He smiled. 'So, *BJ Dai Lo* it is. Welcome to the unit.'

It was everything Smith had expected: tactical training, combat exercises, contingency planning. With each level of expertise mastered, there was always another level to reach. Each day stretched Smith beyond all he had thought possible. But combat exercises are not the real thing. Role-playing SDU colleagues are not urban guerrillas. Blank cartridges are not live rounds. Anxiety about flunking an exercise is not combat stress. What if it were real terrorists writing the script? The question was like an unscratchable itch. Terrorists had spared Hong Kong, probably because they knew of the Special Duties Unit.

But what if... Smith half-wished for the chance to put the training to the test. Not a scripted test, but a proper, life-or-death test of arms. Of course there are problems with wishes, even half-wishes.

Sometimes they come true.

CHAPTER 10
SPIDERMAN

SOME HONG KONG streets specialize in particular shopping themes. In Yuen Po Street there are shops selling only caged birds. Shops in Tung Choi Street specialize in goldfish. In the street market nestled between Battery Street and Reclamation Street, shoppers can find jade both good and bad. In a corner of Kwun Tong district called Mut Wah Street, the traders dealt in gold. They did not handle the high-end stuff carried by fancy outlets in Hong Kong Island's Central district or in Kowloon's Tsim Sha Tsui district, but who cares? Gold is gold.

Kwun Tong was a district of factory blocks and high-rise housing projects. It was not what you would call a crime hotspot and its crooks were mostly small-time. Overall, it was a peaceful place. At least it was until one day in June.

On June 9, 1991, there was excitement in Mut Wah Street as word spread that someone was making a movie. A crowd soon gathered to watch the main players. Earlier, they had arrived in plain white van. The van carried no movie maker's logo but the players certainly looked the part. There were two of them. Each had a realistic-looking Kalashnikov AK47 assault rifle. They wore black hoods and stood back to back, covering both ends of the street. They balanced on the balls of their feet and constantly glanced around as if expecting trouble. As the crowd of spectators grew, no one thought it strange there were no cameras, no lighting gantries and no film crew. The sound of approaching

HONG KONG POLICE: INSIDE THE LINES

sirens stirred a murmur of expectation from the crowd. A police Land Rover squealed to a stop and police officers clambered out, guns drawn. The hooded men reacted in an instant.

BAM-BAM-BAM.

In the confines of Mut Wah Street, each shot sounded like a wrecking ball. *BAM-BAM-BAM-BAM.*

Spent cartridge cases clattered onto the sidewalk. Shards of masonry peppered the crowd. Bullets, *tunk-tunk-tunked into* parked cars. A windscreen exploded. The tang of cordite drifted along the street. People screamed. They turned and ran. Some stumbled and fell. Outgunned, the police darted from doorway to parked car to traffic bollard. They took aim at the two gunmen but could not fire, there were too many people on the street. The van's rear doors swung open. Its engine roared. A group of hooded men ran from a goldsmith shop and jumped aboard. More hooded men ran from another goldsmith. The van's doors slammed shut. There was the scream of spinning wheels and the van careered away.

Detectives from Kowloon East Regional Headquarters put together a picture of what had happened. Armed with pistols and assault rifles, a gang had robbed five goldsmith shops in Mut Wah Street. They escaped with gold and jewelry worth HK$5.7 million, more than US$750,000. They fired fifty-four shots but by some miracle, hit no one.

In the coming months, the gang hit three more goldsmiths, escaping with gold and jewelry worth millions of Hong Kong dollars. They carried Kalashnikov AK47 rifles which they used without compunction. Shortly after the Mut Wah Street robbery, the gang obtained hand grenades, stolen from the British army camp at Tam Mei. Careless of innocent lives, they lobbed the grenades at pursuing police vehicles. In Mong Kok, one of the world's busiest shopping areas, they fired thirty shots, killing a woman passer-by. Slowly, the police pieced together details of the man behind the robberies. He was a thirty year old, career hoodlum called Yip Kai-foon. He should have been in jail, serving an eighteen-year sentence for armed robbery but five years into his sentence he had escaped and fled to China. Now he was back at the head of a gang that included local criminals and mainland ex-soldiers. The mainlanders were combat-trained and had military-grade weapons. The locals were hard men; tough and determined.

After each robbery, the mainlanders fled back to China and the local boys faded into the community. No one knew their names. Even within the gang, it was likely they knew each other only by nickname.

They were the *Dai Huen Jai* – the Big Circle Boys.

Barry Smith was moving up. After five years with the Special Duties Unit, he was a Team Commander with the rank of chief inspector. Smith's replacement was Danny Lawley, a cheery South African.

Despite his elevation, Smith was not having a great day. It started when his washing machine went on the fritz and did not improve when he got to work. After a light workout in the gym, Smith and his old team spent all afternoon and evening practicing a railway hostage situation. The railway operators provided a train and the team did the exercise in a siding, miles from anywhere. By the time Smith got home, it was after midnight. He thought about dropping into the local bar but he was on reserve callout. Any emergency and he would be the first contact. *Emergency? Fat chance.* As Smith drifted off to sleep, his bedside telephone jangled. He swore as he reached for it, probably a wrong number or some half-drunk friends hoping he would join them.

'Smith,' he growled into the mouthpiece.

'*BJ Dai Lo?*' the telephone piped back.

Smith sat up. 'Yes,' he answered. 'Who's that?'

'Here is Kwan Jai at SDU base,' the voice answered. 'Lima Team is called out.'

Smith swung his legs off the bed. 'Where and what?' he asked.

'Not clear. I think criminal case,' Kwan Jai answered. *'The case is belong to Kowloon East but Director police operations has authorized callout. Meet the team at Tsuen Wan police station. Get briefing there.'*

As Smith pulled on a T-shirt, the telephone rang again. It was the SDU's commander, Harry North.

'I'm coming with you,' he said. 'Any idea where Tsuen Wan police station is?'

'No idea,' Smith answered. 'We'll have to ask someone when we get near.'

'Well, you can do the bloody asking,' North said. *'I'll be outside your place in five minutes.'*

An hour later, with the help of a drowsy convenience store clerk, Smith and North rolled into Tsuen Wan police station's compound. Danny Lawley and the team had got there first. Tucked away in the shadows, stood their vehicle. It was about the size of a small removal van and painted an anonymous matt black. Written on the side was the logo, 'Tip Top Industrial Cleaners.'

There was always banter and laughter during tactical exercises. Now, as the team checked their gear, the mood was somber. Smith and North grabbed their gear then Smith checked the rest of the equipment. Stun grenades: *check*. Crowbars: *check*. Disc cutter: *check*. Smoke and teargas devices: *check*. Loudhailer: *check*. Torches: *check*.

'A detective superintendent from Kowloon East is waiting for us in the CID office,' Danny Lawley said. The three of them, Smith, North and Lawley, made their way to the detective office.

Detective superintendent Bob Craig was a seasoned investigator. 'Just local ratbags,' he said. 'But word on the street is they've at least one AK47.'

Local ratbags. Smith had expected more. 'We'll do a quick

reconnaissance,' he said.

'No need for that,' Craig said. 'My woman sergeant's had a good look round. She can tell you all you need to know. We've done a full intelligence review. We've even got their phone number.'

'Can you confirm their firepower?' Smith asked.

'Nothing's one-hundred percent,' Craig answered. 'Like I say, they're local ratbags who might have an AK47.'

North frowned. 'Sounds a bit hit and miss,' he said.

'Director Operations agrees this is ours,' Craig snapped back. 'That means I have final say on how we do things.' He paused for a moment. ' He smiled and spread his hands as if yielding a point. 'Lighten up. It's local ratbags. When they see you lot, they'll come along as meek as you like.' They moved to a table where there was a floor plan of the target apartment block. There were two wings linked by a communal lift lobby. From the air, it looked like a letter 'H.' Each wing had eight apartments. Each apartment had a living area, a bedroom, a toilet and a small kitchen. Craig stabbed his finger down onto one of the apartments. 'This is the target address,' he said. 'Twenty-third floor. Apartment 2305.'

'How do we get in?' Smith asked.

'Nothing unusual,' Craig answered. 'Bog standard wooden door with an external folding grill.'

'We can use a small explosive charge on the door, lob in a *flash-bang* then move in to secure the flat,' Smith suggested.

'You bloody won't,' Craig huffed. 'This is a quiet neighborhood. It's just a bog standard security grill and a wooden door. You can pop them both with a decent crowbar.'

'I still think we need to take a look,' Smith said.

'They're very alert to police,' Craig cautioned.

'The sniper team can set up remote observation posts,' Smith insisted. 'It's what they're trained for.'

Craig shook his head. '*No, no, no.* If they spot you, it'll blow the whole operation.'

As Smith, North and Lawley made their way back to the station compound, their mood was dark. 'I don't fancy going in blind,' Smith grumbled.

'Me neither,' North answered. 'But Director Ops says it's their show.'

In the compound, they kitted up. Black combat overalls, body armor, weapons. The gear weighed more than twenty kilos but it felt familiar. North took Smith aside. 'Don't forget, Danny's the assault group leader,' he said. 'You're to hang back and let him get on with it.'

'But...'

North held up his hand, silencing Smith's objections. 'It's up to Danny to get in and sort it out. You're the chief inspector. It's your job to keep a lid on things and keep me informed. Got it?'

'Got it,' Smith sighed.

Smith gathered the team. 'Covert approach,' he said. 'De-bus at the utilities entrance. Take the stairs to the twentieth floor. Assemble there for final briefing.' The team nodded. 'Snipers take position on the ground floor,' Smith added. 'Watch for anything thrown from the windows.'

They boarded the transport and moved slowly through deserted streets. To passers-by, they were just a night-time service company going about its business. Aboard the transport, Smith was not happy. No reconnaissance, no observation posts, no confirmation of enemy firepower. They were going in blind. He kept his worries to himself; no need to unsettle the men. At 04.50 hours, the van coasted to a halt behind the target block. One by one, the men looked to Smith and gave the thumbs up sign: ready to go. They grabbed their gear and spilled from the van. They moved into the utilities yard. Overflowing rubbish skips lined the walls. There was a stench of rank garbage. A cat crouched then darted away. The team hunkered down in the shadows. Smith pointed to two men and signaled them to take the point position. They raised their MP5s and moved to the lobby entrance. They scanned left and right. One raised a fist: all clear. The rest followed. The point men checked the way ahead: clear. They were silent shadows: black combat overalls, black body armor; their weapons were black. They moved slowly and in silence; conserving energy, maintaining stealth.

So it went, floor by floor. Advance, hold, all clear. Advance, hold, all clear. On the twentieth floor, Smith ordered a halt. He did a final inventory check: weapons, stun grenades, teargas shells, crowbars, disc cutter, loud-hailers, torches.

'Fit respirators,' he whispered.

The team fitted their gas masks. Now they were shadows without faces. Smith beckoned Lawley to him. The gas mask muffled his voice.

'Proceed to the twenty-third floor stairwell and hold position there,' he said. 'When we're all in place, send two men to locate the target apartment and report back.'

Minutes later, two men returned shaking their heads. The outer security door was not a folding iron grill. The upper half was filigree iron lattice; the lower half was iron plate.

'We'll not pop that with a crowbar,' Smith said. 'You'll have to take the hinges off.'

'Noisy,' Lawley answered.

'Then you'd better be quick.' Smith said. 'Two men: one to work the cutter on the hinges; the other to crowbar the lock. Select your assault party. Have them stand by with *flash-bangs* and MP5s. I repeat, *stand by* until I give the order to go.' He went back to the floor below and radioed a situation report to Harry North.

'Wait one,' North replied. There was a pause, then, *'CID will phone the targets and tell them to surrender. Understood? Over.'*

Smith's breath escaped in an explosive hiss. *What?* No recce, no observation posts, no confirmation of enemy firepower and now they were alerting the targets. There was no way this idea had come from North.

North's voice cracked over the radio. *'I say again, do you understand? Over.'*

Smith shook his head. 'Understood,' he replied. But he did not understand, he did not understand at all. He joined the others in the twenty-third floor stairwell. From inside the target flat, a telephone began to ring. It seemed an age before it fell silent. It rang again and again, it fell silent.

Delay, delay, delay. It was crazy. They had to move. Smith went back down the stairs and radioed Harry North. 'No response to the telephone,' he said. 'Any instructions?'

North put Bob Craig on the radio. *'Try something else,'* Craig said. *'Tell them who you are and order them to come out. Over.'*

Smith thought he had misheard. 'Say again, over.'

'I've received orders from my HQ. You will stand outside the flat door and tell them to surrender. Did you get that? Over.'

'Er...yes. Message received.'

'Then get on with it.'

'Roger,' Smith answered. To Lawley he said, 'Did you hear that?'

'Yes.'

'Then we'd better get on with it.'

They climbed back to the twenty-third floor. Smith nodded to Lawley. Lawley made chopping motions towards the target apartment. Two men moved forward and flattened themselves against the wall on either side of the door. They were Tommy and *Chee Jai*. Tommy carried a powered disc cutter; *Chee Jai* had an iron crowbar. The rest of the team moved out of the stairwell. Alert, silent, MP5s leveled at the apartment door. Lawley showed them the palm of his hand: *hold position*.

It's Danny's play, Smith told himself. He hung back, feeling like a boxer shackled to his corner. The team sergeant, *Fu Saang*, adjusted the loud-hailer's volume, raised the microphone and pressed the transmit button. There was a howl of feedback. *'Ngoh dei Fei Fu Dui.'* — this is the Flying Tigers. The loud-hailer made his words metallic and harsh. *'Gui go sau. Chut lai.'* — Raise your hands. Come out. *'Jik haak chut lai.'* — Come out immediately.

Silence.

'Ngoh dei Fei Fu...'

BAM-BAM-BAM-BAM-BAM. Bullets punched though the door's iron plate. They ricocheted along the corridor, peppering everyone with chipped concrete.

Armor piercing shells, thought Smith. *My God, our body armor's useless.*

An SDU man pushed the barrel of his MP5 through the filigree section of gate. *Tak-tak-tak.* A cluster of holes appeared in the wooden door. The disc cutter sang to life. Tommy pressed the blade against the lower hinge. SHIZZZZNNGG. Sparks cascaded from the blade. *Chee Jai* wedged the crowbar into the gate hasp and leaned his weight against it.

BAM-BAM-BAM-BAM. More bullets punched through the gate, inches from Tommy's head. BAM-BAM. Splinters from the inner door *pattered* against the eyepieces of *Chee Jai's* gas mask. BAM-BAM-BAM. A lobby light exploded in a shower of glass. In darkness, the disc cutter sprayed a stream of sparks across the floor. There was a numbing BOOM. The apartment's wooden door disintegrated. Wooden splinters and shards of steel *whickered* overhead.

Adrenaline pumped through Smith. *Grenade! If he lobs one out here, he'll wipe us out.*

From street level, came another BOOM.

Lawley pulled the pin from a stun grenade, dropped it through the filigree section of gate then flattened himself against the wall. Hard light flooded the corridor. A *BANG* battered them. A constable fired pellets of powdered CS irritant into the apartment. A trickle of smoke drifted from the door. There was more smoke, now it was thick and heavy. Smith pressed his radio's transmit button. 'Assault party to SDU Commander.

Over.'

'Send. Over.'

'Targets have discharged a grenade inside the flat, which is now on fire. Over.'

'Understood. Targets have thrown a grenade from the window. We have sustained casualties. Over.'

'Understood. I request...'

BAM-BAM-BAM. Bullets slammed into the wall near Smith's head, showering him with stinging concrete. He dropped to a crouch. '...request fire extinguishers. Over.'

'Roger. They're on the way up.'

The elevator grumbled up from the ground floor. The doors opened. Inside, two fire extinguishers stood alone like little red soldiers.

The apartment's gate groaned as the hinges gave way. It leaned at a crazy angle then clattered to the floor. Smith ran forward, Harry North's orders forgotten. He grabbed a torch, drew his Browning and thumbed the safety catch to *fire*. He stepped through the door. Against a wall, a sofa was ablaze. From behind him, there came the metallic roar of a fire extinguisher and the blaze died. Smith's torch beam probed left and right. The apartment walls were seared black. A three-tier bunk bed stood upended and broken. A shattered television lay in the corner. A shelf had spilt its contents onto the floor. A wall picture hung at a crazy angle. *Where are they?* He crouched, expecting an AK47 to rake the apartment, to rip into his men, to rip into *him*. His foot connected with something. It was a grenade. Strewn across the floor were several more. His torch picked out the gleam of an abandoned pistol. And there, standing by the far wall, were two men. Smith leveled his Browning. *'MO YUK!'* − STAND STILL! he shouted. *'GUI GO SAU.'* − RAISE YOUR HANDS.

The two seemed not to hear. Their eyes were glazed, their shoulders slumped.

'GUI GO SAU!'

Slowly, they raised their hands. SDU men bundled them outside. Smith followed. 'Is that it?' He was incredulous. *'Two?'* It wasn't right; something was missing but he could not put his finger on it. Then, realization. *'Fu Saang,'* he called. 'Where's the AK47?'

'Is it not in apartment?'

Smith shook his head.

Fu Saang spoke to the prisoners in rapid Cantonese. One lowered his eyes and answered. *Fu Saang* shook him by the shoulder. *'Gong m'yeh?'* — What are you saying? *'Dai seng di.'* — Speak up.

The man seemed dazed. He muttered a reply. *Fu Saang* turned to Smith. 'He says...' *Fu Saang* spoke again to the prisoner who nodded. 'He says there were six of them.'

'Six? Where're the others?'

'He says, they went out of the window. They climbed up the outside of the building. One has AK47 strapped to his back.'

'Are the others armed?'

'He says, yes. They have pistols.'

For a moment, anger bubbled inside Smith. *Local ratbags?* Hard men with military grade weapons, more like. Four of them were now clambering around outside the building like bloody Spiderman. He radioed his report to Harry North.

'Bring the buggers down to the ground floor,' North ordered. *'We've got the exits covered. The other four are going nowhere.'*

Fu Saang handcuffed the prisoners and took them to the stairwell. At the head of the stairs, Smith paused. The corridor and lift lobby were a wreck. Gouges scarred the walls and ceiling. The remnants of a neon strip light swung from a single wire. The apartment's gate was a lump of twisted scrap. The doorframe was pockmarked and smoke blackened. God knows what the neighbors had gone through. Gunfire, explosions, the smell of burning furniture. He could only imagine their terror.

On the ground floor, the grenade had left a splash of black

HONG KONG POLICE: INSIDE THE LINES

on the block's wall. The wounded had gone off to hospital. All but one of the injuries were minor. The exception was a young sniper called Benny. 'It's a bad do,' Harry North said. 'We think he'll lose an eye.'

By now, other SDU teams had arrived from Fanling. 'Targets are definitely inside one of the flats,' Harry North said. 'BJ's team will sweep from the top floor down. The other team will sweep from the ground floor up.'

Team leaders and sergeants asked a few questions then it was time to go.

Smith's team made their way back up the stairwell. Advance, hold, all clear. Advance, hold, all clear. *Is there someone with an AK47 waiting at the next landing?* Advance, hold, all clear. On the thirty-first floor, they rested. Just one more flight to the rooftop. Smith sent men to secure the stairwell, lift lobby and apartment wings. The rest went to the rooftop. They searched the water cisterns and service structures: all clear. Then it was back to the thirty-first floor. At the first apartment, Smith stood to one side of the door and knocked. In an instant, it was open. The team pushed their way in and checked the living area, kitchen, toilet and bedroom. All clear. The occupants were pale and wide-eyed. Smith took a few minutes to reassure them then warned them to lock their doors and stay inside. Next apartment — no answer. No time to knock. A constable applied a crowbar and the security grill clattered open. They broke open the main door and moved from room to room. All clear.

Next apartment. Clear. Then the next and the next and the next. If there was no answer, they broke in. Thirty-first floor — sixteen apartments. All clear. Thirtieth floor — sixteen more. All clear. With each knock, came the gut-tightening prospect of an armor piercing AK47 round. The search operation turned into an extended game of Russian roulette. Twenty-ninth floor — clear. Twenty-eighth floor — clear. They moved to the twenty-seventh floor. Smith knocked on the first door. A man answered. His face was ashen, his eyes were wide, his hands shook. *'Mo yeh, Bongban.'* — Nothing here, Inspector. There was a catch in his voice. Smith held up his hand for silence and signaled the man to open the grill. The man eased it open but still, it rattled. He winced and cast a quick look at the bedroom. Smith, *Fu Saang* and two constables stepped past him. The man pointed to the bedroom. Smith held the Browning, stiff-armed before him. He pointed to two constables. They took position on either side of the door. Smith made a chopping motion. A constable gave the door a kick. It slammed open. The men stormed in, MP5s level. *'MO YUK! GUI GO SAU!'* — *DON'T MOVE! RAISE YOUR HANDS!*

Inside the bedroom, three pairs of hands shot up. On the bed were three Chinese army, Black Star pistols. Beside them lay an AK47 assault rifle. The constables bundled the prisoners into the living room. *Fu Saang* supervised their handcuffing and Smith radioed a situation report to Harry North. North's voice crackled back. *'Five down, one to go. Continue the sweep until you meet the other team.'*

And so it continued. Floor by floor. Sixteen apartments to a floor. With each knock, maybe gunfire or a grenade would answer them. Then there was a radio message to all teams. SDU had arrested the sixth gang member.

Eight hours after it started, the operation stood down. Smith and the team gathered on the ground floor. They unloaded their weapons and stowed them in the transport. Someone handed Smith a bottle of water and he drained it in one. He stripped off his combat gear and slipped back into his jeans and T-shirt.

'All done,' Harry North announced. 'You should get yourself home. We'll do the debrief tomorrow.'

'How are the injured?' Smith asked.

North frowned. 'All fine except Benny. He lost that eye.'

'I'd best get to the hospital,' Smith said.

'Good idea,' North said. His voice became a low growl. 'I

ordered you to leave it to Danny,' he said. 'But you were first through the door.'

Smith had no answer.

'It's not good enough,' North continued. 'Disobedience of orders under fire.'

'Sorry,' Smith said. 'It... it was a spur of the moment thing. I forgot.'

'Do you know what happens to people who disobey orders under fire?'

Smith could only shrug.

'Their commanding officer has to decide between a discipline hearing and a medal. Now bugger off.'

Each gunman went to prison for more than twenty years. Yip Kai-foon, the gang's leader, was not there during the raid. He fled back to China and did not surface for another four years. In May 1996, police caught up with him as he tried to sneak back into Hong Kong. He opened fire on the police and in the ensuing gunfight, he suffered injuries that left him confined to a wheelchair. He returned to prison where, eleven years later, he died of lung cancer.

In time, all the injured Special Duty Unit officers returned to work, including the sniper, Benny. Benny trained his good eye and continued to work as an SDU sniper. For Barry Smith and Harry North, there were reports to write. Awards are vexatious things. At each level of command there are senior officers who are not content with the facts they are given. There are endless questions and the answers never seem good enough. But in time, the reports are complete, the recommendations are final and the questions have all been answered. The machinery plods along at a glacial pace but eventually, it gets there.

Three and a half years after the incident, Barry John Smith, BJ to his friends, stood before Her Majesty the Queen and received the Queens Gallantry Medal for exemplary acts of bravery. He was not alone. Also receiving the Queen's Gallantry Medal were Tommy and *Chee Jai* who despite coming under heavy fire, stuck to their task and got the apartment door open.

Barry Smith served with the Special Duties Unit for twelve years. He took part in eighty operations before returning to normal police duties. And that should have been an end to it, but it wasn't. The *Dai Huen Jai* gang had started their Hong Kong careers in the goldsmiths' enclave of Mut Wah Street, which is in Kwun Tong. It is one of life's coincidences, that years later, Chief Superintendent Barry Smith, QGM, took command of Kwun Tong police district.

Old habits do not pass easily and on their release, the gunmen all went on to re-offend. As Smith leafed through his morning crime reports, he was delighted to read that his detectives had busted a burglary gang. For months, the gang had been causing the district some heartache. As Smith read the list of those arrested, he saw two familiar names. He called his detective superintendent. 'Do any of these characters have convictions for firearms offenses?' he asked.

Yes they did, came the answer. Years earlier, two of them had been in a shootout with the Special Duties Unit. Smith thanked the superintendent, put down the phone and leaned back in his chair. *Perhaps I should consider a reunion party*, he thought.

But on second thoughts, perhaps not.

HONG KONG POLICE: INSIDE THE LINES

PART 6
UMBRELLA MOVEMENT

HONG KONG POLICE: INSIDE THE LINES

CHAPTER 11
THE BANQUET

A WISE OLD SERGEANT once said, 'If either side of an argument thinks you're a good fellow, you've handled things wrong. When both sides think you're a bastard, you've got it right.'

In 2014, a lot of people thought the Hong Kong Police were all bastards. For seventy-nine days, there were barricades in Hong Kong's streets, sheltering behind which were political protesters, mostly young people. They believed that with right on their side, they could do whatever they wanted. Bunkered in their tower block offices, government officials tried to please everyone. Of course, they ended up pleasing no one. Abused and battered by one side, rendered powerless by the other, the Hong Kong Police did its best to stay on top of things.

Before going further, I must explain the inexplicable. Well, not inexplicable to Hong Kongers, but close to unfathomable to anyone else. I am talking about Hong Kong's election system.

The top official, the equivalent I suppose of mayor, has the official title of Chief Executive of the Hong Kong Special Administrative Region of the People's Republic of China. Chief Executive for short. The Chief Executive is formally chosen by a committee of twelve-hundred people. The committee is supposed to reflect Hong Kong's broader society, but its membership criteria means that most are Beijing loyalists. The committee first selects candidates for the Chief Executive post then votes on which one gets the job. Not surprisingly, the new

HONG KONG POLICE: INSIDE THE LINES

boss always receives Beijing's blessing.

Now for the hard part. I am talking about the way Hong Kong elects its Legislative Council. The Council enacts local laws, approves budgets, keeps an eye on public expenditure and sets local taxes. It looks like an elected city council in any established democracy but looks can deceive.

In most such societies, voting is simple. Come election day, people visit their local polling station, put an *x* in their box of choice and *voila*, we have an election. Note the caveat...*in most such societies*... because in Hong Kong, the election rules are unlike any other. There are seventy council seats. Five are reserved for elected members of the community-based, District Councils. Of the remaining sixty-five seats, thirty-five are from geographic constituencies that work like geographic constituencies in other Western-based systems. Together, they have an electoral base of three-and-a-half million people, each of whom has a vote.

Now comes the tricky bit. When we take away the five seats reserved for the District Councils, and the thirty-five decided by free and open elections, there are thirty seats left. These belong to a wondrous political entity called 'functional constituencies' for which there are no geographic boundaries. Instead, the Hong Kong government invites various business and professional groups to elect one of their own to sit on the Council. Among these groups are financiers, accountants, industrialists, medical professionals, teachers and, to lend the process an egalitarian shine, three trade unionists. Financiers can vote for another financier but no one else. The same goes for architects, industrialists, trade unionists and the rest. A shade under 240,000 people, or less than seven percent of the electorate, can vote in the functional constituencies. This seven percent chooses who sits in the remaining thirty seats.

The effect of this lopsided voting system is a seventy-seat legislature that boasts eighteen political parties and several independent councilors. It is a mishmash of conflicting ideas and on many days, it looks like a rowdy playpen. As Star Trek's Mister Spock would say, '...*it's politics, Jim, but not as we know it...*'

Despite the divisions, one issue separates the Council into two distinct camps. On one side is the pro-*status quo* group, on the other is the pro-democracy group, known as the pan-democrats, or pan-dems. The pro-*status quo* group believes close ties with Beijing are essential for stability and prosperity. The pan-dems see full democracy as a necessary bulwark against interference from China's leadership.

On July 1, 2004, the seventh anniversary of China's resumed sovereignty over Hong Kong, the pan-dems teamed up with other groups and held a "march for democracy". China's paramount leader, the late Deng Xiaoping had offered fifty years with no change, they declared. Had not Britain and China agreed that Hong Kong should have a high degree of autonomy that included full and free elections? The organizers claimed 530,000 people attended, the police suggested the number was closer to 200,000. Whether it was the higher or lower figure, turnout was impressive. And so it went, every year. Every July 1, pro-democracy rallies attracted tens of thousands, and sometimes hundreds of thousands of people. It was always civilized. Protest organizers met police and discussed their plans. Come the day, the police stopped traffic and escorted the protesters from their rallying points to the protest site. There were no arrests, no disorder, in fact, no problems at all. But neither was there democratic reform. From the sidelines, many of Hong Kong's young people watched in dismay. Nothing was happening. It was if the mass protests never happened. As far as Hong Kong's central government was concerned, everything was fine. There were elected councilors in the legislature, people could speak freely and anyone could exercise their right to protest. But things were not at all fine. There were protests but no one was listening. And when a government does not listen, the voices of protest tend to get louder.

HONG KONG POLICE: INSIDE THE LINES

Detective Sergeant Danny Yu muttered under his breath. His transfer to the Regional Intelligence Unit was supposed to be temporary but that had been three years ago. His job was to piece together bits of seemingly disconnected information. It was like assembling a jigsaw puzzle but without a picture to work with. At first, it had been challenging, but after a while, it all became routine. He reached for his thermos, poured a generous measure of *boh lei* tea into a glass tumbler and opened a day-old copy of the Chinese language newspaper, *Hong Kong Economic Journal*. It always carried thoughtful articles on the economic and political issues of the day. Danny skimmed through the usual investment analyses and his eyes caught a piece by a little-known academic from Hong Kong University's law faculty. As expected, it was nothing new: everyone should have the right to vote, all votes must carry equal weight, anyone should be able to stand for the Chief Executive office. Danny then read the next section, and read it again. This was new. He stood and moved through to his chief inspector's office.

'Boss.'

Chief Inspector Bob Bolling looked up. 'Yes?'

Danny put the journal on the desk. Bolling raised an eyebrow. 'Sorry, Danny,' he said. 'Written Chinese aint my strongpoint.'

'It's a call for democracy,' Danny said.

Bolling pretended to stifle a yawn.

'No, no,' Danny urged. He leaned across the desk and tapped the page. 'This time it's different.'

As Danny gave a rundown of the article, Bolling's face darkened. 'Bloody hell,' he sighed. 'The Regional Commander needs to know.' He picked up the journal. 'Who wrote it?'

'Someone called Benny Tai,' Danny said. 'Benny Tai Yiu-ting.' He shrugged. 'He's a law professor at the university.'

Bolling shrugged. 'Never heard of him.' He folded the journal back so the article was face up. 'Leave it with me.'

Danny went back to his desk. *Benny Tai Yiu-ting*, he mused.

CHRIS EMMETT

Who the hell is Benny Tai Yiu-ting?
It was January 13, 2013. Soon, everyone would know the name.

That spring, Benny Tai Yiu-ting called a press conference. Standing with him were human rights activist, the Reverend Chu Yiu-ming, and sociology professor, Chan Kin-man. Democratic reforms must be in place by July 2014, they insisted. If not, they would call people onto the streets and blockade the Central business district. Tai estimated he could muster ten thousand people.

'What will the police do?' a journalist asked.

Democracy has a cost, Tai answered. If the cost is jail, then so be it. Civil disobedience must be peaceful, he insisted. The movement would occupy the business district not only with peace, but also with love.

The campaign had found a new name: Occupy Central with Love and Peace. In university halls and secondary school corridors, it generated much talk. The Hong Kong Federation of University Students came aboard. So did a secondary school student group called 'Scholarism.' Their leader was Joshua Wong, a charismatic seventeen-year-old who was already a protest veteran. Quick to spot a bandwagon, local politicians got into the frame. Anti-communists lined up with leftists. *'Democracy,'* they cried and some actually meant it.

The Occupy movement did not have everything its own way. Many older Hong Kongers preferred the comfort of the *status quo*. What price democracy at the cost of turmoil? they asked. The teahouses, *mahjong* parlors and street restaurants buzzed with the issue.

In June 2014, Beijing shouldered its way into the debate. Beijing wagged its finger and reminded everyone that Hong Kong had a high level of autonomy only by China's good grace. Along with that came a chilling warning: Hong Kong had a

People's Liberation Army garrison, which was well able to deal with any state of emergency.

The Occupy movement held an unofficial referendum, inviting voters to choose the best way to elect Hong Kong's chief executive. They expected 100,000 to participate. After ten days, nearly 800,000 had voted. Soon, it would be July 1, the anniversary of Hong Kong's return to China. There would be the usual rallies and protest marches, but this time there was a heightened sense of discontent and of challenge.

Detective Sergeant Danny Yu did not feel right. He wore jeans, a T-shirt, a baseball cap and a nifty pair of sneakers. Still, he was not a happy man. He was supposed to be a detective but his cap had a blue and white checkered band. Above its bill was the badge of the Hong Kong Police Force. Over his T-shirt, he wore a high visibility tabard. Displayed on the front and back, were the words:

警POLICE察

What a day. First, the sun had baked the tarmac, making the air shimmer. Then it rained. At first, it was cooling but as it cleared, a steamy haze rose from the road, making the heat even more oppressive. Danny checked his watch. Eight p.m. Twenty-hundred hours in police jargon. He had been here all afternoon. Baked by the sun, drenched by the rain and still nothing had happened. For the umpteenth time, he checked the battery of the Intelligence Unit's video camera. The sun was low but in downtown Hong Kong, there is always enough light to film. Danny's duty post was in Chater Road, on the eastern fringes of the Central business district. It was a pleasant part of town. Danny watched people taking their ease among the shrubbery and water features of Statue Square. Beyond that was the colonnaded grandeur of the Court of Final Appeal. It was just two stories high but had a granite sense of permanence typical of Victorian buildings. To Danny's left was the cenotaph memorial, set in a lawn as flat and as smooth as a championship billiard table. The swanky Prince's Building arcade was behind him.

Traffic was light: a double-decked bus, a few private cars, a taxi or two. The uniform boys had laid out interlinked barriers to separate the marchers from the traffic. For the marchers, they had reserved the sidewalk and a couple of traffic lanes. The rest of the road was for motor vehicles. Bored policemen and women lined the barriers. They wore their day-to-day uniforms of blue shirts with navy-blue slacks. Only sergeants and inspectors carried revolvers. No one expected trouble. Why would they? The democracy marches always went smoothly.

Again, Danny checked his watch. Five past eight. The radio newscasts reported half a million people had gathered in Causeway Bay's Victoria Park. Official reports put the number at just under 100,000. Either way, they were on the march and headed straight for Detective Sergeant Danny Yu. Danny was not too worried. Every year it was the same: teachers, clerks, factory workers, delivery drivers, health carers, even civil servants. They were the middle class and the aspiring working class. There were family groups, work groups, neighborhood groups. Decent people who knew how to conduct themselves.

But where the hell were they?

Danny heard them before he saw them. It was a formless hum that grew to a roar. Now he could see them. Thousands, no, tens of thousands of people, all walking slowly towards him. They jammed the road. There were banners demanding democracy, banners condemning Beijing, banners showing the face of Hong Kong's chief executive, Leung Chun-ying. Some showed him wearing a Mao cap complete with red star badge, others pictured him with vampire teeth dripping blood. The banners were blue, yellow, crimson. Scattered among them were British flags from Hong Kong's colonial past. Danny pressed the camera's record button and squinted through the viewfinder. There were young, old and middle-aged, but mostly young. Some wore headbands emblazoned with pro-democracy slogans. They were singing a popular Canto-pop song, the words changed to a democracy theme. As they came nearer, their voices swelled. Their eyes gleamed. Their faces were hard, determined, expectant.

This is not the usual crowd, Danny thought. His heart raced. *Something will happen. Something will happen soon.*

'Luk-baak-gau,' — Six-eight-nine, a loud hailer bellowed. Six-hundred and eighty-nine, the number of votes it took to get Leung Chun-ying elected to Hong Kong's highest office.

'Luk-baak-gau,' the loud hailer bellowed again.

'Ha toi!' — Get off the stage, the crowd roared back.

'Man jue,' — Democracy, the loudhailer blared.

'Man jue,' the crowd shouted back.

The crowd pushed further into Chater Road. The barriers were a bottleneck. Those at the back could not move. 'Mo wai,' — No room, they shouted. Those at the front grabbed the barriers and shook them. The line of barriers weaved and rocked like an iron snake. Police pushed back, physically holding the barriers in place.

'Mo wai. Mo wai. Mo wai.' The rhythmic chant became a formless roar. A link on one of the barriers snapped and it toppled into the road, dragging two more with it. A young man clambered over it. He raised his arms and danced among the traffic. Others followed. The traffic slowed then stopped. The blare of car horns joined the roar of the crowd. Where the barriers collapsed, a line of police linked arms but they were too few. Protesters barged through them. Hundreds of young men and women surged into the road. Then it was thousands. They were an eddying, swirling torrent. They ran past Danny's position, past the cenotaph, past Prince's Building. And still they came, flattening the barriers, pushing aside the police.

They filled the road, cheering and laughing. A loudhailer

bellowed, *'Choh daai.'* — Sit down. *'Gok wai, choh daai.'* — Everyone, sit down.

They sat. They punched the air. Their voices drowned the blare of car horns. *'Man jue! Man jue! Man jue!'*

A policeman spoke into a loudhailer but no one could hear. Policemen and women moved among them. A word here, a gesture there, cajoling them back to the sidewalk. A policewoman tugged at a young man's arm. He brushed her away.

Danny Yu kept filming. He panned left and right. People filled his viewfinder. There were ten thousand or more. Their voices were joyous. Even from his place on the fringes, Danny felt the carnival sense of it all. The chants grew louder. They carried the ring of triumph.

'MAN JUE! MAN JUE! MAN JUE!'

Police blocked off Chater Road. A circle of blue surrounded the protesters. Night came. Police got ready for the following day. They ordered traffic diversions, prepared press releases and arranged fresh officers to relieve those who had been on duty all day. At three forty-five in the morning, a police loudhailer cut through the night. The gathering was illegal, it announced. The protesters must leave immediately or face arrest. A few protesters jeered but most just ignored the order.

Over the next hour, the police repeated the warning. The protesters answered with laughter, jeers and abuse. The jeers died as police moved into the crowd. People scrambled to their feet. There were cries of, *'Haang faan.'* — Stay back. Then it was, *'Chai yan gung gik.'* — Police are attacking. *'Gok wai, faan dai.'* — Everyone, lie down. Phone cameras flashed. People linked arms and legs. As police picked up and carried passive protesters to nearby police vehicles, there were shouts of, *'Mou chi.'* — Shameless.

Eight o'clock neared and the remaining protesters began a countdown. *'Ng.'* — Five. *'Sei.'* — Four. *'Saam.'* — Three. *'Yee.'* —

HONG KONG POLICE: INSIDE THE LINES

Two. *'Yat.'* — One. *'BAAT DIM.'* — EIGHT O'CLOCK.

They were treating it like some kind of game. Having called time, they expected the game to end. But it was not a game. The protesters had ignored the warnings and now had to face the consequences. As the arrests continued, the carnival mood gave way to sullen silence. Among the younger protesters, there were tears. There were more chants of *'Mou chi,'* — Shameless. *'Mou chi. Mou chi.'*

A protester caught the eye of a British police officer and called out in English, 'You are disgrace. Fuck off back to your country.' From another part of the crowd, 'We will find your kids and kill them.' A constable stood impassive as a dozen protesters pointed at him and shouted, *'Bui bun je.'* — Traitor.

By eight-thirty, police had arrested more than five hundred protesters. Just before nine o'clock, Chater Road reopened for traffic. As things returned to normal, some may have thought the protests were over.

They were not. Chater Road was only a rehearsal ground.

Snuggled between the Harcourt Road and the Lung Wo Road expressway, in Hong Kong Island's Admiralty district next to Central, is Tim Mei Avenue. On a map, it looks nothing special but in fact, little Tim Mei Avenue is a veritable corridor of power. In this narrow stretch of road, stand the Legislative Council chamber and its associated offices and next door is the twenty-six storey edifice of steel and glass that is the Central Government Offices.

Behind that is Tamar Park, a pleasant patch of greenery that stretches all the way to the harbor wall. It is a popular spot and during the working week, many office workers spend their lunchtimes there.

Nearby stands what was once the British Army Headquarters. Today, from the wall on the top floor, a five-pointed star overlooks Hong Kong's harbor. Now, the building's official title is The People's Liberation Army Hong Kong Building. Many Hong Kongers prefer its old name: The Prince of Wales Building. Compared to colonial days, there are few soldiers stationed there, but what few there are make their presence known. Even in the heat of summer, the guards wear full combat gear: camouflage fatigues, body armor, helmets and state-of-the-art automatic rifles.

In front of the government office complex is a little plaza, measuring about one-hundred foot square. At its centre is a dais on which stand two flagpoles, one for the flag of the Hong Kong Special Administrative Region, the other for the flag of the People's Republic of China. Officially, the square's name is the East Wing Forecourt. Since its opening in 2011, the little forecourt had seen a lot of action. Protest groups often gathered there to voice objections to this or that. After a while, the forecourt earned its unofficial title, 'Civic Square.' On most days, there would be some kind of protest. Some were small and silent, others were rowdy. Silent or rowdy, the protests did not bother anyone. After all, Hong Kong protesters know that violence gets them nowhere. Then, two weeks after the Chater Road sit-in, everything changed.

It was mid-July when a group that had nothing to do with political reform started a chain of events that would eventually resonate worldwide. They were protesting plans for high-rise housing projects in a green enclave of the rural New Territories. The group had a history of bad behavior, so when they turned up to watch the Legislative Council debate on the issue, they found themselves locked out. Infuriated, they gathered at Civic Square and tried to force their way into the Council chamber. They smashed glass panels and tried to prize open the doors. Police restored order, but the councilors had to suspend their meeting. The next day, builders erected a ten-foot high fence around the square. At first, it was a non-event, some legislators even welcomed the improved security. Only the secondary school student group, 'Scholarism,' took a stand. *'Higher and harder fences will not block public opinion,'* they cried but no one paid them much mind.

As things turned out, they were the only ones who called it right.

On September 1st, 2014 a senior Chinese official visited Hong Kong. He confirmed that only Beijing-approved candidates could stand in the 2017 election for Hong Kong's Chief Executive. Edict duly issued, he returned to China satisfied he had fired a suitable warning shot. But where Beijing heard a warning shot, Hong Kong's democrats heard only a starting gun.

The Hong Kong Federation of Students declared that starting Monday, September 22, it would boycott university classes for a week. At the same time, Scholarism's Joshua Wong called for a one-day boycott of secondary school classes. On the due day, students and teachers from dozens of universities and colleges crammed the main boulevard of Hong Kong's Chinese University. Rough estimates put the number at thirteen thousand. Many wore white shirts with yellow ribbons pinned to their chests. Others wore black T-shirts bearing the words, 'Democracy Now.' Around the campus, banners proclaimed:

'THE BOYCOTT MUST HAPPEN.
DISOBEY AND GRASP YOUR DESTINY.'

Student leader, soon to be Legislative Councilor, Nathan Law Kwun-chung, addressed the crowd. 'Today is not the last step,' he said. 'It's the first step, and countless resistance campaigns will bear fruit.'

The next day, an article appeared in the tabloid *Apple Daily*. In it, Benny Tai Yiu-ting announced that on Wednesday October 1, which was China's National Day, he would host a celebratory banquet on the streets of Hong Kong's business district. It would be no ordinary banquet, he said, it would be a banquet of democracy. He predicted that people would attend in their thousands.

October 1 was a public holiday. Most businesses would shut and, as normal on public holidays, the police would close the streets to all but pedestrians. The police were not concerned. They planned to surround and contain the protesters until they got fed up and went home.

It sounds simple but when things sound simple, you can bet they are anything but simple. As Benny Tai prepared for his grand banquet, neither he nor the police realized that events were already spinning beyond everyone's control.

Year after year, newer and glitzier office blocks rise along Hong Kong's shoreline. No two are the same. There are glass curtain walls of deep blue, burnished silver and in one case, gold. The International Finance Centre soars eighty-eight floors. Compared to all this, the twenty-nine story Admiralty Centre is quite modest. Strictly speaking, Admiralty Centre is not in the business district. Rather, it is off to one side, in the less fashionable Admiralty district. However, what it lacks in prestige, it gains in location. The Central business district is just a short walk away and Admiralty Centre is a major hub for public transport. Underground, there is a Mass Transit Railway station. There are bus bays, minibus stops and a taxi rank. Running east-west are three urban clearways: Harcourt Road, Queensway and Lung Wo Road. Cars, busses, trucks, taxis, mini busses and goods vehicles stream along these roads delivering people, sales goods, mail, office materials and a myriad other vital services and supplies. Like any urban road network, these roads have their problems. Even normal traffic produces epic jams; breakdowns and minor fender-benders bring traffic chaos.

Of course, people can also cause chaos. And if there are enough of them, they can cause chaos for a very long time.

HONG KONG POLICE: INSIDE THE LINES

Any normal Friday, Detective Sergeant Danny Yu would have been winding down for the weekend, but this Friday, something was happening in Tim Mei Avenue. Students had taken their boycott away from the classrooms and were gathering outside the Central Government Offices. Danny had orders to get down there and report anything unusual. He allowed himself a chuckle. *Unusual?* Never mind unusual, it was downright bizarre. He was tired but felt more at ease. Gone was the cap with its police badge, gone was the high visibility tabard with the, 警POLICE察 logo.

Tim Mei Avenue was a narrow stretch of dual carriageway tucked between Citic Tower and the Central Government Offices. There was a raised central divider. Overhead, footbridges linked the buildings. The buildings and footbridges gave the avenue a claustrophobic feel. They trapped the heat and even after the sun had set, Danny felt the energy sucked from him.

Behind its ten-foot fence, Civic Square was empty save for watchful police and security guards. It was ten-thirty at night and with all office workers gone, Tim Mei Avenue should have been empty, but tonight was different. Tonight, thousands of young people had shoehorned themselves into the narrow strip of road. Everywhere, there was a babble of excitement. Television crews threaded their way through the crowd, their lights harsh white. Cameras flashed. Radio commentators thrust microphones at anyone who would talk to them. There was a speakers' stage, kitted out with professional sound and light systems. Flanking it were two dragon drums. The drummers were naked from the waist up; their torsos gleamed. All day, it had been speeches, speeches, speeches. As speaker after speaker came to the microphone, the drummers hammered out a deep *drubdrubdrub,* ramping up the excitement. The applause grew louder, the drumming heavier. Now, Scholarism's Joshua Wong was speaking. After the day's fiery talk, his speech was quite mundane. It was about plans to print thousands of leaflets...

...At the rear of the crowd, there were raised voices and the scuff of scurrying feet. People were running to Civic Square. Joshua Wong moved to the front of the stage. His voice cracked. The sound system made his words harsh and metallic. *'Yap hui gung man gong cheung.'* — Enter Civic Square. The crowd was a riptide. It surged towards the square, carrying Danny with it. People were scaling the fence. Police and security guards moved to meet them. They spread their arms and jigged from side to side as though rounding up errant chickens. More and more people clambered over the fence. Beside the speakers' podium, the drums beat louder. *DRUB – DRUB – DRUBDRUBDRUBDRUB.* Another student leader grabbed the microphone. Keeping time with the drums, he called, *'Wan ngor gung man gong cheung.'* — Give us back Civic Square. Others took up the chant. *'Wan ngor gung man gong cheung.'* Their voices filled the avenue, echoing from the glass and steel towers. *'Wan ngor gung man gong cheung.'* Television crews hefted their cameras and scrambled after the protesters. Now the chant was, *'Hoi jaam.'* — Open the gate. The crowd pressed against the gate and the fence. *'Hoi jaam. Hoi jaam. Hoi jaam.'* Across Hong Kong, live broadcasts flashed from television sets. Police reinforcements moved into Tim Mei Avenue. Protesters thrust up their hands in a charade of surrender. They formed a human wall across the avenue. They pushed against the police line. Their voices swelled. *'Ging chat chit tui.'* — Police retreat. *'Chit tui. Chit tui. Chit tui. Chit tui.'* An umbrella point raked a police officer's face. He reeled back, blood welling from a four-inch gash beneath his eye. *'Chit tui. Chit tui. Chit tui.'* Raised hands became raised fists. *'Chit tui. Chit tui. Chit tui. Chit tui.'* Outnumbered, the police pulled back. The protesters cheered and clapped their hands.

Inside Civic Square, security guards tended to a colleague. He sat with his back to the fence, his lips twisted in pain. Police surrounded hundreds of protesters huddled on the flag podium.

A police loudhailer squawked an instruction: anyone who wished to leave could leave but once gone, no one could return.

Outside the fence, protesters milled about, unsure what to do next. A young man put his head close to Danny's. *'Dong saam,'* — take care, he whispered. *'Jaap chai hai do.'* — Undercover cops around.

'Wan daan,' — Assholes, Danny growled back.

Rumors raced among the crowd: Leung Chun-ying, old 689 himself, would come to Tim Mei Avenue. Benny Tai Yiu-ting had cancelled his "occupation" of Central. Pro-Beijing gangs were coming to attack us.

Midnight passed. More police arrived. There was a clamor of protest as they pulled people away from the flag podium. The police handcuffed Joshua Wong and carried him away. A cry went up, *'Ging chaat mou chi,'* — Police are shameless. *'Mou chi. Mou chi. Mou chi.'* Police in riot helmets moved into Tim Mei Avenue. They advanced with shields and pepper spray. *Spray — push. Spray — push.* The protesters retreated and reformed. They held their ground. The police advanced by inches. *Spray — push. Spray — push.* The advance slowed then stopped. Outnumbered, the police fell back.

Danny stepped into the shadows and phoned his boss. All around was the clamor of anger and protest. He pressed his phone against one ear and his free hand against the other.

'Are they showing signs of going home?' his boss asked.

'There's still a few hundred here. Danny replied. 'They're angry. Word is, most will stay. Tomorrow, more will come.'

From the other end of the phone, there was silence. Then, 'Okay. Come back to the office and get some sleep. I want you back there tomorrow — early.'

The line went dead. Danny checked his watch: two a.m. There was a taxi rank just a few minutes' walk away. He considered calling his wife but it was late. Best leave it until tomorrow.

Tomorrow.

Tomorrow there would be more speeches, more drumming, more noise and more banners. So far, there had been nearly eighty arrests. Four police officers and ten security guards were injured. Tomorrow, the youngsters would have their protest, then maybe they would go home. But would they? There was something different about this protest, something he could not pin down. In previous protests, there had been resigned dignity, but in Tim Mei Avenue, there was only anger. No, not anger. *Rage.* Danny slipped his telephone into his pocket and made his way to the taxi rank.

Back in Tim Mei Avenue, paramedics and first aiders treated the injured. It would be nearly six weeks before one of the security guards returned to work.

Later, protesters issued a press statement blaming police for the violence.

Day-to-day, the Hong Kong Police does what any modern police force does. It protects life and property, prevents and detects crime and keeps the traffic moving. However, if widespread public disorder looms, the Hong Kong Police can switch into what it calls its *internal security structure*. At the heart of this structure is the Police Tactical Unit. Call it what you like, but do not call Hong Kong's Police Tactical Unit a riot squad, it is much more than that. True, the Tactical Unit is a paramilitary force trained in riot control. That said, it performs all kinds of duties including disaster relief, counter terrorism, crowd management at festivals, and anti-crime operations. You will often see the Police Tactical Unit on the beat, supporting regular officers. You can spot them by their headgear. People call them, 'The Blue Berets.'

What makes the Hong Kong Police Force special is that during his or her service, every Hong Kong Police officer must serve at least one tour with the Tactical Unit. Many serve more than once. That makes each one of them something of an expert on internal security. At short notice, every working police district, like Wanchai, Sham Shui Po, Tuen Mun, and all the others, can muster a paramilitary company of one hundred and seventy trained men and women. Officers manning the emergency response cars can do the same. So can the part-time, Auxiliary Police Force. The Hong Kong police internal security function is the envy of the world, but at the heart of its training is a culture of restraint. Do not think that being restrained means being passive. Officers must use minimum force to achieve their aim, but achieve that aim they must.

At this point, it is worth mentioning a few things about teargas. To be precise, it is not gas, it is smoke but the term *teargas* has long passed into common use. Whatever we call it, it has two effects — physical and psychological. There is no way to play this down: the physical effects are downright nasty. Imagine drowning in a vat of super-spicy curry. It gets in your eyes, your throat, your nose. You cannot see, you cannot breath. One whiff of teargas and all you want to do is run — run anywhere just to get away from those billowing clouds of burning, blinding, choking smoke. That is where the psychological effects come in. When part of a crowd starts to run, the effect is contagious. All those around them also want to run, often without knowing why.

The news on teargas is not all bad because the effects last for just ten minutes or so. Really. Ten minutes after you remove yourself from a teargas environment, you are fine. Of course, it is a bad idea to return to the teargas environment, which, when you think about it, is the object of the exercise.

It is all about the progressive use of force. Stage one — the police arrive in full riot gear, which should be enough to tell everyone they mean business. Stage two — the police issue warnings. They do this by addressing the crowd through a loudhailer. To make sure everyone understands, the police hold up banners displaying messages like, '*Stop Charging or We Use*

Force.' Stage three — now it gets serious. If the warnings go unheeded, the police put on their gas masks. Now the warning banners read, 'Warning — Tear Smoke.' Hopefully, the crowd gets the message. If they do not, the police load teargas canisters into their Federal riot guns and the warning banners go up again. Only then does the commander give the order to fire. Sometimes a single canister does the trick but more often than not, there must be repeated volleys. At this point, the police are committed to ending the situation. It is no good using a bit of teargas in the hope the crowd will be a bit more cooperative. Once started, the police must see things through to the end.

Throughout this, it is crucial for the police to keep a clear distance between themselves and the crowd. Ideally, the distance should be about forty meters. Sometimes, a crowd will press in close to the police. When that happens, the police have to create that essential forty meters. They do this with hand-held, teargas grenades. The grenades produce a sudden eruption of teargas, which forces the crowd back. It is all a matter of common sense. The last thing the police want is direct contact. Direct contact is brutal. In direct contact, the police face flailing fists and feet. There are impromptu weapons: sticks, iron bars, bottles, anything to cause injury. Without teargas to force back the crowd, police can respond only with batons. With batons, the effects do not disappear in minutes, they last for days, weeks and in some cases, they are permanent. Police rules of engagement are simple: use minimum force, give plenty of warning, keep a safe distance between the police and the crowd, fire teargas if necessary and once started, keep going. The rules work. They ensure a return to public order with the fewest possible casualties on both sides.

Then, on Sunday, September 28, 2014, in Hong Kong's Admiralty district, someone changed the rules.

It started at sunrise on Saturday September 27. Inside Civic

Square, there was an informal truce. Police stood outside a circle of metal barriers surrounding about fifty protesters. The police made no move to clear them, instead they repeated the original order: anyone can leave but no one may enter.

In Tim Mei Avenue, there was bleary-eyed resentment. At seven-thirty, police wielding body-length shields moved into the avenue and started to push protesters back from Civic Square's perimeter. As one, they raised their shields, pushed forward and slammed the shields onto the tarmac. They advanced one step at a time. *Lift, push, advance, SLAM. Lift, push, advance, SLAM.* Soon, there was clear space between the protesters and the fence. There, the police stopped and held the line.

More protesters arrived until the crowd numbered thousands. To joyous applause, Occupy Central's Benny Tai Yiu-ting took to the stage. He pledged his support for the protests but the cheers fell silent when he announced he would not bring forward the Occupy Central sit-in.

'Jim Jung,' — Occupy Central, the crowd chanted. '*Yi ga, Jim Jung.*' — Occupy Central now.

Tai smiled, waved and left the stage.

Danny Yu found a quiet spot to phone in his report.

'Got that,' his boss answered. There was a pause. 'How are you feeling?'

'Pretty tired,' Danny answered. He glanced over his shoulder. 'And it cannot be long before someone guesses I'm a police officer.'

'Okay,' the boss said. 'You've done enough. Time to go home. Call later for instructions.'

Danny was light-headed and it seemed his legs had lost their strength. His eyes were sore and seemed full of sand. Time to go home, the boss had said.

So that is what he did.

That afternoon, police cleared Civic Square. Throughout

the whole episode, they arrested sixty-one people for offenses ranging from unlawful assembly to possession of an offensive weapon. In Tim Mei Avenue, speaker after speaker called on Benny Tai Yiu-ting to seize the moment and join them. Night fell. Midnight passed. At one-forty in the morning of Saturday September 28, Tai climbed back onto the stage. This time, he announced the immediate start of Occupy Central. At first, cheers rang along Tim Mei Avenue but as the cheers died down, the movement's first split appeared. Hundreds barracked Tai into silence. The students had acted, they shouted but Benny Tai had only talked. Now he wanted the credit for what the students had done. Hundreds packed up and went home. In that instant, the Occupy Central founders became sidelined. Now, they could only sit and watch as the crowd swell became a storm surge. They looked on as in Tim Mei Avenue, there grew a sense that Hong Kong had reached one of those moments when everything would change.

But not everyone glowed with the spirit of love and peace. Some new arrivals did not look at all joyous. They stuck together, grim-faced and determined. They wore construction site hardhats and industrial goggles. The hardhat newcomers were a small group. In fact, among the thousands of joyous protesters, they hardly figured at all.

Small maybe, but they had a plan.

In Police Headquarters, the senior communications officer powered up the control room's computers and opened an incident log. Radios chattered; telephones *chirruped*. In the windowless command and control centre, neon strip lights glowed hard white. Uniformed police and civilian communications officers sat side by side at their consoles. It had been a good few years since Senior Inspector Andy Cruikshank had seen so many bosses in one place. The Commissioner, the Deputy Commissioner, the Director of Operations, plus a veritable bevy of assistant commissioners and chief superintendents. They bustled through the control room, shut themselves in the conference room and closed the blinds.

Cruikshank moved to the operations console and massaged his temples. Last night there had been a party for one of his sergeants, recently promoted to station sergeant. Celebrations had gone on until late and Cruikshank felt a bit frail. He shook his head and forced himself to concentrate. 'How many?' he asked.

The comms officer scrolled through his screen and shrugged. 'Ten... maybe fifteen thousand,' he said. 'They are arriving faster than Field Commander can count them.'

'So, probably twenty thousand.'

The comms officer frowned. 'Might be more,' he said.

'Get an update,' Cruikshank ordered.

The comms officer leaned over his microphone and pressed the transmit button. 'Headquarters command and control centre to Field Commander, over.'

There was a hiss of static.

'Headquarters CCC to Field Commander, over.'

Nothing.

'Should I try command channel 2?' the comms officer asked.

'No,' Cruikshank answered. 'He's obviously too busy to deal with us. Monitor and keep me informed.' He stepped back and moved to the traffic branch console. 'How's it looking?' he asked.

'Not good,' the traffic comms officer answered. 'The crowd has taken over Harcourt Road. Queensway might be next.'

'How's traffic flow?'

'Harcourt and Gloucester Road's locked solid,' the comms officer answered. 'Traffic is backed up to Causeway Bay. If Queensway closes, we can divert everything along Lung Wo Road but...' he shrugged and fell silent.

Behind Cruikshank, a soft voice spoke. 'Situation report

please, Andy.' Cruikshank turned to see Piers Wu, the Assistant Commissioner Special Operations.

'Seems the crowds are growing by the minute, sir,' Cruikshank answered. 'Can't reach the Field Commander, he's probably too busy to talk. We'll try later.'

Wu rolled his eyes. 'The Commissioner wants answers, Secretary for Security wants answers, the Chief Executive wants answers, bloody press want answers.' He gave a humorless chuckle. 'The canteen manager's chasing me. Wants to know how many need feeding.' He chewed his lip. 'Fancy a trip out?' he asked.

Cruikshank brightened.

'Is your callout bag handy?' Wu asked.

'As always, sir,' Cruikshank answered. 'Helmet, gas mask. All the essentials.'

'Good. Grab a radio and report to the Field Commander. Tell him you're my liaison officer. You'll take no action. Your job is to keep me informed, that's all. Got it?'

Cruikshank had indeed got it.

'And don't look so happy,' Wu growled.

'I'll try not to, sir,' Cruikshank answered. He turned and hurried from the control room before the AC Special Ops changed his mind.

Cruikshank heard them before he saw them. It was a clamor of anticipation, like a crowd waiting to enter a football stadium. Then he saw them. It was crazy. Where there should be lines of free-moving traffic, there were people, tens of thousands of them. A line of metal barriers stretched the full width of Harcourt Road. Behind them were police wearing everyday working uniforms. Further back was a line of parked police vehicles. Cruikshank presented himself to the Field Commander, who passed him on to his deputy. The Deputy Commander waved towards the crowd. 'Sector Commander's somewhere down there,' he said. 'He'll tell you what's happening.' Minutes later, Cruikshank found a weary-looking chief inspector.

'You're Cruikshank,' the chief inspector said. 'Jacobs,' he added, offering a handshake, He nodded towards the crowd. 'They're behaving themselves,' he said, 'In fact, they're behaving very well. They just refuse to leave.'

'I thought we'd blocked all access points,' Cruikshank said.

'We have,' Jacobs groaned. He swept his arm towards the crowd. 'But look at them. Half of Hong Kong is here.'

For as far as Cruikshank could see, Harcourt Road was a mass of people. They were laughing, chatting, singing. A young man caught Cruikshank's eye and waved. 'It looks like a bloody beach party,' Cruikshank said.

'I don't like it,' Jacobs answered. 'They're acting like kids and when kids get boisterous, it ends in tears.' He nodded to the far side of the road where a group of hard-faced men clustered together. Some wore industrial goggles and yellow hardhats. Others wore surgical masks covering the bottom half of their faces. 'That lot's up to no good,' he added.

'Commissioner's put out a press release,' Cruikshank offered. 'He's urging people not to join the unlawful assembly.'

Jacobs' lips twisted in what may have been a smile. 'I guess that'll solve everything,' he said. As he spoke, the hard-faced men moved into the crowd. For a moment, they were out of sight. Then one appeared at the front line. Others joined him. Soon there were clusters of them gathered at the front. One cupped his hands to his mouth. *'Wei, chai lo,'* — Hey, copper, he called. *'Diu lei lo mo.'* — Fuck your mother.

'Ging chat chit tui,' — Police retreat, another shouted.

'Ging chat chit tui,' the rest answered. They punched the air in time with the chant. Their voices rose. *'CHIT TUI. CHIT TUI.'* They advanced on the police line. Their eyes gleamed. They raised their hands in mock surrender. From the rear came the shout, *'Chung fung.'* — Charge. They pressed forward, pushing

against the barriers. *'CHUNG FUNG. CHUNG FUNG.'*

The chants lost their form. The words melded into a cacophony of fury. Umbrella points stabbed at the police, drawing blood from arms and faces. A second line of police pulled on their gas masks, jammed their helmets on their heads and stepped up to the barriers. *'Taan hau,'* — Get back, they shouted. *'Taan hau. Taan hau.'* At the rear of the police line, an orange banner unfurled.

停止衝擊,
否則使用武力
Stop Charging or We Use Force

Water Bottles spattered against police shields. Protesters linked arms. *'CHUNG FUNG.'* They surged forward. They grabbed at the barriers, trying to pull them down. Police forced them back with pepper spray. The protesters unfurled their umbrellas, put down their heads and charged again. The police line buckled but held. Shouts and catcalls hammered at them. Police fought back with pepper spray, batons and water jets but still, the attacks came. First-aiders half-carried an officer to the rear.

Jacobs lifted his radio to his lips. 'Headquarters command and control centre, over.'

'Headquarters CCC receiving.'

'There are severe attacks on my front line. Roger so far?'

'Roger so far.'

Jacobs paused. The radio network was not secure. 'Standby for telephone com.' He fished out his telephone and pressed the command centre's speed-dial button. He jammed the phone against to his ear.

A voice crackled in the earpiece. *'HQ CCC.'*

'Give me the controller, please.'

'This is the controller. Speak up, I can barely hear you.'

Jacobs raised his voice. 'My cordon line is about to be overrun. So far?'

'*Roger so far.*'

'I request teargas at this location immediately. Repeat, immediately.'

'*Wait one.*' Moments later, the controller was back. '*Emergency Unit is proceeding to your location. So far?*'

'Got it,' Jacobs answered. 'Arrival time?'

'*Arrival imminent. I'm sending someone with teargas grenades. Use them at your discretion but issue warnings first. Repeat, warnings first.*'

'Will do,' Jacobs answered.

He closed the connection. A Tactical Unit inspector arrived with a canvas bag full of grenades. A police banner unfurled, white letters on a black background:

警告催淚煙
WARNING.
TEAR SMOKE

There were more jeers. The crowd charged again. A teargas grenade arced overhead. It burst with a *PAP*. A cloud of white gas erupted in the crowd. They fell back, coughing, cursing, eyes streaming. Still, some clustered together and charged again. Another grenade. Another eruption of white teargas.

Jacobs radioed in. 'Tear gas deployed. Crowd falling back. I am advancing. Over.'

The reply was immediate. '*Stand fast and secure the junction. Repeat, do not advance. Reinforcements are advancing from behind your position. Over.*'

The Emergency Unit arrived. They wore their helmets, gas masks and Khaki, flame retardant uniforms. They carried a full complement of weapons: shields, batons, Federal riot guns, shotguns. As they passed Jacob's position, they halted. The crowd closed in on them. Police and protesters were just feet apart. Chanting abuse, the crowd moved around the Emergency Unit's flanks and closed in behind it. Above the road, people jammed the footbridges. Some were laughing. Some were shouting. Some just watched. A CNN television crew bustled to the guardrail, their lights dazzling. At street level, police used their shields to parry away bottles thrown from the crowd. Some protesters called for calm. For a while, the chant was, *'Mo tiu yeh.'* — Don't throw things. *'Mo tiu yeh. Mo tiu yeh.'*

A new chant drowned them out. *'Ging chat chit tui.'* — Police retreat. *'CHIT TUI. CHIT TUI. CHIT TUI.'*

The Emergency Unit's teargas warning banner went up. Moments later, a teargas grenade burst in the crowd, shrouding police and protesters in a cloud. Somewhere, someone was shouting, *'JAU!'* — RUN! *'JAU! JAU!'* The protesters broke and ran. Backs bent, hands clasped to faces. They stumbled into each other, they clambered over the central road divider, some ran towards the police line. Another teargas grenade burst, this time directly overhead. Teargas drifted across the footbridge, clearing it. Teargas canisters slid into Federal gun breeches. An order screeched over a police loudhailer. *'Daai yee section, daai saam goh ging yuen,'* — Number two section, third officer. *'Daai gok dok, MIU JUN!'* — Low angle, PRESENT! An officer raised his Federal and snapped shut the breech. He took aim at the road in front of the protesters. *'FIRE!'* There was a THUMP. The Federal's stock slammed into the officer's shoulder. A canister clattered along the tarmac, spinning like a catherine wheel, spraying teargas. The crowd milled like deer in a thunderstorm. The Emergency Unit advanced again. The crowd moved back. There was the THUMP of a Federal. Another PAP of a teargas canister. More burning, blinding, choking white smoke.

In homes, offices, bars and restaurants across Hong Kong, people watched the television reports in dismay. Unaware of the earlier attacks on police cordons, they saw only helmeted police firing teargas at youthful protesters. In their thousands, they stopped what they were doing and rushed to join the protests. The crowds in Admiralty swelled to tens of thousands. That evening, it numbered as many as 100,000 and stretched all the way back into Wanchai. Thousands more gathered in Causeway Bay and Kowloon's Mong Kok district.

For hours, the crowd in Admiralty district retreated, reformed, retreated, reformed and retreated again. Still, it continued to grow. Pockets of conflict popped up behind the police advance. At ten p.m., police were firing tear gas outside City Hall, on the fringes of Central. At ten-thirty, a phalanx of police faced thousands of protesters outside the Bank of America Tower. The crowd was a shapeless, flowing mass. As police advanced, people retreated to the overpasses and footbridges then rallied and returned to the main roads. There was rhythmic clapping and chants of, *'Heung Gong Yan,'* — Hong Kong People, and, *'Ga yau! Ga yau!'* — Go! Go! They commandeered barriers from road works and set their own defense lines. By midnight, they seemed hardened to the teargas. They retreated, reformed and advanced. On Harcourt Road, some ventured out to taunt the police but retreated when approached. The rest clung to the safety of the overpasses and footbridges. They shouted challenges but what had earlier been a roar of anger was now a growl of weary discontent.

Andy Cruikshank blinked sweat from his eyes. His shirt was damp and it stuck to his skin. His gas mask eyepieces had fogged up. In seven hours of conflict, the police had discharged eighty-seven teargas canisters and arrested eighty-nine protesters. There were forty-one people injured, including twelve police officers. It had been tough but finally, it looked like the end was near. Cruikshank took off his helmet and removed his gas mask. Lingering traces of teargas prickled his eyes and stung an angry rash that marked where the gas mask's rubber seal had chafed his skin. Teargas residue had soaked into his uniform, adding to his discomfort. He jammed the gas mask back into its haversack and sucked in a long breath. He pressed the transmit button on his radio.

'AC Special Ops, this is Cruikshank, over.'

Immediately, the reply crackled back. *'Send, over.'*

'Most of Harcourt Road is clear but crowds still occupy the overpasses and footbridges. Roger so far?'

'Understood.'

'I will stand by here for the next phase, over.'

'Message received. Operation is complete. Return to headquarters. Over.'

Cruikshank paused. Obviously, his message had not got through. 'I say again, crowds still occupy overpasses, footbridges and parts of Harcourt Road,' he said. 'The operation is *not* complete, repeat, *not* complete. Over.'

'Operation is complete,' crackled the reply. *'Officers manning road junctions and cordons will remain in place. Officers engaged in the enforcement sweep to stand down. Do you understand? Over.'*

Cruikshank stared at the radio. No, he did not understand. The operation was not complete. What the hell was headquarters thinking?

'Mister Cruikshank, did you understand my last message? Over.'

Cruikshank pressed the transmit button. 'Er...yes. Yes sir. Message received. Out.'

Received, yes, Cruikshank thought. *Understood? No way, not by a long bloody chalk.*

He headed back to Police Headquarters. Perhaps there would be answers there.

In the command center, most of the staff had crammed themselves into the recreation room where a television set showed reruns of the night's events. There were shots of teargas billowing among the crowd. Panicked young people screaming and weeping. Helmeted police forging their way into the mass of people. A police officer emerged from the smoke brandishing a shotgun. The newsreel was on a loop, showing the same scenes, over and over. The voiceover was in Cantonese. Calm, professional.

'Where's the attack on our cordon lines?' Cruikshank gasped. A comms officer shushed him into silence. 'Where are the bottles? Where's the abuse? Where's the traffic chaos?'

No one was listening.

Cruikshank dropped into a chair at an empty console. Information scrolled across the screen. He clicked onto the most recent situation report. People were pouring into Admiralty district. They came from all directions. Police blocked the road junctions and the footbridges but new arrivals simply walked in along the road. They straddled the central road dividers, they chatted and sang. They were strolling around in the carriageway. The whole district had become a giant street party. Two major thoroughfares were impassable and one was down to two lanes.

Assistant Commissioner Special Operations was at the traffic console. 'Tell the Mass Transit Railway people to close Admiralty station,' he ordered. The comms officer leafed through his briefing folder, searching for the telephone number, but it was already too late to stem the flood of people. Admiralty district belonged to the protesters. Cruikshank shook his head, trying to understand how it had happened. The police had not lost the battle for Admiralty, for some reason they had surrendered it.

In Hong Kong, a long-ignored community fault line finally gave way. People who considered themselves only marginally political, canceled the day's plans and went to Admiralty. By early evening, they were so many, it seemed nothing could move them.

CHAPTER 12
THE YELLOW AND THE BLUE

TROPICAL RAIN — the policeman's friend. It pummels the roads and sidewalks. It turns roads into watercourses and claws potholes into the tarmac. Hillsides become mounds of ooze. For anyone caught outdoors, the rain batters the head, face and body. But to the police, the rain is a blessing. When it rains, the police own the streets. Crime goes down, street traders head for home and sidewalk hoodlums disappear.

On night two of the occupation, it rained. Police officers zipped up their waterproof jackets, tugged their caps forward to protect their faces and waited for the rain to clear the protest. Behind the barricades, protesters sheltered beneath underpasses and walkways. They huddled under makeshift tarpaulin and plastic shelters. Dozens of canny street traders, loaded down with cheap umbrellas, moved through the crowd. Someone made a remark about water cannon. It was not funny but still, everyone laughed. A young man removed his spectacles and stepped out into the rain. He spread his arms, tipped back his head and opened his mouth as if to drink from the downpour.

Renewed comradeship spread through the Admiralty site. Someone was singing, '...*raindrops are fallin' on my head...*' A smiling protester stepped up to the barricade and held an umbrella above a police officer's head. Later, the rain stopped. Dawn broke and Admiralty still belonged to the protesters.

That day, thousands more came from their homes and

HONG KONG POLICE: INSIDE THE LINES

workplaces. Secondary school and university classes stood empty. People skipped work and made their way to Admiralty district. Youth led the way and others followed. There were students, teachers, delivery workers, businessmen and women, office workers, shop assistants, general laborers, civil servants, restaurant workers, company managers. They were the young, the old and the middle-aged, but mostly the young. Someone started to sing the 1990s, Cantonese pop hit, 'Under a Vast Sky.'

> Many times I've been ignored and ridiculed
> Never have I given up my heart's ideals
> A moment of forgetfulness then a sense of loss
> Without realization, it faded. Who is there to understand me?
>
> Forgive me my love of freedom
> Although I'm still afraid that I might fall
> Abandon your hopes and ideals, just like anyone can do
> I'm not afraid if someday there will be just me and you.

Others took up the song. The clearway became a festival of youthful optimism but elsewhere in Hong Kong, society polarized.

The protesters adopted yellow ribbons as their symbol. Just a little loop of yellow silk, worn on the chest, the wrist or in the hair. It became an iconic part of the democracy movement. It was everywhere: in the press, on schoolbook covers, on social media posts, chalked and spray-painted on walls, on protest banners and in pro-democracy literature.

A counter group emerged. People showing support for the police wore loops of blue ribbon. They tied blue ribbons to railings outside of police stations, they delivered gifts, fruit and energy drinks to the police, they staged noisy but non-violent rallies in public spaces and at protest sites. Then, others took the blue ribbon as their own. A united front of pro-Beijing activists drafted in people to counter the pro-democracy demonstrations. They too, wore the blue ribbon. Many spoke with mainland accents prompting accusations that the blue ribbons were paid demonstrators, bused in from China. This new wave was more aggressive and as their strategy took hold, they became violent. Police distanced themselves from the blue ribbon movement but the damage was already done.

The dialogue turned ugly. *Police are Beijing bullyboys*, some cried. The teachers' union branded the police *'...the people's enemy...'* Social media posts declared, *'...Hong Kong Police use poison gas against children...'* No one mentioned the violence meted out to police, but why should they? They were on a roll and the world was watching.

As the days ticked by, the protest became better organized. There were deliveries of food, water, tents, and medical supplies. The protesters set up two more camps, one in Causeway Bay on the east side of Hong Kong Island, the other in west Kowloon's Mong Kok district. With a bit more thought, they might have done things differently. Central district, with its global corporations and fat cat businesses was an easy target. Causeway Bay and Mong Kok were something else. In Causeway Bay and Mong Kok, most businesses were small and family run. To compete with retail chains, they cut their margins to the bone. As the Causeway Bay and Mong Kok occupations took hold, custom dried up. Shopkeepers tried reasoning with protesters but they would not listen. Shopkeeper requests became demands. Demands provoked arguments. Arguments became strident. Then, in Mong Kong, things got downright nasty.

Mong Kok is a dazzling, rowdy corner of west Kowloon. By day, there are fashion boutiques, jewelry outlets, camera shops, electrical goods stores, cafes and teahouses. By night, it is all change. Mong Kok then glitters with crimson, yellow, green and purple neon. At street level, there are restaurants, cocktail bars, karaoke joints and nightclubs. Just a short climb up one of many narrow staircases, there are massage parlors, brothels and short-stay apartments. The protesters did not stop to think that where there are pleasure outlets, there are triad gangsters making money off the pleasure givers.

Westerners think triads are like the super villains we see in James Bond movies. In truth, they are a loose collection of criminal clans that are in constant conflict with each other. In Mong Kok, the main triad groups were the Sun Yee On and the Wo Shing Wo. They detested each other, but as long as the money rolled in, they kept a fragile peace. Each group lay claim to stretches of turf from which they wrung as much as they could. They ran vice dens and squeezed local businesses for protection money. They dabbled in semi-legal business like barroom and nightclub security, and on-street valet parking. God help anyone who messed with a triad bouncer or parked in a space reserved for a triad parking service. Triads organized the unregulated and chaotic network of red minibuses. They set routes, fixed fares and marshaled unofficial termini. For relaxation, the two groups stuck to their own turf. Under a long-established, triad code of territory, anyone venturing out of bounds risked a beating. If that happened, the bosses would call out their soldiers and for a while, there would be street warfare.

At the top of the triad pile are the triad bosses. They live the gangster lifestyle of snappy clothes, fast cars and flash women. Below them are the workers. They manage the vice dens and collect the weekly take from businesses, traders and street hawkers. In short, they look after the odds and ends that keep the bosses in Italian suits and French brandy. At the bottom of the heap are the rank-and-file. They are the foot soldiers and rarely show themselves unless the boss needs a show of force. For these low-level triads, life is mundane. To make ends meet, they have proper jobs. They are taxi and minibus drivers. Some are street hawkers, others run small businesses such as fashion

boutiques, jewelry outlets, camera shops, electrical goods stores and teahouses. Low-level triads look just like Joe Public but never forget, it is a bad idea to piss them off.
Which is exactly what the Mong Kok protesters did next.

Mong Kok's street occupation began on the same evening as the occupations of Admiralty district and Causeway Bay and at first it was every bit as carnival-like. A thousand or more protesters took the Mass Transit Railway from Admiralty to Mong Kok station and piled into the junction of Nathan Road and Argyle Street. As far as causing disruption goes, it was a masterstroke. Nathan Road bisects the commercial part of Kowloon, north-south. Argyle Street does the same, east-west. Within minutes, traffic backed up in four directions. Cars, delivery trucks, minibuses and taxis had to find new routes that took them through narrow side streets already clogged with street hawkers and parked cars. The protesters commandeered barriers and sandbags from nearby road works. Soon, they controlled a three-quarter mile stretch of Nathan Road, plus some of the adjoining side streets. The press arrived. There were reporters and photographers from local and foreign newspapers. Television stations set up cameras and microwave links. The presence of the press did not go down well with Mong Kok's evening punters, whose nearest and dearest may not like them enjoying the district's sleazy side. Girls working the brothels and massage parlors found time to catch up on their favorite TV soap operas. Local businesses pulled down their shutters. Parking valets were at a loose end. Minibuses reverted to their old, unregulated chaos. Triad finances dried up and some unpleasant people started to lose patience.

It started with something and nothing. Five days into the Mong Kok blockade, a shopkeeper stepped into Argyle Street, picked up one of the protesters' sandbags and moved it to the side of the road. A protester recovered it and returned it to the barricade. In silence, the shopkeeper carried it back to the roadside. It did not take long for spectators to gather. *'Jau la,'* — Go away, they shouted at the protesters, all the time making shooing motions with their hands.

'MAN JUE,' — DEMOCRACY, the protesters roared back. They cheered as one of their number recovered the sandbag.

By now, Argyle Street was starting to look like a bad-tempered game show. A protester sat on the sandbag. The shopkeeper tried to push him off but the protester gritted his teeth and held on tight. The police arrived. The shopkeeper fell to his knees, clasped his hands together and begged the heavens to drive away the protesters. He waited a few moments but the gods were in no mood to help. His prayers unanswered, the shopkeeper left.

In the afternoon, a woman went from lamppost to lamppost, ripping down pro-democracy posters. More locals came out. Some wore surgical masks. They shook the barriers and chanted, *'Tsing tseung,'* — Clear the area. Their numbers grew but not all of them objected to the protest. Some clambered over the barriers and joined the protesters. Opposing groups stood nose to nose, waving their arms and shouting abuse. Undercover detectives reported that there were triads on both sides.

More people arrived. At the Nathan Road-Argyle Street junction, hundreds of jeering, chanting people surrounded a group of protesters. When police formed a protective circle around the protesters, they too came under attack. The police line broke and the crowd swarmed into the protest site. They shouted obscenities, destroyed tents, ripped down banners and attacked anyone who got in their way. As the violence spread, the police called for backup. When the answer came, there was good news and bad: reinforcements were on the way but were stuck in the gridlocked traffic. Finally, the besieged police linked arms and forced a corridor through the crowd. They took more than a hundred protesters to safety.

Evening fell. There were clashes along the whole three-quarter mile length of the protest site. Locals threw bottles and taunted protesters with shouts of, *'Chun choi, faan hui.'* — Idiots, go home. It was as if thousands of opposing football fans had come face to face in a frenzy of passion and violence. Sun Yee On and Wo Shing Wo triads moved through the crowd, punching and kicking protesters. When opposing triads came face to face, they punched and kicked each other. There was no front line. Violence broke out on the fringes and in the body of the crowd. Outnumbered police shouldered their way through the crush only to find trouble had flared somewhere else. With each troublemaker dragged from the crowd, it seemed that a dozen more stepped in to stir thing up. As police struggled to force pathways from one trouble spot to the next, protesters claimed the police had abandoned them. More protesters travelled from the Admiralty site. By nine o'clock, they outnumbered the locals. Shortly afterwards, police reinforcements arrived. A loudhailer ordered everyone to leave the area. A thousand voices jeered back. At eleven o'clock, more police arrived and at last, Mong Kok became calm.

Police made nineteen arrests, eight of whom were triads. There were twenty-four people injured, including six police officers. As police brought calm to Mong Kok, student leaders addressed the crowd at Admiralty. Police had stood by while triads and pro-Beijing groups attacked the protesters, the speakers claimed. Martin Lee, a long time democracy activist and the protesters' honorary legal counsel, told the crowd that police had used triads to, *'...create a scene and threaten the people...'*

The next day, a pan-democrat legislative councilor told reporters that government had recruited triads to shut down the protests. He had no evidence to back the claim but no one cared. Gleeful bloggers pumped the story into every social media platform and it grew with the telling. Soon, it was a case of volume triumphing over reason. At the protest sites, there was another slogan to hurl at the police.

HONG KONG POLICE: INSIDE THE LINES

'Ging chaat haak se wooi.' — Triad police.

Two days later, Andy Cruikshank rode his bicycle along the stretch of Lung Wo Road linking Wanchai to Admiralty. Earlier, rain had left a gloss of water on Admiralty's road network. When the skies cleared, the sun turned the water into a skein of mist that clung to the tarmac. It did not take long for the mist to burn away, but the air remained humid and close. Sweat stung Cruikshank's eyes, his T-shirt stuck to his back but despite the heat, he was at peace with the world. A breeze blew from the harbor and in the unfamiliar silence, Cruikshank could hear water slapping against the seawall. He made ready to signal a lane change then remembered there was no traffic. *It is the most perfect of days,* he thought and for moment, was half-glad of the street occupation. The sight of a barricade dampened his mood. Behind the barricade, a group of young people watched his approach. One of them grinned. 'Hello,' he said. 'Lovely day, yes?'

'Wonderful,' Cruikshank answered. He paused for moment. 'Is it... is it alright if I come in?' he asked.

'Of course,' the young man answered and signaled two of his colleagues to move the barrier. 'Be careful,' he cautioned. 'Police are on Lung Wo Road.'

Cruikshank nodded his thanks and wheeled his bicycle into what had become a village, set in the heart of the city. Where there had once been a snarl of traffic, there were tents lined up in orderly rows. They were yellow, orange, blue, green, white, grey, and candy-striped. There were art exhibitions, a study area, a kindergarten crèche, a carpentry workshop, a multi-faith religious support station. The Red Cross had a well-stocked first-aid post. There were distribution points for food and water. Groups of protesters collected rubbish in bags marked, 'general,' 'paper,' 'plastic,' and 'glass.' Others with buckets and mops moved around the public toilets. Students clustered around a teacher who was giving an English lesson. More gathered at a podium and applauded the words of a speaker. Cruikshank tried to make sense of it, but it felt unreal. Admiralty district, once a business and transport hub, had the look of an open-air arts festival. Tourists and locals mingled with protesters, chatting and taking photographs. At key road junctions, the police stood behind their barriers. Cruikshank watched as police moved a barrier to let a lorry deliver supplies to the protesters.

'Ah sir,' a voice called. 'Ah Cruikshank sir.' At the barrier, a police officer was grinning and waving at Cruikshank. Cruikshank hunched his shoulders and hurried on.

'Come join us.' The voice belonged to a young woman. She wore a floppy T-shirt and tight leggings. She was smiling. 'Yes, you,' she said. 'We're just starting.' She swept an arm toward a group of young people sat on mats, placed in a circle on the tarmac. 'Yoga,' the women said. She gave Cruikshank the kind of half smile-half frown normally reserved for a hesitant child. 'Come on,' she said. 'It's easy.' She grabbed Cruikshank's wrist and led him to the group.

There is something infectious about the optimism of youth, and Cruikshank found himself drawn into the camp's mood. Among the multi-colored tents, the classes, the speeches and the crowds, there was a joyous abandon he had once felt at a music festival, many years earlier. He stopped at a tent pitched close to the People's Liberation Army Headquarters. Behind an iron gate, four soldiers watched. They wore helmets and thick flak jackets over camouflage fatigues. Each carried an automatic rifle. Their eyes were unblinking, their faces showed no emotion. They were young and it struck Cruikshank that without their uniforms, it would be impossible to tell them from the protesters.

'Don't worry,' one of the protesters chirped. He pointed to where the press had laid claim to one of the footbridges. There were booths bearing the logos of Associated Press, the British Broadcasting Corporation, Al Jazeera and the Japanese public broadcaster, NHK. 'The soldiers will do nothing,' he said. 'Not with so many foreign cameras.'

'Can I take a photo?' Cruikshank asked.

'No problem,' the protester answered. 'But first...' He nodded to the others and they fished surgical masks from their pockets. With the masks fitted, they stood side by side and gave the thumbs up sign as Cruikshank snapped a few pictures.

'Thanks, guys,' Cruikshank said. 'So, what's the plan?'

'Plan?'

'What's the long-term aim?'

They swapped glances then shrugged. 'Maybe... maybe... we wait and see,' one answered.

'For now, we stay put,' another added.

Above their masks, their eyes crinkled in smiles.

Cruikshank headed west along Harcourt Road, enjoying a morning free of diesel fumes and blaring horns. He passed through a barrier and back into the real world. He looked over his shoulder to convince himself he had not half-imagined it all. He had expected a rowdy, ramshackle, unsanitary campsite. What he had seen was a cross between an English country fair and a well-run little town. He mounted his bicycle, looked for a break in the traffic and circled back to Police Headquarters.

CHAPTER 13
UMBRELLA POWER

THE POLICE FORCE'S voice was Chief Superintendent Steve Hui, the officer in charge of police public relations. Hui is a well-spoken man of striking good looks and he became an instant celebrity. He had an endearing style but compared to the protesters' blistering rhetoric, his announcements were a bit flat.

Protester claims of police brutality, political manipulation and triad collusion became more strident. On the barricades, police came in for daily abuse. Off duty, they were harangued in the street, some were assaulted. Anonymous abuse swamped their Facebook accounts. Cars displaying police parking labels were vandalized. Several doctors refused to treat police officers or their families. The young son of a police officer fell victim to a school bullying campaign. It emerged that his teacher had organized it. Some police families became divided when officers and their children chose different sides of the barricades.

Benny Tai Yiu-ting and the other occupy central founders made regular visits to the protest camps. Their welcome was warm but with each visit, it was clear the movement had outgrown them. Occupy Central with Love and Peace was no more. Now, the rally cry was, *'Yu saan gaak meng.'* – Umbrella revolution.

Andy Cruikshank sank into a pit of gloom. The protesters had won the streets, they had won the public relations battle, and so long as central government dithered, they had the police just where they wanted. Cruikshank consoled himself with the thought that it could get no worse.

Then it got worse.

On October 14, there was a disaster. Hong Kong's national football team played Argentina and lost by seven goals to nil. For the police, the loss marred what should have been a good day. Just before six that morning, they had demolished barricades on the westbound carriageway of Yee Wo Street, in Causeway Bay. They left the eastbound section to the protesters and although traffic moved slowly, at least it was moving. Later, they cordoned off Admiralty district's Queensway and set about the barricades with power tools. By lunchtime, the police had opened Queensway to traffic and it seemed that things were getting back to normal.

With Queensway open, the protesters fell back to Harcourt Road and Tamar Park. Most sat in silence and pondered the protest's future. Others had a plan. Queensway was lost but the Lung Wo Road expressway had an underpass that ran directly beneath Tamar Park. Could they take it? At ten o'clock that evening, crowds of protesters charged down footways leading from the park to Lung Wo Road. Ignoring blaring car horns, they ran onto the road and brought traffic to a halt. They formed a human blockade across all lanes then dragged metal barriers into the road, completing the closure. They pulled up concrete drainage covers from nearby roads and carried them into the underpass, laid them out in serried lines, blocking both carriageways. Self-appointed marshals directed vehicles to go back the way they had come. The underpass filled with protesters. Cheers and laughter boomed off the concrete walls. Drawn by the clamor, other protesters crowded the footways and balustrade overlooking the underpass.

A few dozen police rushed from a nearby standby point. They marched into the underpass, then realized that if more protesters came in behind them, they would be trapped. Their commander ordered his men to back away. As they emerged into the open, cheering protesters greeted them with shouts of, *'Jau la,'* — Go away. *'Jau la. Jau la.'* The protesters laughed and high-fived each other. Some taunted the police with chants of, *'Bak Ging. Bak Ging.'* — Beijing. Beijing. Some police stayed to report on developments but protesters surrounded them, shouting, *'Chit tui. Chit tui'* — Retreat. Retreat.

The police fell back to Tim Wah Avenue. Reinforcements were on the way.

Andy Cruikshank massaged his eyes with both hands, trying to drive away the fatigue that seemed never to leave him. He had arrived at Lung Wo Road with the police reinforcements. The police carried batons and pepper spray but kept their helmets clipped to their belts. One man in three carried a Perspex shield. They formed a line across Lung Wo Road and waited, silent, calm, ready.

Cruikshank looked at the underpass and did not like what he saw. A tangle of barriers blocked the entrance. Behind the barriers stood hundreds of protesters. Some wore masks and goggles. They waved the police forward, daring them to advance. That was not the worst of it. Hundreds had gathered on the overhead balustrade. To the left and right, more jammed the footways leading to the park. Police had orders to clear the underpass but to do that, they risked attack from above and from both flanks. Cruikshank was standing next to a weary looking inspector called Jack Chu. 'We should clear the balustrade and footways first,' Cruikshank suggested.

'With what?' Jack Chu answered. 'We're not allowed to use teargas and no one wants a baton charge.' He shrugged. 'There should be plainclothes men up there,' he added. 'They have orders to look out for troublemakers.'

Behind them, a police loudhailer crackled. *'Chin bin yan kwan,*

jun fai lei hoi.' — The crowd in front, leave quickly.
The response was instant. *'Diu lei lo mo.'* — Fuck your mother.
Calmly, slowly, police moved up to the underpass entrance and started to cut away cable-ties binding the barriers together. The protesters rushed forward. They grabbed onto the barriers. Concrete walls amplified their voices. *'Haak seh wooi.'* — Triads. *'Haak seh wooi. Haak seh wooi.'*
The police loudhailer blared its message. *'Jun fai lei hoi.'* — Leave quickly.
The last barrier clattered against the tarmac. The police advanced, shouting, *'Taan hau. Taan hau.'* — Go back. Go back. Police and protesters came together. Lung Wo Road became a swirling, pushing, shouting, cursing melee. Protesters reeled away from pepper spray. Police staggered under punches and kicks.
'Taan hau. Taan hau.'
'Haak se wooi. Diu lei lo mo.'
'Taan hau. Taan hau.'
Up on the balustrade, protesters leaned over the railing and screamed abuse. Down on the road, something wet spattered a constable's shirt, darkening the blue cotton. He shielded his eyes as more liquid splashed his face. He plucked at his shirt. There was a familiar smell. *'Aiiyah. Lam niu jik.'* — Aiiyah. Pouring urine. Up on the balustrade, a man wearing a surgical mask held a one-gallon juice container. To cheers and laughter, he emptied the contents onto the officers below. He dropped the container and stepped back into the crowd. Plainclothes police shouldered their way through and grabbed him. He tried to fight them off but they pepper sprayed him, zip-tied his wrists and passed him to another group of detectives. There were seven in the other group, all members of the elite Organized Crime and Triad Bureau. They were supposed to take the man to a police vehicle in Lung Wo Road but they had other ideas. While uniformed officers battled their way through the underpass, the detectives

took their prisoner to a dark area behind a nearby utility building. There, they threw him to the ground and with his arms still bound, set about him with punches and kicks.

The arrested man was Ken Tsang Kin-chiu. He was a member of the committee charged with electing Hong Kong's Chief Executive. By chance, a local television news crew saw the arrest and sensing something newsworthy, had followed. Within hours, video footage of the beating appeared on television sets locally and worldwide.

By five a.m., Lung Wo Road was clear. When the morning rush hour rolled around, traffic was back to normal. Police made nearly forty arrests. Several people were hurt, including four police officers. As they returned to base, the police may have expected some public acclaim. Instead, they faced public outrage. Images of the beating had flashed around the world. From New York to Buenos Aires; from London to Berlin; from Tokyo to Sydney, the world's press marked the Hong Kong Police as violent oppressors. In Hong Kong, there were rallies, marches and yet more speeches. There were demonstrations outside Police Headquarters and calls for the Commissioner's resignation. Newspaper editorials railed against the police. On TV celebrity chat shows, everyone had something to say, none of it good.

Just as public support started to swing back to the police, an act of madness changed everything.

Chief Superintendent Barry Smith's orders were clear enough. He was to dismantle the barricades in Mong Kok. That should have been good news but he also had orders to leave one lane of Nathan Road to the protesters, which was folly. He said as much during the operational briefing but his boss could only shrug.

'Couldn't agree more,' his boss said. 'But it's politics.'

Bloody politicians, Smith thought. *Put them in uniform and stick* them on the barricades for an hour. He smiled at the thought. Of course, it would never happen and it was no good arguing the point. The orders were intractable.

Smith and his men arrived at Nathan Road before daybreak and found the protest site almost empty. By noon, most of the barricades were gone. Smith still had doubts but the sight of shops reopening and traffic flowing reassured him. All seemed well. At last, the police were taking back the streets. He went home and at seven that evening, was back on duty supervising his officers at Admiralty.

The first inkling of trouble came from local news broadcasts. Thousands were gathering in Mong Kok. A few minutes later, a message came from the headquarters command centre. In Mong Kok, five hundred police faced about nine thousand protesters. Protester numbers were growing. Smith was to leave Admiralty and to take charge at Mong Kok.

In Nathan Road, thousands of protesters pressed in on five-hundred police. The police fought back with batons, shields and pepper spray. As Smith forced his way through, a rage-twisted face turned toward him. 'Hey, fucking *faan-gwai*. Fuck off back to England.' *Faan gwai* — foreign devil. '*Faan gwai, jau laan hui,*' — Foreign devil, fuck off, someone shouted. Others joined in. The chant became '*Faan gwai, jau laan hui. Faan gwai, jau laan hui.*'

Whatever ground the police gained, the protesters took it back. When the message came, Smith's radio operator almost missed it. He was shouting into the transmitter. '*Joi gong.*' — Say again. '*Teng m do.*' — can't hear. 'SAY AGAIN.'

Smith took the radio and pressed it against his ear. '*Withdraw,*' the radio crackled. '*Return to base immediately.*'

The police surrendered Nathan Road. As they negotiated and fought their way clear, protesters cheered, clapped and hurled abuse. A wave of sadness washed over Smith. He was a thirty-one year veteran of the Hong Kong police. He had seen many conflicts but never had he been on the receiving end of such hatred. He climbed aboard the police transport and ordered the driver to return to base.

That evening, police arrested twenty-six people for offenses of assault, criminal damage, disorderly conduct, assaulting police officers, obstructing police, and possession of offensive weapons. First aiders treated fifty protesters. Fifteen police officers needed hospital treatment.

Protest leaders blamed police for the violence.

In Admiralty, a bus company reported losses of HK$3 million, US$400,000 as a result of the protests. Citic Tower's owners complained that the protest camp prevented ambulances and fire engines from reaching the building. In Mong Kok, taxi and minibus operators saw no relief from their fall in earnings. The operators went to the High Court and won an injunction ordering protesters to leave Mong Kok. Admiralty's bus companies and the owners of Citic Tower did the same. Copies of the court injunctions appeared in newspapers. Billposters plastered them on walls in Admiralty and Mong Kok. Court bailiffs read them out at the protest sites. The protesters shrugged them off. What is one more offense? In Mong Kok, protester defiance fueled more local anger and police had to intervene to protect them.

Protest leaders lodged an appeal against all injunctions and everything went back into limbo. A week passed. Then another. Then a third. The police found themselves squeezed between three pressure plates. On one side, a protest movement unwilling to concede anything. On another, a public that demanded action. In the background, a central government paralyzed by indecision but still trying to micromanage everything.

It was twelve-hour shifts for officers working the barricades. Between shifts, some slept on a floor in Police Headquarters, others slept in the street near their duty posts. They waited for clear orders that never came. Rumors filled the information

vacuum.
The head of the civil service ordered the Commissioner to stop firing teargas.
No, the order came from the Chief Executive.
Wrong — China is giving the orders.
Police Headquarters did nothing when protesters stopped and searched vehicles carrying food and water to the police. When the food arrived, it was of poor quality and often soiled with dirt or other contaminants.

In mid November, the High Court rejected the last protester appeal. It instructed bailiffs to clear the protest sites and ordered the police to arrest anyone who obstructed them.
Splits within the protest movement deepened. A group called Civic Passion urged stronger action. Their leader declared, *'...There needs to be escalation, occupation of more areas or maybe government buildings. The campaign at this stage has become too stable...'* Militants launched a night attack on the Legislative Council building. They smashed through the glass doors and briefly entered the lobby. In the public eye, the action undermined the whole umbrella movement. Support for the occupation was on the decline. Now it fell further.

When Andy Cruikshank next went back to the Admiralty protest camp, the place had a different feel. There was no laughter, no singing, no bantering debate. Young men and women sat in silence, some with only their mobile phones for company. The yoga teacher had left. The young men camped outside the Peoples Liberation Army Headquarters had gone. Cruikshank saw a familiar face and tried to remember the young man's name. *'Ho ma?'* — How are you? he asked.
The young man shrugged. 'Arguments. Too many arguments,' he sighed. 'Everyone want to be in charge. Talk, talk, talk. Shout, shout, shout. Too much talk. Too much shout.'

Cruikshank felt a pang of sympathy. 'Maybe it's a good time to leave,' he offered.

The young man shook his head. 'Soon be over,' he said. 'Soon be gone. For what? What have we won?' He cocked his head to one side. 'Why is a foreign *gwailo* interested?' He gave a half smile and poked Cruikshank in the chest. 'Many *gwailo* cops chasing us,' he said. His face split in a grin. 'How about you? Maybe you are *gwailo* cop.'

Cruikshank laughed. 'Not me, my friend,' he said. He pondered the word. *Friend*. Yes, he had found himself liking many of the young men and women he had met in the camp.

'Doesn't matter,' the young man said. He swept his arm to encompass the camp. 'Soon, all be gone.'

Cruikshank nodded a farewell. As he passed back through the barrier, he cast his eyes over the protest camp then turned away.

He never returned.

A week later, police cleared a section of Nathan Road. By lunchtime, traffic was back to normal but that evening, the protesters were back. Some carried clubs and homemade shields. For the next three nights, police fought off attack after attack.

Hong Kong's Chief Executive urged the public to return to Mong Kok and enjoy the late night shopping. The following night, hundreds of protesters crowded Mong Kok's sidewalks. They chanted, *'Gau Wu,'* a phrase that sounds like the Mandarin words for 'shopping,' but in Cantonese street slang means 'trouble.' They blocked sidewalks and repeatedly crossed the road, often stopping to pick up non-existent, dropped coins. Shopkeepers shook their heads and pulled down the shutters.

At Admiralty, things moved up a notch. Organizers mounted the speakers' podium and called on supporters to surround the government offices and stop civil servants from getting to work.

Many had come prepared. Wearing industrial hardhats, goggles and masks, they moved towards the Chief Executive's office complex and the nearby Central Government Headquarters. The police blocked their way. As the protesters advanced, a group of detectives found themselves trapped. They tried to run but there was no escape. Protesters caught one and kicked him unconscious.

Chanting, 'Hoi lo. Hoi lo,' — Open the road. Open the road, the protesters moved closer to the police line. A constable unfurled an orange banner:

停止衝擊,
否則使用武力
Stop Charging or We Use Force

From the protester ranks, someone shouted, *'Yat. Yee. Saam.'* — One. Two. Three. The protesters charged. It was yellow hardhats against blue helmets. Homemade shield against Perspex shield. Punches and kicks against batons and pepper spray. *'HOI LO. HOI LO.'* On the footbridges and around the government offices, police held the line. On Lung Wo Road, protesters broke through. Cheering and leaping about like children at a birthday party, they stopped traffic. Police reformed and advanced. The protesters fell back. As morning broke, police reclaimed Lung Wo Road. They pushed the protesters back from the government offices. Militants darted among the crowd, grabbing arms, shaking people. They shouted, pleaded, begged them to regroup and attack. Fighting flared in pockets. Police dashed from one flash point to the next. They uncoiled a fire hose and jetted water into the air above the crowd, soaking everyone.

Detective Sergeant Danny Yu made his way back to Harcourt Road. Behind him, the clamor had become sporadic and seemed quieter. In Harcourt Road, people were packing their gear.

There were fewer tents. Danny glanced around, glad to see no one paying him attention. He moved to one of the footbridges. The space beneath the staircase was in shadow but still, he must take care. A young man was sitting on the footbridge stairs. At Danny's approach, he looked up. His eyes were red and swollen.

'*Pei bai,*' — Exhausted, the young man said. He backhanded something from his cheek. '*Pei Bai. Sam sui.*' — Exhausted. Heartbroken.

Danny motioned the young man to shuffle aside and sat beside him. The young man's head slumped forward, his shoulders shook and he began to sob. Danny put his arm across the young man's shoulders.

'*Pei bai,*' the young man said again. '*Daai ga do pei bai,*' — Everyone's exhausted.

Danny held the young man close. The situation report could wait.

Hong Kong's weather turned cold and rainy. Sensing, the public mood had changed, some Legislative Councilors distanced themselves from the protests. In Mong Kok, local support dwindled to nothing. At Admiralty, a few hundred die-hards held their ground but at the Causeway Bay site, only a few dozen remained. On December 10, about ten thousand people thronged to Admiralty to attend what everyone knew would be a farewell rally. The following day police announced an amnesty just long enough for people to collect their belongings. When the final clearance started, police arrested about 250 passive protesters.

There was no violent resistance.

Andy Cruikshank hated Tuesdays. On Mondays, he felt rested from the weekend. On Tuesdays, the weekend's memories were still fresh but next weekend seemed far away. Cruikshank could barely remember his last weekend off but it remained a basic truth — Tuesdays were a darn sight worse than Mondays. But not today. Today was a special Tuesday. Cruikshank greeted the senior comms officer and took a seat at a vacant console. He punched in the incident number for the Protest Event Log and the SITREP box blinked onto the screen. He knew what the readout would be, but he wanted to read it again:

TUESDAY 16 DECEMBER	
ROADS BLOCKED	None
TRAFFIC DIVERSIONS	None
PROPERTY DAMAGE	None
ARRESTS.	None
INJURIES PUBLIC	None
INJURIES POLICE	None

Cruikshank linked his fingers behind his neck and leaned back. Yes, as far as Tuesdays go, this was a good one.

EPILOGUE
(PROBABLY NOT THE LAST WORD)

OF COURSE, that was not the end of it. There were more than one thousand arrests during the protests. Police released many without charge but some cases had to go to court. Ken Tsang, who poured liquid, believed to be urine, onto the police received a five-week jail sentence. For disobeying the court order to leave the Mong Kok protest site, teenaged student leader Joshua Wong, was sentenced to prison for three months. For leading the invasion of Civic Square, which left eleven security guards injured, he received only a community service order.

An incredulous police force looked on while the courts treated offenders like juvenile pranksters. Many walked away with community service orders or warnings to keep the peace. As convicted protesters walked free, cheering supporters gave them a hero's welcome. Seeing there was still capital in the protests, politicians wagged their fingers and told the police they must work hard to restore public confidence. Police supporters found themselves branded blue-ribbon triads or *Wu Mao* – fifty-cent Beijing Quislings.

Police officers held their peace but beneath the stoic silence, there was seething frustration. For seventy-nine days, they had been on the receiving end of abuse, violence and public vilification. Now, they felt let down by the courts and by the community they served.

Two-and-a-half years after the last protester left the streets,

HONG KONG POLICE: INSIDE THE LINES

the seven detectives who assaulted social worker Ken Tsang, faced district court judge David Dufton. His Honor sentenced each officer to two years in prison. Despite his actions, the assault on Ken Tsang was a disgrace and the sentences should have surprised no one. The video of the assault appeared on television screens worldwide, bringing shame on the Hong Kong Police. The assault was a public relations gift to the protesters and it made the job of every officer manning the barricades much harder. The prison sentences should have brought closure to this episode. Instead, they lit a fuse to frustrations that had quietly simmered for more than two years. Every word of abuse, every missile that found its target, every kick, every blow, every gob of spittle, every bandwagon-hopping public figure, every front-page image of freed protesters smiling from the courthouse steps, sprang into the force's collective memory. Serving and retired police officers, together with families and friends, thronged to the Police Staff Recreation Club in Kowloon. The organizers put the number at more than thirty thousand. There were pleas for money to pay for an appeal. Speaker after speaker took to the stage and called for laws to protect police officers from abuse.

Umbrella protest supporters condemned the rally as an affront to the rule of law. An officer who attended the meeting provided another view. He told a local newspaper:

> *'This is not a protest against the courts or Hong Kong's judicial system, nor an attempt to undermine the rule of law. It is a deep and heartfelt expression of genuine support for our colleagues and their families, who we feel have been unfairly treated and whose actions came out of a time of highly charged political emotion and stress.'*

Police Commissioner Stephen Lo caused a stir when he expressed sadness at the convictions. He went on to say:

CHRIS EMMETT

'...I fully understand the frustration and disappointment that some of you are feeling...However we must bear in mind that Hong Kong is governed by the rule of law, and our judicial system has an established appeal mechanism.'

Commissioner Lo criticized neither the convictions nor the sentences. He made no concessions and in fact, he said very little but his statement went a long way to diffusing the situation. The event proved cathartic and following the Commissioner's statement, there were no more rallies.

During the protests, 520 people needed hospital treatment. One hundred and thirty of them were police officers. No one knows how many injured protesters or police decided not to bother with hospital treatment. Police veterans put the high injury count down to the decision to stop using teargas. Teargas is vile stuff, of course. It stings the eyes, the throat and, as the manual tactfully puts it, *'...those parts of the body most likely to sweat...'* However, no matter how unpleasant the effects, they are temporary. Recovery takes between ten and fifteen minutes. As part of their tactical training, every Hong Kong police officer must experience the effects of teargas. The impact is immediate but recovery is so quick that officers go right back to normal duty and training. The problem with teargas is that it gets a bad press. Scenes of people fleeing clouds of teargas look bad but the honest-to-goodness truth is, those people leave the area on foot, not by ambulance.

The normal method of delivering teargas is by firing it from a Federal riot gun. The idea is to keep a healthy, forty-meter distance between the police and the crowd. Exceptions occur when the crowd closes quickly on the police. When that happens, police are to use teargas grenades to force the crowd back to a safe distance. When the rules change and teargas is no longer an option, things get messy. Without that forty-meter buffer zone, police must engage in close contact. With a crowd determined

HONG KONG POLICE: INSIDE THE LINES

to oppose the police, close contact means helmets, shields and batons against industrial hardhats, sticks, iron bars, bottles, fists and feet. In close contact, people get hurt. So, on September 28, why did the police stop using teargas?

Word on the police side of the barricades was that senior government officials had ordered the Police Commissioner to stop firing teargas. Hong Kong's civil service chief at the time was Carrie Lam Yuet-ngor. Her answer to requests for clarification was a simple, *'No comment.'* The Police Commissioner's direct boss is Hong Kong's Secretary for Security. His answer to the same request was polite but in essence, another, *'No comment.'* Police Commissioner Andy Tsang Wai-hung retired in 2015. He was a no-nonsense Police Commissioner, which made his order to surrender the streets even more puzzling. His answer was adamant: throughout the protests, he alone decided what level of force to use. Commissioner Tsang's statement matched that of Chief Executive Leung Chun-ying. Two weeks into the Admiralty occupation, Leung stated that it was the Police Commissioner alone who had decided to stop all action against the protesters. He stressed there had been no political interference.

And that should have been that, but it was not. In June 2017, nearly three years after the event, then ex-Chief Executive Leung gave an interview to a Chinese television station. In it, he recanted his earlier statement and admitted ordering the Police Commissioner to cease all action against the protesters. His admission explains why the police surrendered the streets, stopped using teargas and went on to adopt the more dangerous strategy of close contact containment. It also explains why the street occupations ended only when private businesses took out court orders to clear the roads. The admission points to one conclusion: having taken personal charge of police and government strategy, Chief Executive Leung Chun-ying took no effective action. He prevented the police from using a method of restoring order that would have ensured fewer casualties and seen a faster conclusion to events. To make matters worse, Mister Leung then sat back and let the police force take the blame for all that went wrong. This inflicted long-term damage on how sections of Hong Kong society sees its police force. In his book, *'Umbrella: A Political Tale from Hong Kong,'* Kong Tsung-gan sums up how many still feel:

> '...*Since the Umbrella Movement, the force has become more insulated than ever... the police have been used as the guard dogs of the regime...*'

Were the Hong Kong Police Force politicized during the umbrella protest? Answer: Most certainly yes but throughout Hong Kong's history, it was ever thus. During the violent disturbances of 1956, 1966 and particularly during the 1967 Red Guard era, the police have stood accused of being the hard-core, political enforcement arm of the *status quo*. It is an accusation faced by the police in every liberal society. During the United Kingdom's miner's strike, militant strikers branded the police 'Maggie Thatchers' Storm Troopers.' There are similar stories from the USA, Europe and Australasia. It is the mark of a liberal society that people can criticise their police without fear of reprisal.

During the Umbrella Movement's street occupation, all sides played the political game but it was a game in which the policemen and women at the barricades were unwilling players. Sadly, it was they who took the brunt of the protesters' political passions.

More than four years after protesters left Civic Square, a follow-up drama played out in Hong Kong's District Court. As the year 2018 neared its end, Benny Tai Yiu-ting went on trial before Judge Johnny Chan Jong-herng. Alongside him in the dock were the other two co-founders of Occupy Central with Love and Peace, plus six leading figures from the seventy-nine day street protests. All nine defendants stood charged with causing a public nuisance and inciting others to cause a public nuisance. In a controversial move, eight of them also faced the unconventional charge of inciting people to incite others. On Friday December 14, with all the evidence in and final statements complete, His Honor adjourned the case for four months so he may consider the evidence.

On Tuesday, April 9 2019, the trial reconvened. In a 268-page judgment, Judge Chan recognized the notion of civil disobedience, but ruled that it was no defense to a criminal charge. He described Benny Tai and his two co-founders as naive to believe that by encouraging people to block roads, they would force government to bow to political demands.

The verdict: the Occupy Central leaders were acquitted of the charge of inciting people to incite others, but were declared guilty of all other charges. Their six co-defendants were all found guilty.

Years after the last protester left the streets, the fault lines remain deep and wide. They linger in the workplaces, in centers of education and within families. So deep is the mutual resentment, it is hard to see an end to it. The divisions are not just political, they are also generational. The pro-democrats are mostly young; those favoring the *status quo* tend to be older.

This is where there should be suggestions on how to resolve everything but in truth, it is best to leave you with the words of someone else. Now retired, Steve Wordsworth was a police officer who spent time with the policemen and women on the barricades. Their fortitude made a lasting impression on him and he has this to say about them:

I'm up and at them early, before the dawn's first light.
Standing in my uniform, I'm ready, tidy, bright.
I'll hold the line in Central, Mong Kok or Causeway Bay.
I don't do it for the money, but I do it anyway.

CHRIS EMMETT

I'm cursed by the students, abused, my worth made small,
Whilst shameless politicians are stirring up a brawl.
I'll be spat at, kicked and beaten, attacked in many ways.
My every move recorded, edited, contorted,
Made into propaganda to take the press in sway.

And if I raise my baton or stand in self-defense,
I'll be the aggressor although there's no offense.
Held in contempt and hatred, I'm also held in shame,
By people who attack me but who accept no blame.

Though I stand and do my duty, there's bound to be a price,
In pain and in lost dignity, but I don't feel contrite.
I don't expect your sympathy, it's gone past that today.
Just remember, I'm still human. Like you in every way.